The Rise of Cyberbullying: A Challenge for South African Schools

Lewis

Table of Contents

Chapter 1 – Introduction

1.1 Problem statement background

The role of the police in schools is one of the essential attempts in ensuring safety from violence, such as physical fights and shooting, so that schools can focus on the education of children. For this reason the police have been mandated to facilitate safety in schools (Morales, 2020; Prinsloo, 2005). Both in South Africa and abroad, school violence also stems from bullying that ranges from face-to-face to cyberbullying, which leaves devastating psychological effects on children and their academic achievements (Juan *et al.*, 2018; Pittaro, 2020; Smit, 2015). Investigations that followed after the Columbine High School shooting, which on 20 April 1990 was then the biggest murder in school grounds to date, revealed that most school shooters had been bullied and responded to their victimisation in retaliatory actions to victims and those who had not helped prevent their victimisation (Pittaro, 2020). Research shows there is association between cyberbullying with school violence and suicides among adolescents (Jolliffe and Farrington, 2011; Pittaro, 2020; Volk, Dane and Marini, 2014; You and Lim, 2016). The advancement of communication technologies in the recent decades has led to another form of bullying – cyberbullying. Cyberbullying has become prevalent among children aged between 12 and 18 in South African schools (Kyobe *et al.*, 2018). The proliferation of technological innovations implies that research and consequently, legislation, will not keep abreast of addressing technology-mediated violence (Smit, 2015). Notably, in the South African context, response to online risks and harm faced by schoolchildren is lacking, as well as evidence-based prevention strategies (Burton, 2014). Also, studies on cyberbullying interventions are still relatively new and have been increasing for the past decade (Gordon, 2018; Smith, 2019), and Africa in particular is lagging behind (Smith, 2019). However, emerging patterns in the developing countries indicate where parents and teachers have no skills and support regarding Internet use, and children engage in more risky online behaviour, such as contacting, sharing pictures and personal information with strangers (Porter *et al.*, 2016). The prevalence of cyberbullying is increasing in South Africa due to high number of mobile phone owners among the youths, especially in rural areas (Kyobe *et al.*, 2018; Oosterwyk and Kabiawu, 2016). The bullying that is carried out using mobile phones is referred to as mobile bullying.

Mobile bullying is described as a subset of cyberbullying in which aggression is carried out through mobile phones regardless of Internet access (Mtshazi and Kyobe, 2014). Bullies consist of two main categories that include pure bullies and bully-victims (Olweus, 2001). Pure bullies are aggressive and hardly fall victim to bullying, while bully-victims are simultaneously victimised and bully others (Gámez-Guadix, Gini, and Calvete, 2015; Pouwels, Scholte, van Noorden and Cillessen, 2016). It can be seen that bully-victims behaviour swings between the extremes of pure bully and victims, and they may not be easily identified (Olweus, 2001, Juan *et al.*, 2018). Studies show that bully-victims may be a minority group, but face higher risks of poor conduct, academic and peer relationship problems, as well as substance abuse, compared to bullies (Juvonen and Graham, 2014; Protogerou and Flisher, 2012; Sangalang, Tran, Ayers, and Marsiglia, 2016; Smith, 2016).

Most studies focus on traditional forms of violence, while mobile technology is increasingly used for victimisation, which has necessitated investigation of the problem in mobile context (Kyobe and Lusinga, 2018). Furthermore, the use of social networks for bullying in South African public schools is a growing problem and the understanding of mobile bullying is still limited (Smith, Mahdavi, Carvalho, Russell and Tippett, 2008; Ndyane and Kyobe, 2019). This problem is also prevalent, especially in rural areas of South Africa such as the eastern part of the Free State province where Internet access through mobile phones is dominant (Odora and Matoti, 015; Statistics South Africa's General Household Survey, 2017). Furthermore, the cyberbullying aggression has been studied from the perspectives of learners, bystanders, educators, and parents (Cassim, 2013; Craig, Bell, Leschied, 2011; O'Brien and Moules, 2013; Robinson, 2013; Vandebosch, Beirens, D'Haese, Wegge and Pabian, 2012). However, as asserted by Addington (2013), little is known about law enforcement's activities in combating cyberbullying. Sometimes they are viewed as aggravating the already fragile situation in schools by using excessive force (Ryan et al., 2018). The involvement of all stakeholders, including law enforcement, helps to form part of the environment that can help the fight against cyberbullying (Cassim, 2013; Solberg, Olweus and Endresen, 2007; Vandebosch *et al.*, 2012). The Centre For

Justice and Crime Prevention (2015) notes cyber aggression affects many children in South Africa however it remains unexplored. Smit (2015) is also adamant about society's need to protect South African children against the negative effects of cyberbullying. Popovac and Leoschut (2012) also made a call for studies about cyberbullying that are evidence-based in order to discover experiences the children lived in schools. A call is also made to understand the contribution and effectiveness of the law enforcement in the fight against cyberbullying.

Law enforcement can play a paramount role in serving justice and preventing mobile bully-victim behaviour in schools. However, the law enforcement contribution and effectiveness in addressing mobile bully-victim behaviour is not known. There is a need to understand factors that influence the law enforcement effectiveness against mobile bully-victims. Generally, reporting is the starting point and seen as the most essential tool to combat child maltreatment, criminal acts, and bullying; however, it is still lacking, especially in children, due to inadequate or non-existent reporting systems (Blakey, Glaude and Jennings, 2019; Kyobe and Lusinga, 2018). Kyobe and Lusinga (2018) note reporting is important in countries like South Africa where the crime rate is one of the highest in the world; however, schools lack adequate reporting systems. Cognisant of the fact that violence such as school shooting also springs from lack of interventions for bullying from those expected to ensure safety (Pittaro, 2020), this requires capacitating the police and schoolteachers as the go-to for reporting bullying incidents. Learners participate online and are prolific consumers of social media, which determines thresholds for social communication, but educational institutions have been reluctant to include forms of online sexual violence in their policies because these interactions occur online (Shariff and Eltis, 2017). Also, teachers marginalise mobile bully-victims, often viewing their behaviour as provocative and impulsive, and therefore deserving of maltreatment (Popovac and Leoschut, 2012; Yang and Salmivalli, 2015). Hence, the creation of safe environments to optimise the likelihood that those learners feel at ease to disclose maltreatment is imperative, as well as their being believed and provided support through the process (Blakey *et al.*, 2019). When attempting to report mistreatment to such school officials, they may not provide mobile bully-victims a just support, and in turn the latter might seek other ways to take revenge.

Additionally, the use of technology allows bullies to conceal their identity, through anonymity and impersonation in social media (Fraser *et al.*, 2013; Hoff and Mitchell, 2009), and the telegraphic nature of social network communication makes it hard to prove beyond doubt the intention to harm in messages (Fraser, Bond-Fraser, Buyting, Korotkov and Noonan, 2013). Meanwhile, in South Africa the responses to bullying "are fragmented and rely on various pieces of legislation, common-law definitions of criminal offenses, and civil law remedies" (Badenhorst, 2011: 7), and preventive measures are limited.

Furthermore, research on bully-victims groups is still lacking (Ioannou *et al.*, 2018), and studies that seek to develop applications to mitigate cyberbullying are also lacking, except for independent developers aiming to improve safety of social media users (Ashktorab, 2018). Hence, the focus of the proposed study is to develop a mobile application that can aid law enforcement in diagnosing and preventing mobile bully-victim behaviour in high schools.

Also, factors that differentiate bullying from peer aggression include power imbalance, repetition over time and intentions of harm, whereas aggression does not involve repetition (Haslam, 2006; Jolliffe and Farrington, 2011; Olweus, 2013; Olweus, 1999; Salmivalli, and Peets, 2011). The advanced skills to use technology and its affordances such as anonymity and large audience facilitate mobile bully-victims' power imbalance and repetition through rapid widespread harmful contents (Fousiani, Dimitropoulou, Michaelides and Van Petegem, 2016; Fraser *et al.*, 2013; Hoff and Mitchell, 2009; Vandebosch and Van Cleemput, 2009). This view supports the need of an artefact that will enable the law enforcement competency in diagnosing and preventing mobile bully-victim behaviour in high schools.

The development of interventions has focused on whole schools since the bullying behaviour has received attention as a threat to social and public health issues (Smith, Bauman and Wong, 2019). These interventions generally include components of raising awareness, bystanders' roles, and coping strategy enhancements as well as peer support (Smith, Bauman and Wong, 2019). Additionally, technology-mediated interventions have been developed that focus on protecting children's online experiences by blocking profane contents and enabling reporting as well as parental/guardian control (Ashktorab, 2016; Shieh, 2016; Wisniewski *et al.*, 2017). Although whole school or whole class interventions can be valuable, they do not pay attention to some learners that need targeted interventions, and need to be first identified, as well as determination of the kind of intervention needed (Smith, Bauman and Wong, 2019). Also, studies have been conducted from schoolteachers' perspectives, including their confidence and attitude and how parents view their actions towards learners (Smith, Bauman and Wong, 2019). The police have been inserted in schools to help curb violence, but their contribution with regard to curbing cyberbullying has not received much attention (Coon and Travis, 2012).

1.2 Research questions and objectives

1.2.1 Research question

- How can a mobile app be used to aid law enforcement in diagnosing and preventing mobile bully-victim behaviour?

1.2.1.1 Sub-questions

- What is the effectiveness of the proposed app in aiding law enforcement to control mobile bully-victim behaviour?
- What is the law enforcement perception on the use of the proposed app in combating mobile bully-victim behaviour in schools?

1.2.2 Research objectives

- To develop a mobile app to aid the law enforcement in diagnosing and curbing mobile bully-victim behaviour in schools.
- To identify impediments to law enforcement effectiveness in combating mobile bully-victim behaviour.

1.2.2.1 Additional objective

- To understand the process of developing a mobile app for use as interventional tool.

1.3 Research strategy

Pragmatism was adopted as the research philosophy underpinning this study, in order to answer the research questions and meet the research objectives of this study. Following the adopted philosophy, the Design Science Research (DSR) methodology (Vaishnavi and Kuechler, 2004; Vaishnavi and Kuechler, 2015) process model to achieve the goals of this study. The process model consists of five phases, including problem awareness, suggestion, development, evaluation and conclusion. The details of the research strategy are discussed in Chapter 3 – Methodology, Chapter 4 – Study procedure, and in Chapter 5 – Design and development.

1.4 Research contribution

The contributions emanating from this study include theoretical, methodological, and practical contributions.

1.4.1 Theoretical contribution

This study provides a conceptual framework was developed through literature review by considering factors that influence the police's effectiveness in fighting against mobile bully-victims. Also, dominant theories in bullying that explain children's behaviour as influencing factors in dealing with mobile bully-victims were considered. In turn, the "Cyberbullying Continuum of Harm" conceptual framework was extended to enable inclusive (bullies, bully-victims, and victims) and moderated reporting platform for identification of mobile bullies, bully-victims, and victims, in order for culprits to account for their actions. Also, the extension includes severity assessment for determining level of hurt on mobile bully-victims, in order to inform remedial actions.

1.4.2 Methodological contribution

The methodological contribution in this study was the use of the Design Science Research (DRS) method to investigate reporting and severity assessment of mobile bully-victims behaviour, as well as the development of the intervention artefact (mobile application) thereof. The iterative nature of DSR methodology enabled the demonstration of the robustness and usefulness methodologies in this study. Furthermore, the adoption of the pragmatism as a philosophy stance enabled this study to establish and show the use of mixed methods to gain deeper understanding of the phenomenon being investigated, and ensuring research validity of the finding.

1.4.3   Practical contribution

This study provided recommendations that may be helpful for formulating policy and intervention programmes to curb the mobile bully-victims behaviour in schools, since specific legislation that addresses bullying, including cyberbullying or mobile bullying is still lacking (CJCP, 2015). Information regarding policy decisions has been provided in this study. For instance, this book provides information on targeted prevention and interventions programmes towards the most efficient and relevant resources and control of impact. Also, this book provides a way for identification of mobile bully-victims that might be beneficial for criminal law court cases.

1.5   book layout

This book consists of ten chapters that are arranged as follows:

Chapter 1 – presents the introduction to the study as well as the research questions and objectives.

Chapter 2 – presents a literature review on bullying, intervention strategies, behavioural theories and role theory, and discussion. The chapter concludes with the description of the theoretical framework and strategies for addressing with mobile bully-victims.

Chapter 3 – describes the philosophical stance and research methodology that were applied in this study, and the framework for design research activities.

Chapter 4 – *describes the study procedure that was applied in this study, and specifies data collection as well as data analysis methods.*

Chapter 5 – discusses the framework that guided the development of the mobile application, and the rationale for the developing the intervention (mobile application). This chapter also presents the overview of the adapted Design Science Research process model for developing the mobile application.

Chapter 6, Chapter 7, Chapter 8 and Chapter 9 – present the development and evaluation iterations, which apply the adopted Design Science Research process.

Chapter 10 – presents the conclusion of the study and highlights recommendations for future mobile bully-victims interventions.

Chapter 2 – Literature review

2.1   Introduction

This chapter discusses methods for identifying mobile bully-victim behaviour, assessing its impact, and interventions that can aid the effectiveness of law enforcement in combating mobile bully-victim behaviour.

Studies on children who bully others and are also victimised can be categorised into two lines of traditions: the "aggression research" and "bullying research". Aggression research is mainly about general victimisation context with no regard for power differential, and peer nominations facilitate the identification of aggressive victims. Bullying research context stresses the power imbalance along with intention and repetition of aggressive behaviour. The bully-victim concept stems from traditional bullying research. However, the use of bully-victim and aggressive victim concepts are interchanged in the literature.

Adequate diagnosis is essential to deal with mobile bully-victim behaviour effectively in schools. Also, instead of treating symptoms only, levels of effects of the behaviour also need to be identified and treated. The causes can be identified through the designed artefact where student share their personal perceived effect. This could inform the provision of remedies that are aligned to hurt-levels, instead of combing through the thickets of various mobile bully-victim effects.

2.2   Overview of bullying

Bullying is defined as being victimised repeatedly and over time through negative actions of others (Olweus, 1978; Olweus, 1993). The forms of bullying include direct aggressive acts, "such as hitting, kicking or pushing; verbal aggression, such as name-calling and abusive language; or relational aggression, such as spreading rumours or socially excluding peers" (Smit, 2015: 2). Other forms of bullying include indirect aggression (Ortega *et al.*, 2012) and social aggression.

Indirect aggression involves spreading rumours or writing graffiti about the target (Jolliffe and Farrington, 2011; Smith, Cowie, Olafsson and Liefooghe, 2002). Relational aggression includes "harming or threatening to harm the target's relationship" (Salmivalli and Peets, 2011: 324). Social aggression refers to harming the target's self-confidence or social status through social exclusion or demeaning facial expressions and gestures (Fitzpatrick and Bussey, 2014).

Males are more prone to traditional forms of bullying than females, whereas more representatives of cyberbullying are females (Li, 2006; Li, 2007). However, gender differences are not consistently shown in cyberbullying researches (Ang and Goh, 2010).

2.2.1   *Aggression, victimisation and bullying*

Schools are clouded by aggressive behaviours that threaten their ability to facilitate learning in a place of safety (Smit, 2015). Aggressive behaviour is described as harmful acts that are directed to another individual with intention to harm, while the target is motivated to avoid the behaviour (Bushman and Anderson, 2001). The forms of aggression include proactive and reactive aggression. Proactive aggression is a goal-directed and harmful behaviour, while reactive aggression occurs in response to a perceived threat or social provocation (Dodge, 1991). However, bullying is a deliberate act that can occur without provocation (Salmivalli and Peets, 2011).

Aggression and school bullying overlap conceptually, involving a set of intentions. Jolliffe and Farrington (2011) note both bullying and aggression share intentions such as causing fear, misery and hurt to the victim. However, aggressive behaviour does not involve repeated incidents over time (Jolliffe and Farrington, 2011). Meanwhile there is evidence that a harmful incident of bullying need occur only once to have effect (Olweus, 2013). Volk, Dane and Marini (2014) note in other instances victims have committed suicide as a result of a single bullying incidence. Salmivalli and Peets (2011) suggest bullying is a subtype of aggressive behaviour. Clearly there is a fine line in the understanding of aggressive behaviour and bullying behaviour.

Bullying types include pure bullies, victims, and bully-victim (Salmivalli and Peets, 2011). Pure bullies can be regarded as individuals who perpetrate negative actions towards seemingly weaker peers, often to gain a social status or dominance.

Victims are described as children who cannot easily defend themselves against bullies (Troop-Gordon, 2017). Mobile bully-victims are described in section 2.3.2. Bullying behaviour also consists of three universally accepted characteristics: (1) intention to harm, (2) repetition over time, and (3) a power imbalance (Olweus, 1999; Salmivalli, and Peets, 2011: 323). Bullying can also take place among peers, by victimising an individual in a group.

The description of victimisation includes an occurrence of aggressive acts on an individual (Salmivalli and Peets, 2011: 323). Bukowski and Sippola (2001) argue that victimisation is a process of ostracising an individual who may impede a group from attaining its goals, such as maintaining cohesion and homogeneity (Bukowski and Sippola, 2001). Traditional bullies may engage in cyberbullying when retaliating for traditional bullying victimisation (Kowalski, Giumetti, Schroeder and Lattanner, 2014). Burton (2016) notes that in schools, cyberbullying incidents normally originate from offline events. Also cyberbullying is associated with previous in-person bullying and victimisation (Ioannou *et al.*, 2018; Pittaro, 2020).

2.3 Cyberbullying

Cyberbullying occurs through the use of technology to intentionally "bully, harass, hassle and threaten" peers (Goodno, 2011: 641). Cyberbullying includes mobile bully-victim behaviour, and manifest in different forms on various online social networks, making it hard to define (Kao *et al.*, 2019). Cyberbullying is defined as intentional and repeated aggression that is perpetrated through electronic communication technologies such as e-mail, blogs, instant messages, or text messages, towards individuals who may be unable to defend themselves (Kowalski *et al.*, 2014). Hinduja and Patchin (2014: 3) note increasing numbers of children immersed in online interactions causes the cyberbullying problem to grow as well. As a result adolescents cannot avoid being bullied, because defamatory personal material can be posted and become accessible to millions before it is removed whether or not the victim logged online (Smit, 2015).

Although cyberbullying is seen as an extension of traditional bullying, it has distinctive features that permit invasion to all aspects of victims' privacy at any time and any place such as at home or school (Myers and Cowie, 2019). The features that exacerbate challenges to curbing mobile bullying include anonymity, children's skills in using technology, distancing and group effect (Fousiani *et al.*, 2016; Hoff and Mitchell, 2009). Anonymity can be described as the ability of cyberbullies to hide their true identity to their victims. Bullies may also possess an advanced knowledge of using Internet and mobile phones, which may render their victims defenceless (Vandebosch and Van Cleemput, 2009). Distancing relates to a technological device's effect that ensures that cyberbullies do not get to see the consequences of their actions (Donegan, 2012). The group effect relates to rapid spread of harmful material through Internet and mobile phones (Heirman and Michel, 2008). Power imbalance is another feature that encourages bullying behaviour, in that aggressors perceive themselves as superior, while the victims are seen as being inferior (Haslam, 2006; Olweus, 2013). Speculations suggest that physical appearances, differences in opinions or beliefs, relationship problems, and females cite gender as a primary reason for cyberbullying (Faucher, Jackson and Cassidy, 2014; Hoff and Mitchell, 2009).

Bullying and harassment are now commonly carried out via mobile phones (Porter *et al.*, 2015), a phenomenon that is known as mobile bullying. Evident in the description of cyberbullying, mobile phones use represent popular media for bullying conduct (Juvonen and Graham, 2014), and it can form appropriate investigation stance – mobile bullying.

2.3.1 *Mobile bullying*

Mobile bullying is described as a subset of cyberbullying in which aggression is carried out through mobile phones, regardless of Internet access (Mtshazi and Kyobe, 2014). This aggression includes "sending threatening text messages, phone calls or nasty images to others" (Mtshazi and Kyobe, 2014:3). This form of aggression is exacerbated by low accessibility costs, which makes it possible for an individual to own multiple phones and subscriber identification module (SIM) cards (Aker and Mbiti, 2010; Kreutzer 2009). As a result perpetrators enjoy the untraceability of their actions. The other factor that contributes to the untraceability of the perpetrators is that by African norms, sharing of mobile phones is common (Aker and Mbiti, 2010). Therefore, bullies can make sure that they are not directly linked with harassment actions by borrowing their friends' mobile phones.

Olweus (1999) notes that bullying occurs without obvious provocation, however, Pikas (1989) suggests that a category of provocative victims incites bullying behaviour. Another type of bullying that is receiving attention in research is bully-victim behaviour, also called provocative victims (Olweus, 2001). The proposed study will focus on mobile bully-victim behaviour.

2.3.2 *Mobile bully-victim*

Perpetrators of offline school violence may adopt mobile phones and the Internet to continue bullying and dominating their targets, a phenomenon known as mobile bullying (You and Lim, 2016). In other cases, targets may also bully others; this dilemma is referred to as bully-victims (Juan *et al.*, 2018). Bully-victims are defined as children who have been bullied and who bully others (Marini, Dane, and Volk, 2010; Olweus, 1978).

Bully-victims' distinguishing feature is lack of emotional control (Lam, Law, Chan, Wong, and Zhang, 2015; Schwartz, Proctor and Chien, 2001). Bully-victims may seek revenge and gratification by humiliating others despite the presence of an audience (Smith, Mahdavi, Carvalho, Fisher, Russell and Tippett, 2008). The bully-victim behaviour is reactive in nature and may be a result of dysregulation (Volk *et al.*, 2012). This observation implies that mobile bully-victims may resort to violence in order to avenge themselves. The impact of bully-victims may also be linked to impaired relationships between children and teachers (Popovac and Leoschut, 2012).

The elements that make up bully-victims include those of pure victims as well as pure bullies (Juan *et al.*, 2018; Olweus, 2001). Similar to effects on pure victims, bully-victims also tend to be depressed, possess low self-esteem and high aggression inhibition, and feel rejected by peers (Olweus, 2001). On the other hand, bully-victims resemble pure bullies by having heightened levels of dominance, aggression, unsociable behaviour, concentration challenges, hyperactivity, and impulsivity (Bollmer, Milich, Harris and Maras, 2005; Olweus, 2001).

Literature has shown that bully-victims are proactive, reactive and impulsive in their aggression and they have poor emotion control (Lam *et al*, 2015). Also, bully-victims are fewer than pure victims; however, they face a higher risk of social rejection and are subjected to maladjustment in various domains of functioning (Schwartz, 2000).

2.3.3 *Social integration of mobile bully-victims*

A relational perspective of bullying behaviour includes "two social worlds" – social integration and social marginalisation (Farmer *et al*., 2010: 386). Socially integrated bullies try to gain or keep up control of other people through their negative behaviour. These types of bullies fit well into a peer culture, and benefit from peer social support (Farmer *et al*., 2010). This type associates well with friends who commit various levels of bullying and their strengths are easily recognised, which include social skills, attractiveness, and athleticism (Rodkin, Espelage and Hanish, 2015). Rodkin *et al*. (2015) note socially integrated bullies' behaviour is proactive and goal-directed; however, they are perceived as less aggressive and highly esteemed among their peers. These bullies tend to abandon their aggressive behaviour or reconcile with their victims after conflicts once dominance has been established (Pellegrini *et al*., 2010).

Children who are victimised by peers tend to have lower sociometric status (Sentse, Kretschmer and Salmivalli, 2015). That is lower peer acceptance and high peer rejection in school. Bully-victims represent socially rejected children and they "experience significant impairments in behavioural and emotional regulation" (Schwartz *et al*., 2001: 168). Socially marginalised bully-victims may try to bring down a social system that keeps them on the outside (Farmer *et al*., 2010, Rodkin *et al*., 2015). Rodkin *et al*. (2015) note marginalised bullies' behaviour is impulsive and highly reactive to perceived offences, and they are identified as an at-risk group. This group's strength is difficult to identify, but speculations suggest it may come from failed attempts to meet social status or to dominate others through intimidation (Hawley, Stump and Ratliff, 2011). Rodkin *et al*. (2015) suggested that marginalised bully-victims' source of strength may come from efforts to support their attacks through grouping together with children who share similar characteristics. Cook, Williams, Guerra, Kim and Sadek (2010) observed that marginalised bully-victims have externalising and internalising problems, low self-esteem, lack social competence, inadequate social problem-solving skills, poor performance academically, and are negatively influenced by peers they interact with as well as those rejecting them. Clearly marginalised bully-victims embody bullies behaviour (Farmer *et al.*, 2010) and this shows as with Rodkin *et al.* (2015) that bullying behaviour is but one manifestation of a host of problems.

2.4   Interventions

Bullying may take different forms between males and females, but both genders report low affective empathy (Jolliffe and Farrington, 2011). Also Espelage *et al.*, (2013) note categorisations such as bullies and victims may not be useful for cyberbullying preventive interventions, since youth can be both bullies and targets of bullying in different incidents. Therefore, programmes or interventions that aim to curb bullying do so by addressing cognitive and affective empathy (Ang and Goh, 2010; Jolliffe and Farrington, 2011). Cognitive empathy relates to recognition of others' emotions (Hogan, 1969), while affective empathy is associated with the ability to experience and share the emotions of others (Mehrabian and Epstein, 1972). Interventions aim at increasing empathy through explicit or implicit attempts to make individuals understand and be aware of emotional effects of bullying on victims (Jolliffe and Farrington, 2011). Brighi *et al.* (2012) suggest that interventions to fight bullying should commend adolescents to caring and affective relations, while they also work to develop high self-esteem.

Interventions that would be helpful regarding mobile phone uses in bullying need to specify "how to contact mobile phone companies and Internet service providers, and legal rights in these matters" (Smith *et al.*, 2008: 384). This knowledge can help as a damage control of bullying; however, it may not prevent incidents of mobile bully-victim behaviour. The interventions that are tailored to different needs, predispositions of bully-victim behaviour are likely to yield greater success (Volk *et al.*, 2012).

The interventions that apply well to bully-victims are those focusing on empathy training, social justice, fostering bully-victims cooperation, and social skills training (Rigby, 2010; Volk *et al.*, 2012). However, Yang and Salmivalli (2015) argue that attempts to increase empathy and constructive responses towards bully-victims may not be effective, because of the perception among peers and teachers that the bully-victim behaviour is provocative and deserves maltreatment. Therefore these negative perceptions necessitate an investigation of effective intervention approaches, as empirical studies on bully-victim behaviour are limited (Yang and Salmivalli, 2015).

A targeted intervention strategy is helpful, such as KiVa that uses adults to address bullying incidents that are referred to them (Salmivalli and Poskiparta, 2012; Smith, 2016, Smith *et al.*, 2019). However, predicting a targeted intervention for children may be difficult due to multiple facets of bully-victim behaviour including those of pure bullies and victims (Juan *et al.*, 2018). As such, a universal intervention should be directed to all schoolchildren, including bystanders, bullies, victims and bully-victims. Hood and Duffy (2017) suggest children's behaviour improves morally when they perceive that their online activities are monitored, as such effective cyberbullying interventions need to focus on eliminating moral disengagement. A mobile app that facilitates law enforcement monitoring of children's behaviours online could be effective in curbing bully-victim behaviour.

2.4.1 Digital-based interventions

Interventions to antisocial behaviour such as cyberbullying require the use of different modalities, including social, legal, and technological measures (an der Zwaan, Dignum, Jonker, and van der Hof, 2014). The use of technology as intervention to influence behaviour by applying social influence is referred to as persuasive technology (an der Zwaan, Dignum, Jonker, and van der Hof, 2014; Kight and Gram-Hansen, 2019).

Interventions have been prescribed for victims, schools, or potential cyberbullies, which offer education about cyberbullying processes (Reychav and Sukenik, 2014). Such interventions help to identify possible cyberbullying occurrences around specific topics such as "race and ethnicity, sexuality and sexual identity, physical appearance, intelligence, and social acceptance and rejection", and the negative tone tied to messages (Reychav and Sukenik, 2014: 89). Certainty about possible cyberbullying behaviour may be reached when consistent negative tones on messages escalate over time. Other technology-oriented intervention tools include Internet filters and child-friendly web browsers; however, social media issues are not addressed (Reychav and Sukenik, 2014). A suitable solution on social media-based bullying would be filtering nasty messages, and permitting a list of safe contacts; however, this endeavour requires high investment of time and efforts by parents (Reychav and Sukenik, 2014).

A technological intervention was developed to combat cyberbullying by helping to detect possible instances of cyberbullying on social media (Lieberman, Dinakar, and Jones, 2011). This intervention provides role-based intervention for bullies, victims, friends, family and teachers. In the bullying process, bullies are warned of possible consequences of their action, victims are encouraged to seek emotional support and deterred from retaliation, and friends are discouraged from joining in, but to defend victims.

Gordon (2018) notes research on cyberbullying prevention is relatively new and ranges from universal programmes with limited or no specific elements targeting cyberbullying, to whole school approaches and Internet safety education lessons that include cyberbullying. Seemingly, the role of the law enforcement in the fight against cyberbullying, particularly mobile bully-victim behaviour has not been examined. Since the law enforcements' role is to prevent crime, gaining insight about their involvement in curbing mobile bully-victim behaviour would be valuable.

2.5   Law enforcement

The description of law enforcement agencies (police and prosecution agencies) includes: visible police patrols, investigation, intelligence gathering, arresting and prosecuting of suspects and syndicates (Liebermann, Landman, Louw and Robertshaw, 2000: 9). However, the proposed study focuses only on the policing role.

The contribution of South African law enforcement against online and cyberbullying including mobile bully-victim behaviour in schools is not clear. This is as a result of a lack of specific legislation that addresses bullying, including cyberbullying or mobile bullying (CJCP, 2015). The South African judicial system has no dedicated legislation and still lags behind regarding tackling or instituting processes to curb bullying and cyberbullying (Laubscher and Vollenhoven, 2015; Reyneke and Jacobs, 2018). Hence, bullying cases have been addressed through the lenses of the Protection from

Harassment Act 17 of 2011 (Mtshazi and Kyobe, 2014, Reyneke and Jacobs, 2018; Republic of South Africa, 2011; Smit, 2015), since there are similarities between bullying and harassment, such as causing harm or instilling fear of harm (Laas and Boeraart, 2014). The Protection from Harassment Act 17 of 2011 describes harassment as a conduct that is intended to cause harm or anticipated harm by stalking a target at home, work or study place, and communicating with the target in writing, or verbally, or electronically. Harassment also relates to bullying; however, the Harassment act does not cater for a repeated act of harm and time length factors, which are defining elements of bullying (Laas and Boeraart, 2014). The problem with the Protection from Harassment Act 17 of 2011 may be that it falls short in addressing and preventing mobile bully-victim behaviour. This observation necessitates finding alternatives such as using a mobile application to diagnose and prevent mobile bully-victim behaviour.

2.6 Cyberbullying law

In an attempt to address cyberbullying, South Africa pieces together legislation, common-law about wrongdoing and civil law solutions, which are non-preventive (Badenhorst, 2011; Smit, 2015). Globally, starting from 2016, anti-bullying laws have been enacted in all states of American (Dasgupta, 2019). These laws generally require adoption of effective measures against bullying, including age appropriate sanctions against bullies, equipping teachers with skills to deal with bullying, and record keeping of incidents' details (Dasgupta, 2019). For instance, "New Jersey's Anti-bullying Bill of Rights Act", comprehensively addresses harassment and bullying that interferes with rights of individuals or causes school disruption (McCarthy, 2014:812). In this law, schools are accountable to timely resolve bullying incidents, even those originating outside the schools (McCarthy, 2014). Clearly, the law enforcement's quick response to reported incidents and knowledge to address cyberbullying is paramount.

Additionally, Dasgupta (2019) notes the availability of cyberbullying law influenced victims' likelihood of reporting cyberbullying incidents at school. Also, Dasgupta (2019) suggests addressing cyberbullying through punitive measures may increase reporting for victims. However, bully-victims may not report incidents because they are also involved as bullies, as noted by Walgrave (2013), bullies will try to avoid facing consequences of their actions. Also, cyberbullying incidents may vary by degree, making it difficult to address using same standards (Rigby et al., 2004). Hence, the law enforcement may need to be able to differentiate cyberbullying from threats and harassment, and minor incidents such as name calling (Broll and Huey, 2015). These observations show that antibullying laws may not be effective in addressing mobile bully-victims. Hence, other ways are needed to encourage reporting, such as the proposed mobile application in this study.

2.7 Factors influencing the law enforcement's effective fight against mobile bully-victim behaviour

Anti-bullying policies could be provided in legislation to bring resources and authority to address the problem of bullying particularly cyberbullying (Dayton and Dupre, 2009). However, there are several notable impediments to law enforcement roles against mobile bully-victim behaviour. These include lack of a common definition of cyberbullying (Betts, 2016), and no available cyberbullying or mobile bully-victim offence. Judicial systems also attempt addressing current technology issues, particularly cyberbullying, by applying old laws (El Asam and Samara, 2016; Smit, 2015). Hence, the law enforcement face challenges in deciding which offence a suspect may be charged with (El Asam and Samara, 2016).

The use of technology in cyberbullying makes it hard to tell a real situation from fabrication, which requires skills to discern. As noted by Zetter (2013), a mother and daughter created a fictitious MySpace account of a 16-year-old named "Josh Evens" to lure emotional fragile Megan, in order to learn what the girl would say about her own daughter. Once Megan bought in, "Josh" dashed verbal abuses until she committed suicide.

Lack of surveillance may be attributed to inadequate skill of tracking cyberbullies. As noted by Kwan and Skoric (2013), in some instances perpetrators of cyberbullying are never found, forcing the police to inform the victim that nothing else could be done. As such the community may lack trust to law enforcement in helping against cyberbullying victimisations. Hai-Jew (2006) notes that trust enhances cooperation and accurate information. Trust may be attributed to dependence on another person's competence to deal with a situation, as well as protection by not publicising information shared in confidence (Anwar and Greer, 2011). Seemingly, trust is influenced by expectation of privacy, and possession of necessary skill for a particular situation. "Trust is the willingness to depend on another person or institution based on the belief in the integrity, ability, and benevolence of the other party" (Bansal, Zahedi and Gefen, 2016:1). The dependent expects the other party to fulfil the expectations (Gefen, Rose, Warkentin, and Pavlou, 2005).

The degree to which a person is willing to depend on others, as well as her behaviour across situations, is determined by trust (Bansal *et al.*, 2016). Trust is a social phenomenon that is valuable in social interactions because it can reduce the complexity of assessing behaviour and motives (Bansal *et al.*, 2016).

Bullying is still a challenging behaviour in which perpetrators try to avoid penalties from authorities by intentionally remaining undetectable or misrepresenting (Volk, Veenstra and Espelage, 2017). Also, in criminal law addressing cyberbullying requires the presentation of evidence that proves beyond doubt that the threat was intentional. However, the telegraphic nature of much online communication such as "LOL" for "laugh out loud" and "TTYL" for "talk to you later" presents a challenge in presenting amicable evidence for intention to cause harm (Fraser *et al.*, 2013: 32). Social media communication slang allows cyberbullies to engage in hostile activities figuratively and without literally spelling them out (Fraser *et al.*, 2013). Although bullies and victims may understand the meaning of the messages, "proving a definite meaning and intentions can be more difficult" (Fraser *et al.*, 2013: 32-33). As such, the problem with contents that have various meanings makes evidence weak (Fraser *et al.*, 2013).

The persisting challenge in fighting bullying has been lack of reported incidents (Mishna, Saini, and Solomon 2009; Smith *et al.*, 2008; Troop-Gordon, 2017). Children do not report bullying experiences because they fear that their mobile devices will be confiscated or lose Internet access privileges (Perren *et al.*, 2012). Also the lack of confidence in law enforcement hinders reporting of cyberbullying incidents (Cross, Monks, Campbell, Spears, and Slee, 2011). This may be a reason the law enforcement is not readily involved in the fight against mobile bullying. Perren *et al.* (2012) also note that children feel that their parents are not accustomed to cyberspace, as such they may not be able to help against cyberbullying. Also, schools personnel feel that the police sometimes use excessive force on learners (Ryan *et al.*, 2018), which could lead the teachers to be protective for bullies and choose not to report case to the police. This implies that the fight against mobile bully-victim behaviour requires technological skilled roles that do not threaten access to mobile phones for children, but ensure a safer use. As such, the law enforcement role may also be to entice children to report bullying incidents.

The primary solution in South Africa would be legislation specifically enacted to protect learners against all forms of cyberbullying (Smit, 2015). It seems the lack of appropriate legislation hampers law enforcement's role against mobile bully-victim behaviour. Smit (2015) notes the true challenge of cyberbullying lies in finding ways that prohibit criminal actions against children in schools. Interestingly, Thaxter (2010) suggests the use of legislation in dealing with mobile bully-victim behaviour should be the last alternative. Therefore law enforcement success in combating mobile bully-victim may need the use of technology as a platform for fighting mobile bully-victim behaviour.

2.8   Dominant theories

Theories that mainly address cyberbullying are limited, as studies still rely on amalgamation of theories. Espelage, Rao, and Craven (2013: 49) note, "discussion of explanatory theories of cyberbullying involvement among youth are sparse and piecemeal, and conclusions have been based largely on cross-sectional studies". As also noted by Smith *et al.* (2013) the absence of a complete theoretical approach still haunts the cyberbullying field. Espelage *et al.* (2013) note dominant theories in the cyberbullying field include social-ecological theory, social information processing theory, general strain theory, social learning and social norms theories as presented in the following subsection. These are reference theories that provide knowledge about a phenomenon, which served as a motivator for constructing artefacts to solve existing problems (Patas, Milicevic and Goeken, 2011).

2.8.1   *Social-ecological theory*

The law enforcement can be aided with a thorough understanding of mobile bully-victim behaviour's environmental context. The social-ecological framework is mainly valuable for understanding bullying behaviour in schools (Swearer, Espelage, Vaillancourt and Hymel, 2010). "A theoretical understanding is needed to link the nascent and most relevant theoretical and/or casual factors within a social–ecological conceptual framework, to explain why some young people perpetrate cyberbullying behaviours" (Cross *et al.*, 2015:1). In the area of school bullying and peer victimisation, the social ecological model seeks to explain how personal traits of children interact with system or environmental context to promote or curb victimisation and perpetration (Espelage, 2014). The context that may be particularly relevant for the involvement of law enforcement in the fight against mobile bully-victim behaviour in school is exosystem. 'Exosystem' refers to a social system "such as parent's workplace, school administrators and institutional infrastructures" which a child does not interact with but still influence children through a microsystem (Cross *et al.*, 2015: 2). Microsystems relate to contexts or structure such as family, community and schools, which a child has direct contact with (Espelage, Rao, and Craven, 2013). Social-ecological framework provides a holistic view of bullying phenomenon, and consists of process-oriented theories of attitude and behaviour change in children (Swearer *et al.*, 2010).

Espelage (2014) notes that the likelihood of bullying involvement is influenced by risk and protective factors such as lack of parental control, exposure to violence, microsystems and exosystems. Influences on cyberbullying aggression at community level can be addressed through awareness of school policies and laws as regulatory environment means (Cross *et al.*, 2015). As such, law enforcement's role could be to make youth aware of the existing laws, and set guidelines for acceptable behaviour within society or schools.

Also, social identity theory (SIT) posits groups to which an individual identifies with influence decision-making. SIT "argues that human behaviour can be explained in part by viewing people as irrationally but naturally biased in favour of those whom they perceive as belonging to the same sociocultural group (i.e., others who are perceived as sharing the same values)" (Gefen, Rose, Warkentin, and Pavlou, 2005: 61). That is, individuals rely on members of a socially esteemed group when making decisions (Gefen, Rose, Warkentin, and Pavlou, 2005).

2.8.2   Social learning and social norms theories

Deviant behaviours are learnt through social interactions and communications with other people. Social learning theory posits the external environment largely influences the acquisition and maintenance of aggression and other risk behaviour (Espelage, Rao, and Craven, 2013). People learn from each other beliefs and attitudes that endorse misbehaviour and methods of offending (Holt and Bossler, 2015). This is experienced through exposure to deviant behaviour and reinforcement of cyberbullying such as viewing nasty messages posted on social network sites (Freis and Gurung, 2013; Rodkin *et al.*, 2015). As noted by Cross *et al.* (2015) children who are pro-bullying are more likely to engage in traditional bullying as well as cyberbullying. This observation could also include mobile bully-victim behaviour.

Bullying is a dyadic phenomenon whose psychological mechanisms can be understood by considering who is bullied and why (Rodkin, Espelage and Hanish, 2015). The fundamental causes and motivations for school bullying and cyberbullying particularly mobile bully-victim behaviour are similar. Similarly, the role theory can assist law enforcement's involvement in detecting and monitoring behaviours that lead to mobile bully-victim behaviour.

2.8.2.1 Social rank theory

Social rank theory or social dominance theory suggests that many societies support aggressive behaviour of individuals, who have higher rank, status, or power within a group (Espelage *et al.*, 2013). Also social rank theory "posits that the peer group becomes established as a hierarchy whereby some students use aggression to dominate their peers as a means of gaining prestige, power, and access to resources" (Beran and Li, 2007: 18). Children engage in bullying behaviour to gain reputation and navigate dominance hierarchies such as promoting group solidarity (Volk *et al.*, 2014; Rodkin, Ryan, Jamison, and Wilson, 2013). Kwan and Skoric (2013) note schoolchildren that bully others to gain social status continue their behaviour in cyberspace, such as mobile bully-victim behaviour on Facebook. Meanwhile bullies receive more positive affirmation than negative feedback from peers (Juvonen and Graham, 2014).

The social rank theory can be used to conceptualise the link between schools bullying particularly mobile bully-victim behaviour. As suggested by Beran and Li (2008), children who submit to school bullying may be at risk of further bullying in cyberspace and they may attempt to retaliate through technology. As such, law enforcement's role-based interventions need to understand that mobile bully-victim behaviour and traditional bullying are interrelated. The effects of cyberbullying relate to development of psychological distress and poor psychosocial adjustment such as low self-concept (Raskauskas and Stoltz, 2007). Studies focusing on preventive efforts against cyberbullying could be informed by self-concept theory (Espelage *et al.*, 2013).

2.8.2.2 Resource control theory

Bullying may be used to gain privileges for using resources in schools (Volk, *et al.*, 2014). Resources include "material, social, and informational things that are generally seen as desirable by children" (Espelage *et al.*, 2013: 52). Reijntjes *et al.*, (2013) posit bullying behaviour may start as an attempt to gain social status and then continue for consolidating high status and defending the in-group boundaries. Acquiring dominance and social status is important and serves as an indirect means of gaining tangible benefits such as resources or desired opportunities (Volk *et al.*, 2014). Bullying behaviour within a group is seen as a strategy to gain control of social resources (Postigo, González, Montoya, and Ordoñez, 2013). These observations map the link between bullying to gain social rank and bullying to control resources.

2.8.2.3 Self-concept theory

Cyberbullying studies use self-esteem as a distinguishing factor between bullies, victims and bully-victims (Brack and Caltabiano, 2014). Self-concept, or self-esteem, is defined as a positive or negative perception of the self (Rosenberg, 1965). Bullies attack targets to enhance their self-concept (Okoiye, Anayochi, and Onah, 2015). While bystanders reinforce bullying and bullies' self-concept, on the other hand victims' self-concept is adversely affected (Espelage *et al.*, 2013; Okoiye *et al.*, 2015). Okoiye *et al.*, (2015) propose orienting schoolchildren on the need to possess good virtues, discipline and positive self-control. Self-concept theory suggests that altering schools attitude thereby diminishing cyberbullying reinforcement, and employing cognitive approaches for bullies, targets and bystanders, cyberbullying will cease to sustain positive self-concept (Espelage *et al.*, 2013). Thus the self-concept theory is deemed an appropriate construct to aid law enforcement's fight against mobile bully-victim behaviour. Normative beliefs are influential in social processing as in social information processing theory (Nicol and Fleming, 2010).

2.8.3 *Social information processing theory*

Lack of social problem-solving abilities may be one of the factors that drive children's engagement in antisocial behaviours. Social information processing theory suggests that aggressive behaviours are mostly driven by impairment in social problem solving (Clavete and Orue, 2011; Espelage *et al.*, 2013). As such, children who lack proper interpretation of social information may behave unbecomingly in ambiguous situations (Espelage *et al.*, 2013; Nicol and Fleming, 2010). In ambiguous social situations, children tend to attribute hostile intents to others and react aggressively (Pornari and Wood, 2010). This observation implies that mental processing of social situations is directly related to a child's behaviour (Espelage *et al.*, 2013).

2.8.4 *General strain theory*

People may engage in deviant behaviour as a result of experiencing strain (Holt and Bossler, 2015). General strain theory (GST) contends "that individual who experience significant strain will develop anger and frustration in response, which then place them at risk of engaging in deviant behaviour" (Espelage *et al.*, 2013: 51). Staksrud (2016) notes that bully-victims of cyberbullying are more associated with a tendency to react to stimuli with anger towards perpetrators. Bully-victims choose cyberbullying as a means of avenging themselves, as technologies such as mobile phones help to avoid direct contact, thus eliminate injury (Holt and Bossler, 2015). Staksrud (2016) notes anger as a most critical emotional reaction for the purpose of GST, asserting wish for revenge, and forcing individuals to take action without reservations. GST is concerned with crime and has successfully explained a wide variety of antisocial and deviant behaviour (Staksrud, 2016). This theory could provide an understanding of why mobile bully-victims may continue with their behaviour despite the risks of being penalised.

2.8.5 *Theory of planned behaviour*

In order to change actual behaviour of teachers, learners and other involved officials, school culture must be aligned with its climate (Smith 2016). School climate relates to bullies and victims prevalence. Smith (2016) notes Hawley and Williford's (2015) use of the Theory of Planned Behaviour (TPB) to provide the theoretical underpinning for interventions to curb bullying, stating that the intervention should aim for changes in (1) perceptions about the nature of bullying; (2) attitude regarding bullying conduct and towards victims as well as reporting and intervening of bullying; (3) subjective norms (SN) about thoughts and expected behaviour by other people; (4) efficacy beliefs, about assurance of a safe reporting platform. Also, interventions should target popular individuals to bring about behavioural change (Smith, 2016). Pabian and Vandebosch (2014) discovered that attitude, as a component of the TPB, was positively influenced by the effectiveness of cyberbullying as a way to vent negative feelings. The SN and attitude towards cyberbullying are the most influential elements in designing preventive interventions (Auemaneekul, Powwattana, Kiatsiri and Thananowan, 2019; Jafarkarimi, Saadatdoost, Tze Hiang Sim and Mei, 2017). The TPB is suitable at the developmental period of adolescents, since peer influences contributes significantly to them as a strong subjective norm towards their intention to engage in cyberbullying (Auemaneekul *et al.*, 2019). Hence, identification of mobile bully-victim influential learners can help to reduce the behaviour. This can be done through courses and talks to enlighten the identified learners about the negative impact of cyberbullying behaviour on other learners (Jafarkarimi *et al.*, 2017).

2.8.6 *Role theory*

Role theory is concerned with organisation of social behaviour. Roles are formed according to work responsibilities, as well as group and society participation. As such, "role theory is one key element in understanding the relationships between the micro-, macro-, and intermediate levels of society" (Turner, 2001:233). This theory refers to roles as a behaviour that complies with predefined positions instead of players who enact them (Biddle, 1906). Turner (2001) notes that role is defined as the dynamic aspect of status, such that a role is attached to every status in society and every role is attached to a status. Status is described as a position in a society that includes a designated collection of rights and obligations (Van der Horst, n.d). Coon and Travis (2012) note there are three components of roles: the prescribed role (expected behaviour of an actor), the subjective role (how the actor believes he should behave), and the enacted role (how the actor actually behaves). Given the nature of cyberbullying such as anonymity of perpetrators as discussed in section 2.7, the role of the police in combating mobile bully-victims is jeopardised. Role focuses on a limited set of actions that characterise people in a context (Masolo *et al.*, 2004). Other studies have extended the definition of role to include social status, and expected behaviour, which also includes exhibited behaviour (Sesen, 2015). Masolo *et al.* (2004) note social role includes a set of rights, an act carried out by a person, and set of expected behaviours.

Role theory describes the expected behaviour from individuals based on their social position (Banto, 1996; Bazana and Dodd, 2013), which provides predictive information about how well individuals carry out their work (Friedman and Allen, 2011). In this proposed study, role theory can assist in determining what the law enforcement is doing in fighting mobile bully-victim behaviour in schools. Prinsloo (2005) notes that police officers have been invited to help prevent crime in schools. As such the police's role is to provide protection for the society; however, there is disagreement about what the role of the police is in schools that stems from prescribed and subjective roles (Coon and Travis, 2012). Role strain also related to role stress pertains to challenges that are encountered in performing a given role and that an individual may not be well equipped to perform that role (Henning and Weidner, 2008). The source of role strains can be associated with role conflict, role overload, role ambiguity, role incompetence, and role incongruity (Henning and Weidner, 2008; Mobily, 1991). The law enforcement agents need to keep gaining a working knowledge about new technologies and their uses to successfully prevent mobile bully-victim behaviour (Thaxter, 2010). Role strain in this case will help to draw inferences on difficulties that the law enforcement experience in combating mobile bully-victim behaviour. Little is known about the enacted role of the police in schools (Coon and Travis, 2012). The identification of those challenges can help to ameliorate the identified difficulties for law enforcement in dealing with mobile bully-victim behaviour.

2.9   Theoretical integration – Suggestion

While the theories discussed above shed light on the phenomenon of mobile bully-victim behaviour, the aims of this study are not adequately supported. Wieringa (2014) described the relationship between Design Science and a knowledge context, stating that the knowledge context that initiates a Design Science Research includes scientific theories, design specification, useful facts, practical knowledge and common sense. This knowledge context is known as prior knowledge. "The set of scientific theories used as prior knowledge in a design research project is called its theoretical framework" Wieringa (2014:93). The functions of scientific theories include the use of conceptual frameworks to frame phenomena (Wieringa, 2014). Therefore, theories were used to construct a conceptual framework that will guide the design and development of proposed mobile app. "In addition to framing a design problem, conceptual frameworks can be used to frame a research problem" (Wieringa, 2014: 86). Figure 1 depicts the proposed conceptual framework to enhance the effectiveness of law enforcement in fighting mobile bully-victim behaviour. This framework argues the need for a *mobile bully-victim behaviour app* tailored to aid law enforcement agents as the main aim of this study. The framework presents constructs from the literature review and the role theory, the primary factor along selected behavioural theories in this proposed study.

The dependent variable is "the effectiveness of law enforcement in combating mobile bully-victim behaviour" and constructs on the left are the independent variables. Role theory helped to identify requirements to make the law enforcement effective in fighting mobile bully-victim behaviour (see Role theory in section 2.8.6). These include maintaining a working knowledge of new technologies and social networking sites to deal with mobile bully-victim. Thus *diagnose mobile bully-victim behaviour* construct arises from the challenge to successfully identify mobile bully-victim behaviour (see section 2.1), which is worsened by the anonymity provided in using technology. Additionally, social information processing theory suggests children may interpret ambiguous situations as threats (see Social information processing theory in section 2.8.3). Therefore, confirmation and *severity assessment of mobile bully-victim behaviour* will help to inform a suitable way to *resolve mobile bully-victim behaviour incidents*. Law enforcement agents can use the proposed app to verify ambiguous incidents, and prevent possible retaliation in valid situations.

Children are concerned about entertaining their online friends so much that they do not think about the effects of their actions on others (Shariff, 2015). Sometimes children may be enticed to share personal information or semi-nude pictures with online friends, which can incite bullying from their peers if publicised (Shariff, 2015). In this case, the incited cyberbullies would simply be reacting with disgust to the sighting. Shariff (2008) notes children know how to use technology appropriately, but not efficiently, so they get into trouble while seeking fame. Therefore, adults should observe how children use technology, work with them and provide coaching so that children can be proud of how they use it, instead of paying attention to children's use of technology only when they get into trouble. However, teenagers avoid being friends with their parents on social media (Shariff, 2015). Probably this is one of the reasons children fall prey to cyberbullying because they lack supervision. The Theory of Planned Behaviour (see section 2.8.5) is seen as one of the vehicles that enable targeted interventions against cyberbullying by soliciting influential individuals' support for victims. With regard to the proposed framework in this study, the identification of mobile bully-victims' influential traits could initiate interventions to curb this behaviour. This can be achieved by identifying influential mobile bully-victims for targeted intervention. The social status of influential mobile bully-victims could be safely and effectively identified using sociometrics (Cillessen and Marks, 2017; García Bacete and Cillessen, 2017), in order to enable targeted intervention.

Children need to be assured of their safety so that they can report mobile bully-victim behaviour incidents without fear of negative repercussions (see Smith in Mobile bully-victim in section 2.3.2; General strain theory in section 2.8.4). Hence, *enabling safe bully-victim disclosure* is imperative, and this process will in turn help to *instil trust on mobile bully-victims.*

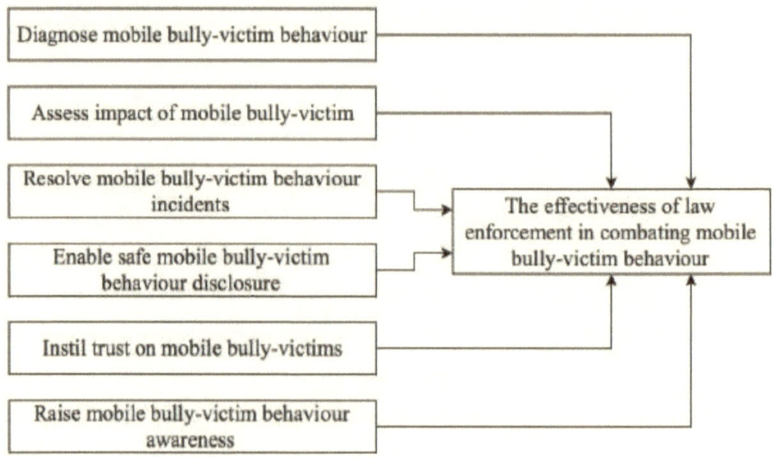

Figure 1: Conceptual framework for effective mobile bully-victim behaviour combat (adapted from Mtshazi and Kyobe, 2014)

The social ecological theory posits that personal traits of children interact with environmental context to promote or curb victimisation and perpetration (see Social-ecological theory in section 2.8.1). Thus *raising mobile bully-victim behaviour awareness* can help to discourage misbehaviour among children and identify pitfalls in school systems that permit mobile bully-victim behaviour. Also social learning theory posits that deviant behaviours are learnt through interactions and communications with other people (see Social learning theory in section 2.8.2). Counter measures can be enabled through law enforcement interactions with school system to discourage mobile bully-victim behaviour stemming from needs to gain social status, resource control, and to rid negative self-esteem (see Social rank theory in section 2.8.2.1; Resource control theory in section 2.8.2.2; and Self-concept theory in section 2.8.2.3).

Social information processing theory suggests children, especially those who are bullied (Lereya, *et al.*, 2015) may interpret ambiguous situations as threats (see Social information processing theory in section 2.8.3). Law enforcement agents can use a mobile app to help verify ambiguous incidents. A successful and valid diagnosis of such incidents will help *instil trust in victims* and *encourage reporting mobile bully-victims behaviours*.

These constructs serve as the basis for the design requirement, which also translates into the design specification of the artefact. Overall, the solution's process for mobile bully-victims starts with identifying mobile bully-victim perpetrators, and then assessing the impact of their behaviour. Burton (2016) notes in the South African context, most of common cyberbullying perpetrators are peers of learners, within and outside schools, and are generally known to their victims. Hence, the identification process involves polling students' participation (these will include reporting incidents) in mobile bully-victim behaviour. García Bacete and Cillessen (2017) note rating is less amenable to identification of sociometric groups than nominations. Hence peer nomination and self-nomination are used for this study. A sociogram will be created to identify learners with high proximity prestige for mobile bully-victim behaviour. Then the mobile bully-victim assessment matrix will be used to evaluate the impact of mobile bully-victim incidents on the identified learners. Also learners will be afforded an opportunity to confirm nomination along the assessment matrix. In the end, the report of the process can be used to inform corrective and remedial steps on identified mobile bully-victims.

Children often do not realise that their impulsive and joke actions of online postings could land them with legal liabilities, risking turning every youthful regret into a criminal act (Shariff and Chan, 2013). Therefore, realisation of a proposed solution to develop a mobile app artefact that can be used to facilitate peer- and self-nominations, severity evaluation on nominees, and produce reports, in order to enable resolving the mobile bully-victims behaviour restoratively. While child pornography offenders are often predators, adolescents who supposedly from flirting and joking intents commit sexting should not be subjected to the same legal actions (Shariff, 2015; Shariff and Chan, 2013). This suggests that a different approach is required to address teenage offenders, such as the application of restorative justice. As also suggested by Thaxter (2010), bringing charges against mobile bully-victims should be considered only after preventive interventions and awareness attempts have failed. Similary, Reyneke and Jacobs (2018: 78) posit, "the law is only one of the vehicles that can be used to address bullying and it should in all likelihood be regarded as the last option that should be used to address the issue" of bullying. Therefore, the Bullying Prevention

Advisory Group (2015) suggest using restorative justice to resolve the bullying incidents, and raising awareness about unacceptable uses of mobile device.

Although online interventions provide support for victims with others that experienced the same problems, they should be complemented with adults to oversee, verify, and provide guidance should suicidal or inappropriate ideas arise (Tłuściak-Deliowska, 2018). Literature suggests that interventions that work well are those fostering cooperation of bully-victims (Rigby, 2010; Volk *et al.*, 2012; Tłuściak-Deliowska, 2018). Hence, this study seeks to explore the moderated (cooperative) intervention where the police moderate the reporting of learners' involvement in cyberbullying. Hence, this framework assumes that "the presence and cooperation" of the bully-victim with the adult – in this case the police – is required in order to address mobile bully-victims behaviour (Tłuściak-Deliowska, 2018: 40-41).

Hence, while the app's report will provide entry points to addressing mobile bully-victims incidents, the app usage will also help to raise awareness. The app reports will also be used to strengthen evidence of reported cases as well as advising schools to include policies to regulate mobile bully-victim behaviour in their code of conduct. Additionally, the app will provide a platform for learners to report mobile bullying, without fear of being victimised.

An Information Technology (IT) artefact is defined as "an object, or a bundle thereof, intentionally engineered to benefit certain people with certain purpose and goal in certain contexts" (Zhang, Scialdone and Ku, 2011: 3). IT Artefacts can be categorised as product and process artefacts (Farib, Asadullah, and Mior Nasir, 2017; Venable, Pries-Heje and Baskerville, 2012). Product artefacts include tools, diagrams, and software used by people to complete tasks. On the other hand, process artefacts are methods and procedures providing guidance for accomplishing tasks. Furthermore, artefacts can be purely technical, requiring no people to operate, while socio-technical artefacts require people to use them in order to complete tasks (Venable *et al.*, 2012).

2.10 Strategies for dealing with mobile bully-victim behaviour

The literature is clear about the difficulty of identifying mobile bully-victim behaviour, and lack of clarity about the role of law enforcement activities in addressing this phenomenon. Therefore, a possible way identify mobile bully-victims is to measure mobile bully-victims' social network, along with the bully assessment matrix (Cool School Programme, 2001; Volk, Veenstra and Espelage, 2017). This approach could inform the design and development of a mobile bully-victim app as an intervention instrument. This section presents discussion on the mobile bully-victim sociogram and bully-victim assessment matrix.

2.10.1 *Diagnosing mobile bully-victim behaviour*

Researchers usually measure learners' involvement in bullying using data from those who are closer to the action through self- and peer-reports or peer nomination (Solberg and Olweus, 2003; Veenstra *et al.*, 2005; Volk, Veenstra and Espelage, 2017:37). The Olweus' global measures use a two-item questionnaire with a two- or three-month cut-off. Self-report methods rely on personal experience instances and provide indications of bullying prevalence, but they lack an indication of involved children (Phillips and Cornell, 2012). On the other hand, peer-reports rely on observed experiences, and help to avoid "single-source biases" (Volk *et al.*, 2017: 37). Peer-reports can be used in conjunction with self-reports as a diagnosis method; however, the accuracy of peer-reports needs to be validated (Phillips and Cornell, 2012). Volk *et al.* (2017:38) proposed a synergy of the two report measures, combining their strengths while balancing their flaws. Also, Phillips and Cornell (2012) suggest, with some validation measures, such as nomination confirmation, peer nomination and self-reports can be used to identify victims of bullying. This combination is known as "principle of aggregation" that could "offer more breadth, reliability, and construct validity" (Volk *et al.*, 2017: 38; Ossenkopp and Mazmanian, 1985). Lee and Cornell (2009) note data elicitation from multiple sources reduces measurement error and increase reliability for peer nomination. Also, confirmation is essential for the reports; however, custom ways such as use of counsellors are confined by lack of time (Phillips and Cornell, 2012). Similarly, bullies can be identified by providing their victims with a list of names of all their classmates, and asking them questions that lead to identification of their bullies (Huitsing and Veenstra, 2012; Volk *et al.* 2017). This way, bullies can also identify their bullies, and according to the definition of bully-victims their status may change from pure bullies to bully-victims. Similarly, learners can reciprocate nomination (Huitsing and Veenstra, 2012), which can in turn indicate mobile bully-victims. Basically, learners who are nominated as bullies "as well as reporting being victimized themselves" can be an indication of bully-victims (Volk *et al*. 2017: 38).

2.10.2 Mobile bully-victim sociogram

Similar to the measurement of groups' social relationships, the identification of mobile bullies, victims, and bully-victims can be done using sociometrics. Sociometric measurement is facilitated through peer nominations within a group, such as a class or grade (Cillessen and Marks, 2017). The questions that are used on sociometric measurements are called criteria, and they include affective and reputational criteria (Cillessen *et al.*, 2017).   The affective criteria are subjective to the nominator personally, and they seek to reveal interpersonal feelings or relationships whereas reputational criteria measure perceived behaviour instead of personal evaluations. Sociometric statuses of learners such as "popular, rejected, controversial, neglected, and average", are used to infer learners' acceptance among their peers (Coie, Dodge, and Coppotelli, 1982; Rytioja, Lappalainen and Savolainen, 2019). The data emerging from peer nomination can be used to visualise results in a sociogram.

Similarly, sociograms (social networks) can help authorities to identify bullies and victims in classrooms (Huitsing and Veenstra, 2012). A sociogram is a sociometric diagram that depicts patterns of groups' relationships, and usually indicates which person is preferred to interact with (Salcedo, Salcedo, Pinningho, and Contreras, 2011). Sentse, Kretschmer, and Salmivalli (2015) note sociometric status is conceptualised by peer acceptance and rejection. Sociometric status is commonly assessed through peer-nomination, self-nomination, teacher rating, parent rating or observation (Cillessen and Marks, 2017; García Bacete and Cillessen, 2017). In peer- and self-nomination, learners select others or themselves from a list of names based on certain criteria. The Cool School Programme (2001) describes bullying sociogram as method as asking individuals a series of questions intended to reveal social dynamics in a group, thus uncovering favourable and unfavourable influences in the group. The aims of the bullying sociogram include:

- To prevent bullying by raising awareness of the undesirable behaviour in the group, even if no problems are discovered.
- To provide a safe disclosure of emerging and existing bullying incidents.

- To identify at-risk students, power structures between students, and their involvement.

- To investigate reported bullying instances and to reduce the possibilities of retaliation.

- To provide guidelines to ease the process of noting, recording and investigating bullying.

A study by Salced *et al.* (2011: 150) investigated "a mechanism that can help to distribute students in a classroom, based on their potential bullying capabilities". They identified troublesome learners based on learner's perception and teachers experience, and created a sociogram depicting structures of relationships within small groups. Álvarez-Bermejo *et al.* (2016) also studied the prevention and detection of bullying incited by racial stigma in schools using a gamified system which stored interaction data between students on the application server, and used sociograms to infer the interactions among students.

The construction of a sociogram takes about 15 minutes, and includes asking students which peers they would like to associate with in a specific activity, or with which they would rather not meet (Salced *et al.*, 2011). A node on a graph represents each student, and lines between two nodes represent a relationship (Zhang *et al.*, 2014). Nodes can have a direct relationship, and a relationship linked through another node (indirect relationships). A percentage of influence is obtained through direct links and indirect links in a group (Zhang *et al.*, 2014). Similarly, a high number of in-degree connections indicate a menace based on student perceptions (Salced *et al.*, 2011). Also, in social networks this method is referred to as centrality or proximity prestige, "a composite representation of the quantity and the closeness of children's direct and indirect friends" (Zhang *et al.*, 2014: 513).

2.10.3 Mobile Bully-victim assessment matrix

In addition to polling to identify mobile bully-victims, learners can be asked about the intensity, power imbalance, and whether the victimisation was intentional, goal-directed, proactive or reactive (Volk *et al.*, 2017). Once mobile bully-victims have been identified through a mobile bully-victim behavioural sociogram, a bullying assessment matrix is used to confirm bullying behaviour, evaluate its severity, and inform corrective steps. The bullying assessment matrix provided by Bullying

Prevention Advisory Group (2015: 8) is used "to assess the severity and impacts of bullying behaviour that requires a formal response". This matrix involves three assessment factors about bullying instances: (1) severity, (2) impact, and (3) frequency. Each factor has three rating scales: (1) moderate with a yellow tag, (2) major with an orange tag, and (3) severe with a red tag. The sum of all these rating scales for the assessment factors is 9. Incidents that score between 8 and 9 are severe, while those that score between 6 and 7 are major, and scores between 3 and 5 indicate moderate incidents. However, any factor rated as severe (3) is automatically tagged red (severe). Amid the lack of professionals' availability to authenticate identify mobile bully-victims necessary in peer-nominations (Phillips and Cornell, 2012), the assessment matrix can be used to evaluate and infer the severity effect of the behaviour.

Chapter 3 – Research methodology

3.1   Introduction

This chapter discusses the methodology that was followed to investigate and test the application that is designed to aid the role of law enforcement in combating mobile bully-victims behaviour in high schools. A methodology is described as application of system of principles, practices, and processes to a particular division of knowledge (Peffers, Tuunanen, Rothenberger and Chatterjee, 2007), while "embracing philosophy, assumptions about validity, and sometimes preferred methods" (Bazeley, 2013:8). Generally, Information Systems (IS) research methodologies consist of three categories, namely, quantitative methodology, qualitative methodology, and design science methodology (Nazir Ahmad, Colomb and Ibrahim, 2012). Then the paradigm and philosophical stance from which the current study was conducted, as well as methods, strategies and purpose are presented. Also, data collection and analysis, the sampling technique, research instruments, ethical concerns, and time-line are presented.

3.2   Philosophical stances: Ontological and epistemological

Philosophy is derived from the Greek word meaning "love of wisdom" (Warburton, 2012: 26), and is described as "a way of thinking about certain sorts of question using logical arguments". Brier (2015) states the primary aim of philosophy is creation of a particular knowledge, through critical examination of the basis of beliefs, prejudices, and methods used in sciences. Deleuze and Guattari (1994) note philosophy as a practice of creating, discovering, and producing concepts. Also "philosophy is primarily concerned with rigorously establishing, regulating and improving the methods of knowledge-creation in all fields of intellectual endeavour" (Partinton, 2002).

Knowledge creation involves actively cutting, drawing out and constructing social reality from an initially unintelligible fluid of interactions and sense impressions. These isolated parts of social reality are then identified, labelled and causally linked to other parts of our experiences in order to form a coherent system of explanation. It is, thus, through this process of differentiating, cutting out, naming, labelling, classifying and relating that modern knowledge is systematically constructed.

In essence "knowledge is therefore produced through this process of selective abstraction, identification and recombination" (Partinton, 2002: 223).

"Philosophical thinking revolves around the four pillars of metaphysics, logic, epistemology and ethics" (Partinton, 2002). Metaphysics attempts to comprehend the reality of phenomena (Brier, 2015). Morgan (2007) refers to the tripartite linkage of ontology, epistemology, and methodology as metaphysics paradigm, and notes that it includes axiology. Axiology is associated with the study of values. Logic is concerned with methods used to capture and extract universal generalisations about how things interact in reality (Partinton, 2002). Ontology originates from metaphysics and philosophy, and its use explains the nature of the reality (De Vasconcelos, Gouveia, and Kimble, 2016).

Ontology is a knowledge repository that provides definitions of concepts and terms as well as how these concepts are linked (Li, Xu, Zhang and Lau, 2014; Nazir Ahmad, Colomb and Ibrahim, 2012). Gruber (1993) defines ontology as a consensual and explicit specification of a shared conceptualisation. Bishop (2015) notes two distinct ontologies, realist and relativist. The realist ontology entails a knowable reality that is independent from our creation of it (Smith, 2006). That is the technology of knowing is the only limit to attaining unbiased knowledge. As such the discovery of universal laws that govern behaviour requires objective measurements. On the other hand, relativist ontology entails the belief that the world is only knowable through conceptual frameworks embedded in different cultures, individuals, and research process (Bishop, 2015), and this knowledge is subjectively uncovered. Another research paradigm branch known as pragmatism posits, "objectivist and subjectivist perspectives are not mutually exclusive" (Wahyuni, 2012: 71). As such pragmatism guides a fruitful mixture of approaches such as ontology and epistemology to understand social phenomena (Wahyuni, 2012). Therefore pragmatism is selected as the ontological stance for the proposed study. While ontology is a study concerned with being – "the nature of reality", epistemology focuses on knowing (Partinton, 2002: 2; Symon and Cassell, 2012; Ramaprasad, Syn and Thirumalai, 2014; Simon, 2015). Epistemological studies involve reflection about methods and standards used to produces reliable and verifiable (Partinton, 2002).

The philosophical stances known as competing research approaches are positivism and constructivism epistemologies (Morgan, 2007). Traditionally quantitative research approaches are positivist or post-positivist inclined epistemologies, while qualitative research approaches take constructionist or interpretive epistemologies (Bishop, 2015). The challenge between researchers who adopt positivist paradigm versus constructionist paradigm stem in distinctions between realism and relativism beliefs, which influence the design, process, and evaluation of researches (Bishop, 2015). Although interpretivist and pragmatism are two possible and important research paradigms for qualitative research in information systems (Goldkuhl, 2012). These research paradigms do not drive towards a practical problem solving. However, pragmatism is not concerned with the epistemological differences between realism and relativism, it advocates "a shared research – to produce positive change in the world" (Bishop, 2015: 7).

Pragmatism views scientific truths as conditional and can be obtained through various sources of experience and experimentation, and knowledge is constructed and grounded in the world (Bishop, 2015). Morgan (2007: 66) proposes that pragmatism definitions concentrate on three "concepts such as lines of action and warranted assertions, along with general emphasis on workability". Lines of actions relate to actual behaviour, warranted assertions relates to beliefs that support those behaviours, and workability is associated to the consequences that are likely to be produced by different behaviours.

Researchers have not yet reached consensus about the definition of cyberbullying (El Asam and Samara, 2016), except noting the use of electronic communication technologies (Kowalski, *et al.*, 2014) particularly mobile phones. Also cyberbullying researches are still at infancy "most studies are mere reports of prevalence rates and concurrent relationships among factors with cross-sectional data" (You and Lim, 2016:173). Since a pragmatic approach focuses not on notions of perfect understanding among people on earth, but on how much shared understanding can be accomplished and kinds of shared lines of behaviours possible from the consensual understanding thereof (Morgan, 2007). Also mobile bully-victim behaviour is an ever-changing phenomenon, hence pragmatism is a suitable epistemological stance for this study.

3.3 Overview

This study followed the framework by Hevner (2007), which consist of three iterative cycles as shown in Figure 2. The framework starts off with the relevance cycle, which helps to understand end-user environment through interactions such as focus groups and interviews. The *rigour cycle* involves evaluation of artefacts and theories to make contribution in design science and application domain knowledge base. The *design cycle* focuses on artefact creation and its evaluation.

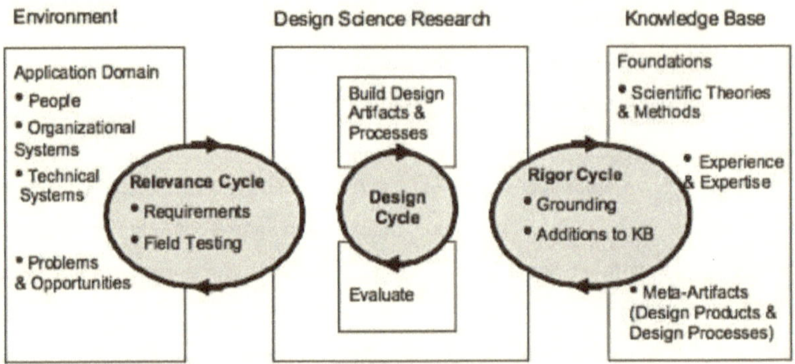

Figure 2: Design science research cycles (Hevner, 2007)

DSR approach allows construction of a new artefact stemming from specific requirements and underlying theory (Turber and Smiela, 2014). Defining requirements helps to review prior approaches (Turber and Smiela, 2014). Following the design cycles (Hevner, 2007), the checklist regarding the structure and sequence of activities in this study is presented in Table 1. The sequence specifies the Design Science Research Methodology (DSRM) activities, design science phases, applied methods and selected tools, activities with methods, and output (Wieringa, 2014).

Peffers *et al.* (2008) describe the knowledge base for each of the DSRM activities:
In the problem identification and motivation activity, the knowledge base includes literature review of studies that investigate about the phenomenon and a series of papers that explore the identified problem. This can help to understand the problem's relevance, its existing solutions and their limitations (weaknesses). A well-defined

problem assists in developing an effective artefact to optimise the problem, while a suitable justification of the artefact' value encourages the researcher to attempt to find solution and accept the outcomes thereof (Farib *et al.*, 2017). The definition of the problem helps to infer objectives.

Table 1: Study Structure

DSRM Activities	Phase	Methods/ Techniques	Activities	Output
Identify problem and Motivate	Problem awareness	Literature review Workshops	Systematic literature review	Research problem and questions Conceptual framework
Define objective of a solution	Suggestion	Expert evaluation Case study - *Exploratory focus groups*	Discuss concepts with book supervisor (Turber and Smiela, 2014) Analyse focus groups transcripts Confirm preliminary requirements	Concepts validation Design requirements
Design and development	Development	Prototyping	Create use case diagrams, UML and code	Artefact
Demonstration and Evaluation (summative and formative)	Evaluation and Validation	Action research - *Surveys* - *Experimentation* - *Confirmatory focus groups*	Assess artefact's design using triangulation	Requirements and design refinements Descriptive analysis of reports, focus groups transcripts, and surveys. Action research validity Utility evaluation results
Communication	Conclusion	Findings compilation	Document result	Discussion, conclusion and recommendations. Research results are disseminated to the intended audience, both as academic output and artefact usage guidelines.

The *definition of objectives activity* knowledge base includes knowing how possible and feasible the solution is. Also the knowledge of available methods, technologies, and theories that could be used to define objectives is essential. The output of this activity include design requirement for the proposed artefact solution (Mtsweni, Biermann and Pretorius, 2014; Farib *et al.*, 2017). These requirements are created as an attempt to address the research question: What are current problems faced by the police in addressing mobile bully-victim behaviour in schools? The artefact requirements were first based on the conceptual model for diagnosing mobile bully-victims in schools, and were further refined through usability tests and focus group discussions with the target users.

The *design and development activity* require knowledge for applying methods, technologies, and theories in the creation of an artefact that addresses a problem. The artefact in this study was built based on agile methodology with rapid prototyping methods, as also recommended by Koppenhagen *et al.*, (2012). Agile methodology is an adaptive software development life cycle that focuses on artefact creation and clarifying requirements simultaneously. Koppenhagen *et al.*, (2012) suggest using artefact concept version and artefact prototype version (APV) as a method to build artefacts, which support DSR iterative approach. This approach allows staged development that continuously adds functionalities on the artefact until completion. The innovative artefact in the form of a mobile application was designed and developed based on the conceptual model for diagnosing mobile bully-victims in schools. Attempts to balance norms in academic rigour against the practicalities of real-world development limit innovation in DSR (Conboy, Gleasure and Cullina, 2015). Conboy *et al.* (2015: 169) note the solution to this limitation is "agile development, in which design practices react and adjust to changing user requirements while maintaining more dynamic structures for managing resources and software quality". Also, Kirmani (2017) notes agile development is suitable for small to medium sized projects. Agile approaches use a develop-deliver-feedback cycles, which accommodate changing requirements by facilitating communication between the developer and users (Flora and Chande, 2013). The iterative nature of agile approaches reduces the risk of developing software that is misaligned to the market needs. Also agile processes are suitable for mobile applications (app) development, and adhere to customer satisfaction through early and frequent delivery of working software as primary measure of progress (Flora and Chande, 2013; Kirmani, 2017). The adjustments of agile enable flexible software processes, continual learning and adaptations to changing requirements and technologies (Kirmani, 2017). The method adopted for the current study is lean software development (LSD), which focuses on continual learning and development while reducing waste, such as a waiting time (Kirmani, 2017). LSD avoids cluttering products with nice to have features that do not add value to users, and unnecessary code and functions (Kirmani, 2017). Lean software development consist of five principles (Rodríguez, Partanen, Kuvaja and Oivo, 2014):

- *Value* focuses on producing artefacts that have value to the organisation, and avoids waste by removing items that consume resource, but producing no value.
- *Value stream* ensures that each activity produce customer value, through end-to-end collection of required action.
- *Flow* avoids value stream discontinuity by organising activities as a continuous flow to foster smoother delivery.
- *Pull* implies that products or parts thereof are made available just in time as required by the customer.
- *Perfection* focuses on continuous improvement to ensure zero defects.

The *demonstration activity* requires knowledge for using the artefact to solve the problem. The use of the artefact in solving the problem or achieving its contextual purpose is demonstrated with regard to feasibility, using ex ante evaluation (Venable, Pries-Heje and Baskerville, 2012).

The *evaluation activity* depends on knowledge of relevant matrices and evaluation techniques. Also the feasibility of the solution is compared to the original goal of the artefact. Evaluation requires knowledge of suitable matrices, and appropriate data collection and analysis, in order to demonstrate artefact's utility and efficacy (Hevner, March, Park and Ram, 2004).

The *communication activity* requires knowing about the discipline's culture. In this study the presentation of the book clarifies the contributions to knowledge base.

Relevance cycle

For this cycle the problem relevance was established through literature review, from which a conceptual model was developed. This conceptual model was validated by developing a mobile application that was also validated through focus group discussions, usability tests, and a survey (Koppenhagen, Gaß and Müller, 2012; Lowdermilk, 2013; Schnall *et al.*, 2014). The analysis of focus groups was carried out using thematic analysis, while usability data was quantified in analysis, and the descriptive statistics was used to analyse the survey data. Also, Social Network Analysis was conducted on reports (digital trace data) that were produced through learners' interactions with the mobile app (Zorrilla and de Lima Silva, 2019). Within the relevance cycle the requirement analysis was performed, which helped to establish requirements for the identified (proposed) solution. Requirements entail statements that pinpointed "necessary attributes, capabilities, characteristics, or quality of a system for it to have value and utility to a user" (Koppenhagen, Gaß and Müller, 2012). Requirements description is necessary to inform design decision of the solution, in short they are design guidelines. The constructs of the conceptual model that emanated from Literature review (see Theoretical integration in Chapter 2) were in turn transformed into the initial set of the artefact requirements and design principles. Then participants' comments from focus groups discussions and artefact tests helped with refinement of the initial requirements and design principles (Koppenhagen, Katz, Maedche, and Müller, 2011). A decision about what to do refers to design principles, while documentation of decisions refers to requirements specification (Wieringa, 2014). Also relevance is concerned with determining whether the research outcomes are useful, to theory, practice, or further research (Venable and Baskerville, 2012).

Rigour cycle

The focal point of the rigour cycle is selecting methods (Gregor and Hevner, 2013). Therefore rigour focused on the reliability of research and ensuring that established research methods are followed (Venable and Baskerville, 2012). This cycle helped to identify theories and methods for the design and evaluation of the artefact. The theories and methods were identified through a review of existing studies that used or designed mobile technologies and applications to address cyberbullying or mobile bullying in schools (Gregor and Hevner, 2013). Also, as discussed in section 5.2, the researcher conducted an ecological scan of existing applications that are used to address mobile bullying in schools.

3.4　Design science research methodology

Research is a process of systematic inquiry that is designed to collect, analyse, interpret, and use data (Mertens, 2010). Some of the characteristics that differentiate research from acquiring knowledge purely by experience and reasoning include (William, 2001):

- Research is systematic and controlled, rather than acquiring experience in uncontrolled and haphazard manner.
- Research is empirical and leans on experience and the surrounding world for validation, instead of abstract reasoning that is not linked to reality.
- Unlike experience and reason, research is self-correcting allowing rigorous testing of results, and public scrutiny and criticism of methods and results.

Design Science Research (DSR) is a new paradigm that was recognised in the Information System mainstream in 2004 (Gregor and Hevner, 2013; Hevner, March, Park and Ram, 2004). DSR is defined as creation and evaluation of IT artefacts to offer solutions to understood research problems (Peffers, Tuunanen, Rothenberger, and Chatterjee, 2007). Researchers who use design science paradigm, mainly choose design-theory or pragmatic-design methods (Gregor and Hevner, 2013). DSR is pragmatic in nature as it places emphasis on relevance with a clear contribution to the application environment (Hevner, 2007). Epistemologically, Design Science researchers are pragmatists, supported by information on predictably functioning artefacts (Vaishnavi and Kuechler, 2015). That is the evaluation of an artefact's behaviour against information – the description of components interaction, by the degree the artefact behaves predictably confirms the information.

Iivari (2007) states design science research is basically done at three levels: (1) a conceptual level, (2) a descriptive level, and (3) a prescriptive level. Hence, each research level produces different kinds of knowledge and truth-values (Sonnenberg and Vom Brocke, 2012). Conceptual knowledge captures "what things are out there" in terms of concepts, constructs, conceptual frameworks, classification, taxonomies, or typologies. Descriptive and prescriptive researches build upon the foundation formed by conceptual knowledge (Sonnenberg and Vom Brocke, 2012). Descriptive research is concerned with describing, understanding, and explaining, "how things are out there". "Prescriptive research yields prescriptive knowledge in the form of IT artefact (design product knowledge) and recommendations for practice (design process knowledge)" (Sonnenberg and Vom Brocke, 2012: 382).

Hevner and Chatterjee (2010) describe design in information systems as developing software artefacts that address a human problem in an efficient and useful way. Also design is an innovative creation of non-existent artefact using new knowledge (Vaishnavi and Kuechler, 2015). Innovative design involves conducting research to fill the gap and result in research publication, that is design science (Vaishnavi and Kuechler, 2015). In essence, DSR constitute learning along the creation and implementation of an artefact. Thus the fundamental principle of DS is that knowledge and understanding of a design problem and its solution are acquired in building and application of an artefact (Hevner and Chatterjee, 2010). Lukka (2003) states constructive research approach includes:

- Addressing real-world problems that are identified as relevant.
- Innovation drives the construction of artefacts that solve the identified real-world problem
- Implementation of the artefact is also used to test its efficiency and utility
- Experiential learning takes place along a team-like co-operation between the research and practitioners
- A clear and detailed prior theoretical knowledge is inherent, and
- Then empirical findings are reflected back to theory.

DSR consists of two parts, design and investigation, that correspond to two kinds of research problems, design problems and knowledge questions (Wieringa, 2014). Design problems' aim is to change the world and involves analysis of real or hypothetical stakeholders. On the other hand, knowledge questions search for knowledge about the world in its current state. Table 2 provides heuristics that differentiate design problems from knowledge problems.

A problem can create new and different kind of problems, which form iterations over design problems and knowledge problems in DSR (Wieringa, 2014). This allows a sequence that starts from a design problem, then asking knowledge questions about the artefact. For instance, probing the artefact's performance and effects on entities in the problem context. "The knowledge-question-answering activity returns knowledge to the design problem-solving activity" (Wieringa, 2014: 6). Similarly, a quest to answer a knowledge question can lead to new design problem, such as creating a prototype, to stimulate its context.

Table 2: Heuristics to distinguish design problems from knowledge problems (Wieringa, 2014)

Design problems	Knowledge questions
Inspire to change the world	Search for knowledge about the world
Design is seen as a solution	Answer is reached by proposition
Many solutions may be designed	Only one answer
Evaluation focuses of utility	Truth informs evaluation
Stakeholder goals informs utility	Stakeholder goals do not inform truth

DSR consists of seven steps for carrying out research, and ensuring validity and rigour in the development of IT artefact and its evaluation (Hevner, *et al.*, 2004; Peffers *et al.*, 2007). These guidelines include (Hevner *et al.,* 2004):

(1) *Design as an artefact*: artefact refers to an instantiated object, an existing artificial model or process such as models and software (Gregor and Hevner, 2013).

The objective of the current study was to create a mobile application for law enforcement agents (South African Police) to aid combating mobile bully-victim behaviour in schools.

(2) *Problem relevance* deals with clear articulation of the research problem to real world practice (Gregor and Hevner, 2013). Design science research's objective is to develop technological artefacts to address essential and relevant problems (Hevner, March, Park and Ram, 2004).

DSR's objective is to develop technological artefacts to address essential and relevant problems (Hevner, March, Park and Ram, 2004). The problem relevance in this study is centred on the difficulty of diagnosing mobile bully-victim behaviour. As noted in the problem definition in this study, mobile bully-victim behaviour swings between pure bullies and victims. Also, this phenomenon has been studied from learners', teachers' and parents' perspectives. However, research about law enforcement's involvement in South Africa is lacking.

(3) *Design evaluation*, Hevner (2007: 91) notes "the essence of Information Systems as design science lay in the scientific evaluation of artefacts". Design science research involves multiple iterations of the design cycle before output is passed to relevance and rigour cycles (Hevner, 2007). The artefact must be tested in experimental situation and laboratory before it is released for testing in the field.

A prototype of a mobile application (app) was designed by the researcher and iteratively improved. The usefulness and functional effectiveness of the mobile application were then evaluated through a questionnaire, focus groups and the app's reports (Goodhue, Klein and March, 2000; Jungherr, Schoen, Posegga and Jürgens, 2017).

(4) *Research contribution* of DSR paradigm is mainly in a form of design theory or artefacts, which Gregor and Hevner (2013) view as complementary perspectives. DS contribution to knowledge may include theory development. Also, "contributions to knowledge could be partial theory, incomplete theory, or even some particularly interesting and perhaps surprising empirical generalization in the form of a new design artefact" (Gregor and Hevner, 2013: 339).

The contribution of this study was the development of the mobile application as a reporting platform for identification of mobile bully-victims and measurement of severity this behaviour caused on the identified learners. Other contributions were theoretical, including a conceptual framework regarding law enforcement needs in their fight against mobile bully-victims behaviour, and documentation of the design process based on DS was valuable for practice.

(5) *Research rigour*, Hevner (2007) posits a good DSR is defined by the synergy between relevance cycle and rigor cycle as well as their contributions. Also, "research rigour in design science is predicated on the researcher's skilled choice and application of suitable theories and methods for constructing and evaluating the artefact" (Hevner, 2007: 90).

In this study, rigour will be ensured through the selection and application of appropriate methods and theories within the DSR methodology (Peffers *et al.*, 2007).

(6) *Design as a research process*, "design is inherently an iterative and incremental activity" (Hevner *et al.*, 2004: 85). It involves a cyclical generation of design alternatives and testing the alternatives against requirements until a satisfactory design is produced (Hevner, 2007). As such design is a process of discovering an effective solution to a problem (Hevner *et al.*, 2004). Problem solving involves the use of available means to achieve expected outcomes while adhering to existing laws of the environment (Simon, 1996).

This study included the design of a prototype that seeks to improve current applications. The design process of the application was continuously subjected to evaluation for improvement feedback.

(7) *Communication* of research pertains to presentation of research effectively both to managerial and technical audiences (Hevner *et al.*, 2004). The completed book will be presented both to managerial and technical audiences in a clear manner.

There are different models available for use in DSR (Vaishnavi and Kuechler, 2015; Wieringa, 2014). Vaishnavi and Kuechler's (2015) model provides a collection of propositions that articulate construct relationships. That is suggestions for how things are or should be. Unlike natural science model, which traditionally focus on truth, design science models are utility centred. The steps and procedure adopted for the proposed study are based on Vaishnavi and Kuechler's (2015: 17) model as depicted in Figure 3 below.

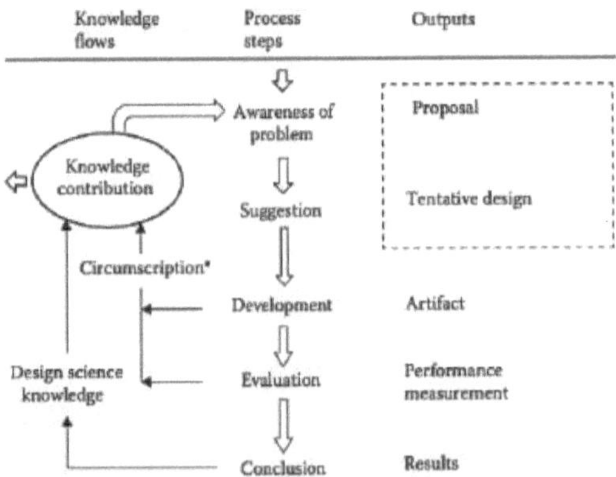

Figure 3: Design science research process model (Vaishnavi and Kuechler, 2015)

3.4.1 *Awareness of problem*

The goal of a Design Science Research is to investigate a problem before an artefact is designed and no requirements on an artefact have been established yet (Wieringa, 2014). In a research seeking "to improve a problematic situation, the first task is to identify, describe, explain and evaluate the problem to be treated" (Wieringa, 2014: 41). This study conducted a literature review to identify, describe and explain the problem. The goal of problem awareness, also referred to as problem investigation, is to create a scientific theory of real-world problem (Wieringa, 2014). Hence the outcome of this activity is a conceptual framework that frames the research question.

Awareness of problem can be inspired by various sources, including application of new findings in other disciplines to one's field, and is concerned with producing a research proposal. Braun, Benedict, Wendler and Esswein (2015) argue the problem formulation in DSR is informed by principles of practice or theory. Practice refers to knowledge that is created through interactions with organisations. Theory refers to creation of knowledge such as artefacts by means of generalisable principles – a theory-ingrained artefact. Furthermore, the description of a problem should enable reasonable consideration of innovativeness, application of existing theories and existing work (Braun *et al.*, 2015).

In the current study the problem was identified through literature review (Gacenga, Cater-Steel, Toleman, and Tan, 2012; Wieringa, 2014; Gregor and Hevner, 2013).

Also a workshop, to define mobile bully-victim phenomenon, was conducted, from which participants' comments, revealed that awareness of the mobile bully-victim was lacking. The literature review helped to create a conceptual framework to frame the research problem. This framework was also confirmed through requirements analysis in the application domain to ensure effectiveness of the prescribed intervention. The requirement analysis involved focus groups discussions with law enforcement personnel and schoolteachers.

3.4.2 *Suggestion*

The output of this phase is tied together with the proposal, and includes a tentative design and possibly a prototype based on the design. The DSR views support the aims of this proposed study, which is designing a mobile app (interventional tool) consistent with contextual environment requirements and law enforcement opinions (Hevner, 2007). Since literature indicates a need to understand the law enforcement's contribution and effectiveness, and clear legislation to inform activities against mobile bully-victim behaviour. The innovativeness of the proposed tool is to provide an alternative approach to aid law enforcements in combating mobile bully-victim. The *suggestion* phase follows the abductive process to verify the problem (Johnson and Onwuegbuzie, 2004). Similar to Gregor and Hevner (2013) in the suggestion phase prototype solutions were developed and tested in practice.

3.4.3 *Conceptual framework*

The design and investigation of an artefact requires the use of a conceptual framework to define artefact structures and its context (Wieringa, 2014). A conceptual framework consists of a set of concepts or constructs that describe artefact's phenomena and context. Conceptual frameworks "can be used to frame design problems and knowledge problems, specify and describe phenomena, and generalize about them" (Wieringa, 2014:90). Additionally, Bazeley (2013) notes a "conceptual framework (literature, theory, paradigmatic foundations) provides a foundation, focus, and starting point for the analysis". Chapter 3 (Literature review – Awareness of problem) presents the conceptual framework.

In order to substantiate the identified problem and to appreciate the underlying sources of the problem an exploratory study was conducted (Koppenhagen, Katz,

Maedche, and Müller, 2011). During this phase, data was collected through exploratory focus group discussions, in order to validate the identified problem and inform the design. This allowed for collection of a detailed domain and problem definitions from police who are responsible for social crime prevention in schools, and schoolteachers as well.

3.4.4 Development

The *development* stage focuses on developing a tentative design and implementation of an artefact.

In the proposed study the implementation of the design will be a software development. Android Studio development package will be used to develop an app that will aid law enforcement officers in fighting against mobile bully-victim behaviour in schools.

3.4.5 Evaluation

Design Science Research involves creation of innovative artefacts as a solution for important problems. These artefacts should have demonstrable capabilities, whose potential benefits and risks are well evaluated and predicted (Hevner, March, Park, 2004). The development of guidelines for conducting and criteria for evaluating design science research in IT is important (Hevner, March, Park, 2004). March and Smith (1995: 254) define evaluation as "the process of determining how well the artefact performs." Peffers *et al.* (2012) identified five purposes of evaluation:

i)   Evaluating an instantiation to establish utility and efficacy of designed artefacts. This involves a rigorous demonstration of artefact's utility, and the assessment criteria seek to expound if the artefact works. Primarily, the aim is to determine whether or how well the designed artefact achieves its purpose.

ii) Evaluating the formalised knowledge about utility of an artefact in achieving its purpose. "When an artefact is evaluated for its utility in achieving its purpose, one is also evaluating a design theory that the design artefact has utility to achieve that purpose" (Peffers *et al.*, 2012: 3). Hence, evaluation in Design Science Research also confirms or challenges the design theory.

iii)	Evaluating the artefact against other existing artefacts' ability to achieve like purpose. A new artefact's utility should exceed existing artefacts' that can be used to achieve the same purpose.

iv)	"Evaluating the artefact for side effects or undesirable consequences of its use" (Peffers *et al.*, 2012: 3). Another purpose of artefact evaluation centres on unintended impacts over time.

v)	Evaluating a designed artefact formatively to discover flaws and improvement areas while an artefact is developed. Formative evaluation helps to identify areas of improvement and refinement on an artefact under development.

Evaluation is emphasised as crucial for artefacts contribution, as well as how design science research is conducted (Peffers, Rothenberger, Tuunanen, and Vaezi, 2012; Hevner, March, Park, 2004). Peffers *et al.* (2012) note context requirements where the artefact is implemented inform the criteria for evaluation. The artefact's evaluation may be "in terms of functionality, completeness, consistency, performance, reliability, usability, fit with the organisation and other relevant quality attributes" (Hevner, March, Park, 2004: 13). Empirical work is needed to aid construction and evaluations, while "constructs, models, methods, and instantiations" are done in a suitable environment (Hevner, March, Park, 2004: 9). The aim of the methods is not to prove why the artefact works (as in behavioural science), rather to determine how well an artefact works (Hevner, March, Park, 2004).

The evaluation of an artefact may include functionality, accuracy, reliability and usability (Hevner, March, Park and Ram, 2004). Hevner *et al.* (2004) summarised five design methods and matrices for evaluating an artefact:
- *Testing study* to discover failure and defects (functional testing), as well as coverage testing all function of artefact (structural testing).
- *Observationally studying* of artefact in depth in the business environment (case studies)

- *Analytical evaluating* studies static qualities of the artefact's structure (static analysis), and studying the artefact's fit into Technical Information Systems – architecture analysis.
- *Experimental evaluation* studies the artefacts qualities in a controlled environment (experiment), and simulation that uses artificial data for artefact execution (Simulation).
- *Descriptive evaluation* uses knowledge-based information such as relevant research to justify the artefact's utility (informed argument), and using detailed *scenarios* to demonstrate the artefact's utility.

The usability testing and focus group methods were adopted during the development of the artefact, while the experimental evaluation was employed at the end of the development.

Upon the completion of the development, the artefact was *evaluated* against the proposed conceptual framework. The conceptual framework was first evaluated through expert reviews (Gregor and Hevner, 2013), and preliminary prototype versions were evaluated and revised through testing and experimentation using designated participants (Hevner *et al.*, 2004). Gibson, and Arnott (2007) argue that in order to test the worthiness of an artefact, the focus group discussions method should be included in Information Systems' Design Science Research. The results of the evaluation were used to reiterate the process starting with the *suggestion* phase. Thus the cognitive process adopted for the *development* and *evaluation* phases is deductive.

3.4.6 Conclusion

In the *conclusion* phase the results of the process are documented as either firm or inexplicable. While the firm knowledge may include learned facts that could be replicated, or behaviour that could be induced again, the inexplicable knowledge may be used for further research. In this phase the researcher will reflect on learned experiences and derive abstract concepts that were observed throughout the DS processes (Gregor, Müller and Seidel, 2013). Essentially, the accumulated knowledge will be shared with the community.

3.5   Design theory building

The basic elements of a Design Science Research project are IT artefact and design theory. The feasibility of the design process and design product is essentially demonstrated by instantiation of artefact from theory (Niehaves, Ortbach and Tavakoli, 2012). Theory specifies how something is done, that is, it is prescriptive in nature and focuses on form and function along methods and appropriate theoretical knowledge that are used in creating IS artefacts (Niehaves *et al.*, 2012).

The formalisation of the knowledge that result from Design science research is done through design theory (Venable and Baskerville, 2012). Venable and Baskerville (2012) noted seven components that are included in design theory, as shown in Figure 4: (1) *meta-requirements* that are to be addressed by the generalised solution, (2) *meta-design* that is adaptable to a specific problem space, (3) *design method* that is applied to adapt meta-design to a specific problem space, (4) *kernel theories* guide meta-design based on meta-requirements, (5) *kernel theories* that inform design method based on meta-design and meta-requirements, and (6) a *testable hypotheses* for testing meta-design and (7) another *testable hypotheses* for testing the design method.

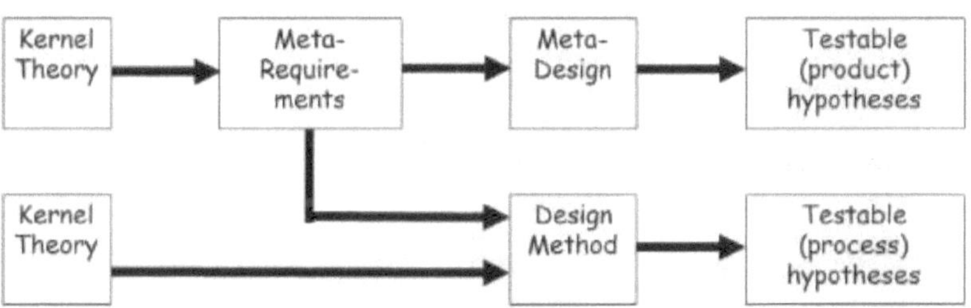

Figure 4: Design theory structure (Venable and Baskerville, 2012)

"A design theory is prescriptive theory on theoretical underpinnings which says how a design process can be carried out in a way which is both effective and feasible " (Walls, Widmeyer and El Sawy, 1992). Therefore, design theories tell how to achieve goals, such as specifying the properties an artefact should have in order to achieve certain goals. There are simpler structures of design theory that consist of only components. Simpler non-prescriptive structures for design theories, which focuses on meta-requirements and meta-design (Baskerville and Pries-Heje, 2010; Venable and

Baskerville, 2012) include: (1) the problem area that is applicable to a design theory (related to meta-requirements), (2) a solution area that specifies a design (relates to meta-design), and (3) relationship between meta-requirements and meta-design that assert some kind of utility of the design, such as effectiveness and efficiency, to satisfy the requirements. Venable and Baskerville (2012) assert theory specifies how to meet general requirements such as applying meta-design.

3.6   A framework for design research activities – Research methods

Pragmatism is "a school of thought that considers practical consequences or real effects to be vital components of both meaning and truth" (Hevner, 2007: 91). Pragmatic approach employs paradigm of choices to clarify how theory and methods can be connected in a research (Morgan, 2007). The three major schools of thought that evolve from quantitative to qualitative paradigms are: purists, situationalists and pragmatists (Onwuegbuziw and Leech, 2005). The purists consist of two categories, namely the qualitative purists also called constructivists and interpretivists, and the quantitative purists also called positivists (Johnson and Onwuegbuzie, 2004). These sets advocate the incompatibility book (Howe, 1988), which states that qualitative and quantitative research paradigms, and their associated methods, cannot and should not be mixed. As a result, the purists maintain mono-method studies. The situationalists support the mono-method studies stance, but further believe that certain research questions are more quantitative inclined, whereas other research questions are best answered with qualitative methods (Onwuegbuziw and Leech, 2005).

Pragmatism is one of the main schools of thought that can be used to guide Information Systems studies (Onwuegbuzie and Leech, 2005). Johnson and Onwuegbuzie (2004) note pragmatism employs a combination of methods or procedures to effectively and efficiently answer research question. As such, qualitative and quantitative methods can be integrated within a single study (Creswell, 2009). Pragmatism upholds the philosophy that the selection of methods is driven by the research question (Onwuegbuziw and Leech, 2005). Johnson and Onwuegbuzie (2004) state that mixing of research approaches should be done in ways that provides the best opportunities to address important research questions. Thus the mixed methodology is deemed suitable for the proposed study, to allow integration of qualitative and quantitative methods within a single study (Creswell, 2009). As such, data collection will include both qualitative and quantitative methods such as surveys, mobile application uses reports, and focus group discussions.

Pragmatism adopts abduction as a logical reasoning (Aliseda, 2006; Morgan, 2007). Abduction is thinking sourced from evidence to explanation, reasoning characterised by different situations including incomplete information (Aliseda, 2006). Abduction construction is based on several tests, of which each provides one or a few best explanation pending subsequent testing (Aliseda, 2006). Morgan (2007: 71) notes traditional use of abduction "is often treated solely as using theories to account for observations". Simply put, abduction is "the logic for synthetic reasoning, that is, a method to acquire new ideas" (Aliseda, 2006: 171). Similarly deduction is described as "the process of drawing conclusions about a phenomenon or behaviour based on theoretical or logical reasons and an initial set of premises" (Bhattacherjee, 2012: 14-15). The deductive process intentionally increases knowledge by refining and testing existing knowledge (Lee, Pries-Heje, and Baskerville, 2011). In comparison with induction, deduction "involves arguing from the level of the general to that of an exact instance, whereas induction moves in the opposite direction from the particular to the more general" (Bryant, 2017). However, Reichertz (2007) views abduction as "a cerebral process, an intellectual act, a mental leap, that brings together things which one had never associated with one another: A cognitive logic of discovery." Unlike more careful and considered processes of deduction and induction, abduction is seen as a logical "leap" (Bryant, 207). Hence, abductive and deductive inferences are used in this study.

Chapter 4 – Study procedure

4.1   Introduction

This chapter discusses the study procedure that was followed, which consists of three phases, including an inference on teachers and police's nuances in resolving pupils misconduct, especially mobile bully-victim behaviour, in order to inform study design. Another is role-playing by teachers' for assessing the mobile app's utility and efficacy, and its live roll out in a school.

The first phase, involved focus groups with teachers, and police who are responsible for social crime prevention, was conducted to inform study design. Information elicited regarding the involvement of teachers, police and parents, and especially approaches used to handle learners misconduct in schools (see Exploratory focus group A in Appendix 1).

The second phase pertained to the application test. The purpose of this approach was to enable testing the app's utility and efficacy in order to evaluate and guide the design of the artefact. The teachers that took part in phase 1 were requested to also participate in the second phase, as well as pupils who own mobile phones.

The third phase, pertained to live testing of the app in school classrooms and a follow-up to solicit learners' perceptions on the use of the app. In order to alleviate the risk of involving police in the live testing of the application, teachers were requested to take part in the study as role players. The police that took part in phase 1 were requested to participate in the third phase, as well as pupils who own mobile phones. Data collection involved a survey questionnaire with learners, and focus group with the police (see Evaluation Questionnaire in Appendix 2). The third phase also concluded the study.

4.2   Mobile bully-victims identification procedure

Sociometry was used in the identification process through the M-BRS. Sociometry constitutes one of the quantitative tools for investigating individuals' status within a group (Gutiérrez et al., 2016). Sociometric matrix help to infer quantitatively how each member perceives and is perceived by others in the group. The criterion used for classification of learners as bullies, victims, and bully-victims is based on bullying and victimisation relationship in classrooms. The resulting data was analysed using sociograms and social network analysis (Howison, Wiggins and Crowston, 2011).

4.2.1 Sociometric criteria (nominations)

Social choices can be done subjectively or objectively and consciously. Subjective choices are guided by intuitive feelings, such as liking or disliking others on first impression. On the other hand, objective and conscious choices are based on experience and knowledge, such as knowing that a person has or does not have skills for particular group tasks (Leung, Silberling, 2006). Since bullying and victimisation is an objective and conscious action (Thompson, 2019). In this study, the researcher chose objective and conscious criterion for identification of mobile bully-victims in classrooms. "When members of a group are asked to choose others in the group based on a specific criteria, everyone in the group can make choices and describe why the choices were made" (Leung, Silberling, 2006: 59). Learners were asked to nominate their peers who have bullied them, or nominate themselves if they had bullied their classmates.

Limiting the number of questions is essential for guarding against respondents fatigue (Grunspan, Wiggins and Goodreau, 2014). Hence learners completed the nominations by answering only two questions:

- Question 1. *Please select the name of the learner that bullied you in the past three months.*
- Question 2. *Please select the peer's name in the list that you have bullied in the past three months.*

In this way survey fatigue was not an issue because there was no need to ask learners a long list of question about their classmates' attributes. However, learners' nominations were not limited, but each nomination removed the learner from the list in order to avoid duplicate nominations by a single learner.

Although the purpose of nominations was to identify mobile bully-victims, identifying bullies and victims through either self- or peer-reporting led to the desired result (van Dijk *et al.*, 2017) since the definition of bully-victims behaviour includes being bullied and victimised as well. Victims' nominations were used to differentiate bullies from bully-victims (van Dijk *et al.*, 2017). Learners' behaviour is determined by noting nominations as follows (van Volk *et al.*, 2017):

- Learner A nominates learner B and learner B nominates learner C, which makes learner A a pure victim, and learner B both a bully and victim (i.e. bully-victim), and learner C a pure bully.
- Learner A nominates B and B nominates A, which make both learner A and B bullies and victims.
- Learner A nominates B and no nomination is made for A, which makes learner A a victim, and B a bully.
- If a learner is not nominated and did not nominate other learners, is regarded as non-involved learners.

In order to ensure learners anonymity, in terms of nominators' identity, names were never revealed to the nominees either by the police or the client app. This helped to minimise risks to participants by implementing confidential social network data collection (Grunspan *et al*, 2014), which is discussed in more details in section 4.3.4.

4.3 Data collection

Data collection is a systematical process of gathering and measuring relevant information to address research questions by evaluating outcomes or testing hypotheses (Peerman, 2014). Furthermore, Peerman (2014) emphasises that data collection should be done accurately and honestly across disciplines and methods of research.

In Information Systems research, the case study research is the most widely used method (Orlikowski and Baroudi, 1991). The case study enables studying information systems development and implementation, and is suitable to understand the interactions between information technology (IT) products and organisational contexts (Darke, Shanks, and Broadbent, 1998). A case study is an empirical enquiry that draws evidence from multiple sources (triangulation) in order to investigate a contemporary phenomenon within its application context (Yin, 1994). Thus data collection and analysis can use qualitative and quantitative methods. In this proposed study, data collection included focus group discussion, surveys and artefact reports.

This study used a combination of data collection methods that is referred to as triangulation (Carter *et al.*, 2014). The following subsections present data collection with reference to problem awareness, suggestions, and artefact evaluation phases as depicted in Figure 3 of section 3.4.

4.3.1 Group interviews

Data collection from the police was done through group interview, in which the researcher asked a set of questions, and participant gave responses (Parker and Tritter, 2006). In focus group interviews the researcher takes the role of a facilitator, whereas with group interviews the researcher plays an investigative role. The investigator takes centre stage "asking question, controlling the dynamics of group discussion, often engaging in dialogue with specific participants" (Parker and Tritter, 2006). In this case, participants respond to the researcher's question. However, where focus group is concerned the researcher moderates group discussion between participants.

4.3.2 Appreciative Inquiry

The broad aim of appreciative inquiry approach is to enable mutual inquiry into a topic to reveal strengths and capacities that exist in the group and organisation as a whole (Kandola, 2012; Stratton-Berkessel, 2010). Participants reflect on what works well as a starting point – the positive core, and envision adaptation or enhancing the existing technology. As such appreciative inquiry "orients practitioners to look for the positive core, build relationships, recognize assets, challenge underlying assumptions that take energy from cooperative capacity, and actively engage participants in creating preferred futures" (Lewis and Winkelman, 2017: 63). The positive core is central to organisation's values, such as teaching people to recognise their strength to achieve specific outcomes. Also, appreciative inquiry facilitates collective change in an organisation.

Appreciative inquiry consists of five phases, including "(1) topic selection, (2) discovery, (3) dream, (4) design, and (5) destiny" (Ludema, Cooperrider and Barrett, 2006: 189). The topic selection helps the researcher to determine positive and well-working procedures in the organisation. Following the topic selection is establishment of existing aspiration (dreams) for enhancement, then the creation of the solution to realise the dreams, and finally the destiny is achieved.

In this study, a set of eight questions was created to facilitate discussions with participant about the phenomenon (Kandola, 2012). Participants were given opportunities to express their experiences and strategies to achieve objectives. Since appreciative inquiry focuses on positive thinking only about an organisation, it was deemed unsuitable for addressing the researcher's questions.

4.3.3   *Focus group discussions*

The design and evaluation of the application used data collections known as exploratory and confirmatory focus groups (Tremblay, Hevner and Berndt, 2010). Exploratory focus groups (EFG) were conducted during the design and refinement of the artefact. A confirmatory focus group (CFG) was employed to evaluate the artefact's utility. Tremblay *et al.* (2010) note focus group is a useful technique for both exploratory and confirmatory methods, when little is known about the phenomenon, as well as improving validity and generalisability of the design. As advised by Tremblay *et al.* (2010) this study conducted altogether one pilot test, three EFG and one CFG. Also, in order to avoid social loafing in social group discussions, sample sizes were kept at no more than six participants.

The context of the socio-technical environment of South African Police personnel was uncovered during the initial exploratory study. Also, human factors concerning the use of technology to diagnose mobile bully-victim behaviour among school children were determined. Focus groups were also used to gain familiarity with the context in which the artefact would be used.

A focus group discussion can be conducted as a serial interview, "where all comments are directed back to the moderator", when time is limited and the purpose is to identify different points of views (Krueger and Casey, 2015: 374). Alternatively the moderator encourages conversations between participants, as in unstructured interviews, in order to learn how participants respond to each other in the group, which might be a predictor of how participants respond outside the focus group.

Following the problem awareness phase, in literature review, an EFG discussion was conducted to establish identified problems with law enforcement (Tremblay *et al.*, 2010). The literature review helped to construct a conceptual model, and informed the set of discussion probes for the EFG discussion. Then the collected data was analysed to clarify the research problem, refine the initial set of requirements and design principles, as well as justify and show artefact's originality (Braun *et al.*, 2015).

4.3.3.1 Focus group procedure

In DS, research problems can be transformed into artefact's objectives through requirements analysis (Peffers *et al.*, 2007). Requirements analysis also helped to address wicked problems (frequent shifting requirements and constraints), as well as describing the problem and domain, and problem conceptualisation (Braun *et al.*, 2015; Gaceng, *et al.*, 2012). During the suggestions phase of the design science, exploratory focus group discussions were used to draw law enforcement's opinion on preventing and diagnosing mobile bully-victim behaviour (Hevner, 2007), and to inform the design for the development phase. Due to the police's limited interactions with learners in schools, and since the artefact would be used with learners, schoolteachers were also involved in data collections. Schoolteachers were involved to fill gaps that could exist in the design and developing an artefact that would be suitable for the police and learners' use. The appreciative inquiry method was also used to guide focus group interviews, in order to gain understanding of participants' contexts (Kandola, 2012). The researcher acted as the moderator during each focus group discussion, while adhering to important skill requirements noted by Tremblay (2010):

- *Respecting participants*, to afford all participants the opportunity to share their views,
- *Communicating clearly* both in writing and verbally,
- *Listening skills* and *self-discipline* to control personal views,
- *Friendliness* and sense of humour, and
- *Encouraging participation* from all group members.

Having designed the artefact's prototype based on the conceptual model that is informed by the literature review in this study. Tremblay *et al.* (2010) suggested the following procedure to facilitate evaluation and design revision of the artefact through group discussions:

- Begin with explanation of motivation behind the design of the artefact;
- Followed by broad explanation of scenarios on where and how the artefact could be used, and a description of design details of the artefact;
- Finish with a task where participants are asked to use and evaluate the artefact.

As already mentioned (see Group Interviews in section 3.9.1), focus group discussions can be conducted in a similar fashion as in unstructured and serial interviews. The initial data collection from the police was done through a group interview, in which the researcher asked a set of questions, and participants gave responses (Parker and Tritter, 2006). In focus group interviews the researcher takes the role of a facilitator, whereas during group interviews the researcher plays an investigative role. The investigator takes centre stage, asking questions, monitoring and controlling the dynamics of group discussion, and often probing participants to clarify their comments, and engage in a dialogue with specific participants (Parker and Tritter, 2006). In this case, participants responded to the researcher's questions. Also, the researcher moderated group discussion between participants.

In some Design Science Research projects, instruments may be created and used to answer knowledge questions (Wieringa, 2014: 21). The goal of focus group discussions was to gain insight about diagnosing mobile bully-victims, inform necessary design revisions, and evaluate the utility of the artefact in identifying mobile bully-victims. Therefore, a questioning route that is closely aligned to the research objectives was developed to direct group discussions at each stage of design and development (Gibson and Arnott, 2007; Tremblay *et al.*, 2010). The questions ranged from general to specific, and were ordered by importance in each topic (Krueger and Casey, 2015).

Table 3: A sample focus group probe and route

Route	Probes
Opening	1. Tell us your name, which area (sector) you work in, and what you enjoy most about crime prevention in schools.
Introduction	2. What was the first thing that came to mind when you used the app?
Transition	3. Think back when you first used the mobile app as a bully-victims diagnosis tool. What were your first impressions?
Key	4. What was using the app features (definition and instructions, or questions) like for you?
	5. What was particularly frustrating about the app?
	6. What was particularly helpful about the app?
Ending	7. If you could pick one feature between the nomination, and confirmation and assessment to fight mobile bully-victim behaviour. Which one would you pick?
	8. We want you to help us further develop and evaluate the app. We want to know how to improve the functions of the app. Is there anything we should have talked about but didn't?

After the participants gained usage experience of the artefact, discussions about the artefact features were conducted by following the adapted Krueger and Casey's (2015) guidelines in Table 3.

4.3.4 *Mobile bully-victim diagnosis report*

In this study the researcher developed an artefact called mobile bully-victim response system (M-BRS) and used it to produce data to help address the research questions. Learners' interaction with the M-BRS produced social network or digital trace data where the system acted as a data collection tool (Howison *et al.*, 2011; Jungherr *et al.*, 2017). This data is a by-product of learners' interactions with the digital service (Jungherr *et al.*, 2017), in this study it consisted of peer- and self-nominations among learners.

This section presents the procedure that was followed in using the M-BRS to diagnose mobile bully-victims in this study. The M-BRS was developed as a solution to aid mobile bully-victim diagnoses for the police. The M_BRS consists of the server and client applications. The client application contains a mobile bully-victim definition, to enable learners to nominate culprits according to the provided definition of mobile bully-victims behaviour. The nomination is facilitated through the list of learners' names in a particular school classroom. On the other hand, the server receives and records nomination to determine learners that are perceived as mobile bully-victims.

The M-BRS diagnosis process consists of three steps as presented in Table 4. Step 1 starts the registration by allowing client devices to connect to the server. The official can also choose to register learners solely (without learners' involvement), using the class register. Then the identification codes (IDs) are provided for learners to use on the system during nomination and assessment.

In Step 2, the police start the nomination session, and invite pupils to join the session and nominate mobile bully-victims according to the provided definition. While pupils send nominations, the server receives and saves nomination reports. The report includes an indication of how many pupils were nominated, as well as how many nominations each pupil received.

Right after the nomination (Step 2), the client application proceeds to the assessment, (Step 3).

In this step, all learners who did nominate their mobile bullies and/or victims are afforded an opportunity to deny or assent to accusations, and rate effects' (impact, severity, and frequency) experience of the mobile bully-victim behaviour. The police stop the session, and the system would have aggregated reports including that of nominations, to help determine learners' behaviour in relation to mobile bully-victim behaviour, and its effects on each learner. The nominations report consists of the in- and out-degree which help to determine if a learner is identified as a mobile bully-victim, bully, victim, and uninvolved. The assessment reports provide the degree of effects as well as recommendations of remedial actions for learners. The police conclude the diagnosis process by using the report to invite the affected learners for remedial actions.

Table 4: M-BRS diagnosis process

Activities	Rationale
Step 1	
SAP personnel	
Start registration (Optional)	Enable client device connection to the server for registration.
Pupils/ SAP personnel	
Register names (initials and surname), age, gender and grade on the system.	Create class list for nomination o the system
System	
Create identification (ID) code.	Allows tracking pupils' actions on the system, and confidentiality of pupils.
Pupil	
Note ID	Allow pupils to authenticate into and use the system
SAP personnel	
Stop registration session	
Step 2	
SAP personnel	
Start nomination session.	Allows the server applications to accept Wi-Fi connections from clients.
Pupils	
Read bully-victim definition, and its forms.	Aid understanding of phenomenon to enable nominations.
Join session. (Once off)	Allows client applications to join the nomination session.
Read nomination instructions	Guide learners to nominate other learners or themselves according to the definition.
Nominate mobile bully-victims from class list.	Allow pupils to anonymously nominate peers or themselves.
SAP personnel	
View nominations	Monitor progress
Stop nominations session.	End session.
System	
Save results	To allow creating reports.
Step 3	
Pupils	
Read confirm question and select answer.	Allow pupils to deny or assent to accusations.
Read assessment cues and rate effect.	Cues exemplify effects, and allow pupils to rate their experience (impact, severity, and frequency of mobile bully-victim behaviour).
System	
Determine impact levels and save data.	Determine needed support, and save data for reporting.
SAP personnel	
Stop session.	End session.
View results.	Inform required remedial actions.

4.3.5 Survey

During the artefact evaluation phases, a survey instrument that consists of closed-ended and open-ended questions, and focus group discussions were used to acquire both quantitative and qualitative data. The survey questions were adapted from Lewis' (1992) Psychometric evaluation of the post-study system usability questionnaire, and IBM standardised questionnaire Post-Study System Usability Questionnaire (Lewis, 1991c). While a survey was used to uncover opinions and attitudes ascribed to the M-BRS and mobile bully-victim behaviour by participants (Moser and Kalton, 2017), a focus group discussion was conducted to comprehensively explore the discovered perceptions (Carter *et al*, 2014: 545). The other set of data was based on user interactions with the app, including the indication of task success rates by participants, and diagnosis results of the app.

4.3.6 Usability testing

A usability testing also known as user testing, is a scientific procedure to measure user's behaviour in order to infer the effectiveness artefact features (Lowdermilk, 2013; Bastien, 2010). Metrics such as time of task completion or number of errors, and the study can be combined with other methods such as surveys and focus group discussions to measure difficult to observe aspects like satisfaction or perception of value (Lowdermilk, 2013; Neilsen, 2001). This enables exploration of artefact's design and its user experience (usability). Tasks are metrics to be measured, therefore the bases of the usability testing (Lowdermilk, 2013). The tasks are then quantified to represent complete or partial completion and failure rates as indications of artefact usability (Neilsen, 2001).

Usability testing can be done in a natural setting and a controlled environment (lab). Lab-based testing has many drawbacks, including high costs, time and effort taken to set up, and represents unnatural testing environment (Lee, 2007).

4.3.7 M-BRS reports

The app's reports will be used in support (triangulation) of survey and focus group data. The M-BRS reports' data include results of user interactions with the application, and can be interpreted to discover its meaning (Peña-Ayala, 2014). The report will include statistical data about a number of pupils who participated in each diagnosis session. Also, the data included the number of nominated pupils, as well as the number of positively identified mobile bully-victims, bullies, victims, and uninvolved learners.

Data collected through the application includes a list of nominated learners together with their nominators, and severity assessment. In order to solicit this data, learners were asked to do any of the two nominations from name list (1) peers that they perceived as mobile bullies, (2) peers that they had bullied (in this case, learners were also encouraged to nominate themselves – self-nomination). Self-nomination could also serve as a form of confirmation of identified mobile bully-victims. While the confirmation assessment was meant to verify learners agreement with report. The severity assessment results were used to reveal the effects of mobile bully-victims behaviour on learners. The reliability of the selected peer nomination is not only based on the multiple constructs, but also on multiple reporters' data. The combination of two sources of data, peer- and self-nomination, can produce data with more breadth, reliability and construct validity (Volk *et al.* 2017).

4.4   Data analysis

Analysis is described as "close engagement with one's text or transcripts, and the illumination of their meaning and significance through insightful and technically sophisticated work" (Antaki, Billig, Edwards, and Potter, 2003: 30). In this study, different strategies were employed for the analysis of quantitative and qualitative data. Thematic analysis was conducted to validate the problem definition. Template analysis was conducted to inform the artefact design, as well as establishing its utility. Quantitative data analysis was also conducted on surveys and app reports.

4.4.1   Qualitative data analysis

The research conducted thematic analysis on transcripts of focus group that sought to validate the problem definition. Thematic analysis (TA) is an umbrella term covering different approaches for themes or patterns identification in qualitative datasets (Braun, Clarke, Hayfield and Terry, 2018). TA is a method that is neither prescriptive on data collection nor tied to any framework whether epistemology or ontology

(Braun and Clarke, 2013). In their study informed by the design science framework, to develop an information dissemination mobile app for persons living with HIV, Schnall *et al.* (2014) used thematic analysis on focus groups data. The framework for conducting thematic analysis was based on Braun *et al.*'s (2018) six phases, presented in Table 5, familiarisation, generating codes, constructing themes, revision and definition of themes, and producing a report.

Table 5: Thematic analysis phases and descriptions (Braun *et al.*, 2018)

No	Phase	Description
1	Familiarisation	Read and reading transcripts, and jotting down early impression.
2	Creating code	Reducing data into small meaningful chunks.
3	Creating themes	Collating related codes, together with their associated data chunk, into clusters that signify meaning of a particular dataset.
4	Reviewing themes	Reviewing, revising and building themes that were created in phase 3. Verifying if themes make sense. Thematic maps can help to visualise themes relate and succinctly communicate overall story about data.
5	Defining themes	Identifying clearer theme names that signify their essence and scope. Names can be lengthy or just one word.
6	Producing report	Includes weaving existing research and literature with analytic narrative about data extract into report.

The researcher adopted a specific form of thematic analysis for the purpose of assessing the artefact's utility. Template analysis is a thematic analysis style which focuses on hierarchical coding, while adhering to an organised process of textual data analysis and allowing adaptations to the needs of a specific study (Brooks, McCluskey, Turley and King, 2015). Tremblay, Hevner and Berndt (2010) suggest that template analysis can be used on focus group data in Design Science for artefact refinement and evaluation. The researcher "looks for common themes and variations within the transcripts that would provide rich descriptions of the participants' reactions to design features" (Tremblay *et al.*, 2010:605). The quality of data analysis can be ensured through "independent coding and critical comparison among researchers and by expert panels; respondent feedback; and the provision of audit trails." (King, 2012: 433). In this study the researcher coded independently and used member check (respondent feedback) to ensure data analysis quality. Table 6 presents the guiding steps for creating a template as provided by King (2012).

Table 6: Template analysis steps (King, 2012)

No	Phase	Description
1	Prori themes and preliminary coding	• Familiarisation with transcripts, and checking for transcription error. • Coding sections of text, or marking text with encapsulating prori themes in first transcript.
2	Initial template	• Clustering initial codes into meaningful group allows clear definitions of hierarchical and literal relation. • A provisional set of themes is produced to organise the initial template.
3	Modifying template	• Systematically coding the full set of transcripts, while identifying inadequacies and revising the template towards a final form.
3.1	Insertion	• Adding new themes that serve the aims of the research.
3.2	Deletion	• Removing themes that do not serve the aims of the research.
3.3	Merging	• Integrating themes into one
3.4	Changing the scope	• Changing the scope of themes. This may be as a result of deletion.
3.5	Changing the higher order classification	• Changing the hierarchical order of themes. This may be as a result of deletion.
4	The 'final' template	• The final form of the template is reached when no sections of text that are relevant to the research question are left uncoded.

The report accounts of results will consist of identified themes and text drawn from transcripts as illustrative examples (Tremblay, Hevner and Berndt, 2010). Text from transcript can be presented as short quotes and long quotes, and serve two purposes in the report. Short quotes help in points of specific interpretation, while longer quotes provide essence of original discussions. Also, displaying evidence or counterevidence of the artefact's utility as a summary table (Tremblay *et al.*, 2010).

Qualitative analysis involves three simultaneous and continuous activities: "data reduction, data display, and conclusion drawing/verification" (Miles and Huberman, 1994: 10). Qualitative analysis employs interpretive analysis to produce themes that facilitate understanding of the phenomenon being studied (Sargeant, 2012), with interpretive analysis generally being conducted in three steps – deconstruction, interpretation and reconstruction (Miles and Huberman, 1994). The deconstruction step helps to break data into themes or categories that describe the content, the interpretation step helps to make sense of the themes that emerge in the deconstruction step by comparing the results to those of similar studies and exploring theories that explain the relationships between themes, and finally, the reconstruction step helps to reconnect the themes in a manner that makes their relationships visible in order to regain insight that was derived from the interpretation stage. Thus the data that emerged from the focus group discussion notes, and open-ended questions of the survey will be coded in order to uncover the meaning that the law enforcement agents attached to their experiences with the mobile app (Hoekstra 2008).

4.4.2 *Quantitative data analysis (survey)*

The data from the survey will be quantitatively analysed by constructing frequency distributions (based on participant responses) to determine law enforcements' perceptions of mobile bully-victim. Frequency distribution can be described as the organisation of data by indication of counts and percentages of responses on each survey item in a tabular form (Taylor-Powell 2003). The data description will be provided by means of descriptive statistics to calculate the mean, standard deviation and percentage (Mateo 2010; Boone and Boone 2012).

The quantitative data from the survey will be analysed by constructing frequency distributions (based on participant responses) to determine law enforcements' perceptions on mobile app uses against bully-victim behaviour. Frequency distribution is the organisation of data by indication of counts and percentages of responses on each survey item in a tabular form (Taylor-Powell, 2003). The data description will be provided by means of descriptive statistics to provide mean, standard deviation and percentage (Boone and Boone, 2012; Rajathi and Chandran, 2015).

Content analysis will be used on the data from open-ended questions in the survey. Cole (1988: 53) describes content analysis as "a method of analysing written, verbal, or visual communication messages". The responses to open-ended questions will be condensed to a series of canonical quotes, such that each quote represented one phrase or theme (Hall, Collier, Thomas and Hilgers, 2005). However, themes are a product of coding, categorisation, or analytic reflection (Saldaña, 2013). As, such the

First Cycle Coding process focus is to retrieve and categorise data chunks relating to a research question, construct, or theme (Miles, Huberman, and Saldaña, 2014).

Interpretive analysis will also be conducted on qualitative data obtained through group interviews to produce themes that facilitate understanding of the phenomenon being studied (Sargeant, 2012). Thus the data that emerge from group interviews, and open-ended questions of the survey will be coded in order to uncover the meaning that the participants, especially law enforcement agents, attached to their experiences with the mobile app (Hoekstra, 2008). Bryant (2017) notes coding as the process of uncovering what the data is about. Once the data is coded, codes that form common themes and patterns will be categorised and then transformed into concepts. Concepts constructed from inductive data, then developed and checked through abduction (Charmaz, 2014). Concepts are abstract ideas that represent data and consist of specific properties and limits (Charmaz, 2014).

4.4.3 *Quantitative data analysis*

Social network analysis was conducted on the nomination results of the artefact. In network analysis, actors' relations are the main focus, and not attributes of individual actors. Given that the nature of bullying interaction between learners is inherently social, the researcher deemed Social Network Analysis (SNA) theory as perfectly suitable for this purpose (Zorrilla and de Lima Silva, 2019). The core of SNA is the analysis of ties that link network vertexes to reveal network patterns that connect different elements (Contandriopoulos, Larouche, Breton and Brousselle, 2018). Using social network analysis and sociogram helps to understand mobile bully-victims interaction patterns. The quantitative data generated from graphs can be qualitatively described (Volk *et al.*, 2017).

In this study, learners' perceptions of their peers' mobile bully-victim behaviour was measured using the sociometric status procedure. Similar to Zhang *et al.* (2014), a sociometric procedure was used in which learners nominated classmates who were perceive as mobile bully-victims, according to the definition thereof. Learners could also nominate their victims – to indicate which of their peers they had bullied. Learners' perceptions of their peers' status on mobile bully-victim behaviour were measured using sociometric peer- and self-nomination procedure (Cillessen, 2011).

The number of nominations received indicated whether or not that learners are mobile bully-victims, pure bully, or pure victim. Conversely, learners are identified as non-involved, if no nominations are received for that learner. Also, sociometric status was calculated by adding the number of nominations each learner received and then divided by class size, and finally transformed into a PageRank within each class (Coie, Dodge, and Coppotelli, 1982). The researcher found sociogram, PageRank centralities suitable for the exploratory analysis. Furthermore, the nomination data was used to draw social network diagram (sociogram) depicting relations and proximities between mobile bully-victims, pure bullies, and pure victims. This diagram helped to visually identify learners' behaviour in relation to bullying behaviour, and evaluate the effectiveness of the artefact in helping the law enforcement to diagnose mobile bully-victim behaviour in schools.

Quantitative data analysis is recommended for its impartiality (Volk *et al.*, 2017). Quantitative network analysis was used to quantify participants' prominence and the value of nominations in a group (Saqr, Fors and Nouri, 2018). Self-generated identification code (SGIC) was used to enable anonymous data collection from learners (Volk *et al.*, 2017; Vacek, Vonkova and Gabrhelík, 2017). Characters including initials, first letter of the surname, and a three-digit number were user to form SGIC for each participant.

Graph (sociogram): A graph, also called a sociogram, is composed of vertexes (actors) that are connected by arcs (relations) (Zorrilla and de Lima Silva, 2019). Actors in the graph represent learners, while arcs represent actors' relationship (choice) in a directed graph. In this relationship data can be graphed with arcs to represent choices (who is directing a choice toward whom as a bully), and no arcs represent the absence of choice. In the same way, looping arcs (arcs that start and end at the same vertex) represent actors' self-choice. Also, choices may be reciprocated between two vertexes, and are represented by double-headed arcs.

The force-directed algorithm was chosen for rendering the sociogram on the app. In this way, vertexes mutually repel each other, while arcs force attraction between vertexes. Force-directed algorithms balances repulsive and attractive forces to position interconnected vertexes are closer to each other. As a result, highly interconnected vertexes are located to the centre of the sociograms and clusters of interconnected vertexes (cliques) become more visible. There are many force-directed algorithms, some of which have customisable parameters. In this study, the Fruchterman-Reingold algorithm is used as the mathematical bases of this model for presentation of sociograms (Contandriopoulos *et al.*, 2018, Fruchterman and Reingold, 1991).

Centrality

The geographical importance of a node within a graph is referred to as centrality in graph theory (Spizzirri, 2011). The node's centrality can be obtained through degree centrality. Centrality is the measure of prominence, not particularly due to the receiving or the making many nominations; what is essential in this measure is that the actor is simply involved (Wesserman and Faust, 1994). On the other hand Prestige makes distinction between sent and received nominations in directional relations. Hence a prestigious actor is defined as one who has large nomination, thus focusing solely on the actor as a recipient (Wesserman and Faust, 1994). PageRank is an algorithm used in any graph and domains such as biology, neural network and social network analysis (Tan, 2017). There are many variations of centrality measures including degree, betweenness, closeness, eigenvector centralities and PageRank centrality.

Degree

Wesserman and Faust (1994) describe degree of a vertex as the number of lines that are incident with that vertex. Also, the degree of vertex is the sum of the in-degree and the out-degree of vertex, and a vertex with a degree equal to zero is called isolate. Degrees can be very informative in many applications (Wesserman and Faust, 1994). For example, if we ask schoolchildren to nominate their bullies in a class and represent children by vertexes, then a vertex with a large in-degree would indicate a child who bullied many other children, and a vertex with small in-degree would indicate a child who bullied few other children, whereas an isolate or a vertex with zero in-degree would indicate a child does not bully other children.

Vertices' significance depends on their degree – in- and out-degree (Wijayanto and Murata, 2017). Mobile bully-victims exhibit both pure bullies' and victims' behaviour (Poon, 2016; van Dijk, Poorthuis and Malti, 2017). Hence, measuring in-degree and out-degree of their representative vertexes can facilitate mobile bully-victims' identification. The degree of vertices was interpreted in relation to bully-victims, bullies victims, and uninvolved learners (Leung and Silberling, 2006), as show in the decision Table 7 with bully, bully-victim, victim as dependent variables (dep. var), and in- and out-degree as independent variables (indep. var). Tallying the result helped to identify four (4) learner types:

- A vertex's in-degree that is greater than zero and out-degree that is equal to zero, indicates that the represented learner is a *bully*.
- A vertex's in- and out-degree values that are greater than zero indicate that the represented learner is a *bully-victim*.
- A vertex's in-degree and out degree values that are equal to zero, indicates that the represented learner is *uninvolved*.

Table 7: Decision table

Behaviour (Dep. var)	In-degree (Indep. var)	Out-degree (Indep. var)
Bully	**Yes**	No
Bully-victim	**Yes**	**Yes**
Victim	No	**Yes**
Uninvolved	No	No

In terms of degree, a vertex centrality indicates visibility or the potential for activity. A vertex with a relatively high degree can be seen as the major channel of communication as it permits direct contact with many others (Freeman, 1979). In some sense, such a vertex is the focal point of communication among others that connect with it. On the other hand, a vertex with low degree may see itself and be seen by others as marginal, and isolated from direct involvement with most of other vertexes in the network, and is cut off from active participation in the on-going communication process.

Betweenness
The frequency with which a vertex falls between pairs of other vertexes on the shortest or geodesic path connecting them, is referred to as *betweenness*. A central vertex is strategically located on communication paths linking pairs of others. Such a vertex can influence the group by withholding or distorting transmitted information (Freeman, 1979). Also, such vertexes are responsible for communication maintenance, and group processes coordination. The vertex that falls on the

communication paths between other vertexes exhibits the potential for control of their communication (Freeman, 1979). This potential for control defines the centrality of these vertexes. "Betweenness is useful as an index of the potential of a vertex for control of communication."

The geographical importance of a vertex within a graph is referred to as centrality in graph theory (Spizzirri, 2011). The vertex's centrality can be obtained through degree centrality. Google applies a variant of eigenvector centrality named PageRank to rank search results of webpages in their search engine (Spizzirri, 2011). Spizzirri (2011) suggests the strength of eigenvector evaluation is its dependence to collective evaluation instead of expert evaluation.

Closeness
Closeness centrality is an average measure of how close one actor is to other actors along geodesics (Grunspan, *et al*, 2014). This centrality measure is not suitable for a disconnected graph with nodes at zero degree (Grunspan, *et al*, 2014). In this current study closeness centrality is not include, as some graphs were disconnected.

Eigenvector and PageRank
Eigenvector centrality is the measure of a vertex' influence in a network. The centrality indicates the most central vertex in the network against other vertices. Eigenvector centrality focuses on being connected to other nodes that are well connected (Grunspan *et al*, 2014). That is, a link to well-connected nodes results in a higher eigenvector centrality than linking to the same number of nodes who are less well connected. Hence, the strength of eigenvector evaluation is its dependence to collective evaluation instead of expert evaluation (Spizzirri, 2011).

Google applies a variant of eigenvector centrality named PageRank to rank search results of webpages in their search engine (Spizzirri, 2011). The number of votes to a participant translates to the in-degree of the corresponding vertex (Chen, Xie, Maslov, and Redner, 2007). A fuller picture of participants' influence than in-degree impact alone can be shown using the Google PageRank algorithm (Chen, Xie, Maslov, and Redner, 2007). A node's PageRank represents accumulated values from other nodes (Theocharis and Bekiari, 2017). In this study, Google PageRank is used to measure victims, bully-victims, and bullies' behavioural importance (reputation) in classrooms. Google PageRank algorithm seems to produce a useful measure of scientific quality (Chen *et al.*, 2007). PageRank is calculated through a simple iterative algorithm, and corresponds to the eigenvector's calculation steps (Brin and Page, 1998; Tan, 2017). Chen *et al.* (2007) explain the concept of Google PageRank as follows: Google PageRank is a better measure of importance (reputation) than the number of in-degree alone in two parts: (1) being nominated by influential participants contributes more to the Google number than being voted for by unimportant participants; (2) being voted for by a participant that itself has few references gives a larger contribution to the Google number than being voted for by a participant with hundreds of votes. The Google's number of a participant represents a measure of its influence that is then equally transferred to all of its references.

The researcher chose the PageRank centrality because it surpasses other centrality measure discussed in this study (Aggarwal, Sharma, Jain and Jain, 2018), and it is based on the concept of "voting" (Souma and Jibu, 2018), which supported one of the features of the proposed artefact – nominations.

4.5   Risks

As noted by Brewer and Kerslake (2015), cyberbullying causes emotional distress. Therefore foreseeable risks in this study include emotional distress that pupils may experience when requested to think and recall bullying incidents in order to identify mobile bully-victim perpetrators (see section 6.5.4 – Instantiation). The mobile bully-victims diagnosis process required learner's recollection of their bullies, which also led to recounting unpleasant experiences. As also noted by Hoover and Morrow (2015), recollection of unpleasant experience also affects participant interest in the research, while other participants may feel empowered to share their experience and help to address their challenges.

Additionally, pupils' names will be used in the diagnosis process of mobile bully-victims, and pupils may falsely accuse one another. For possible false accusation risks, pupils will be discouraged from accusing others unjustly. Also, in order to deter pupils, they will be informed that bullying is a serious problem with adverse effects on those involved, and unjust accusation is in fact considered bullying as well (Östberg, Modin and Låftman, 2018). The diagnosis process will also provide pupils with an opportunity to deny or assent to accusations. Additionally, professional counselling will be provided to emotionally distressed and false accused pupils if a need arises.

In order to mitigate the risk of using student names with police when testing the app, teachers will be asked to participate as role players for police. Once familiarity with nuances of the app's implementation is gained, the police will be involved in the study.

4.6   Sample

4.6.1   Study's setting

The schools in the Free State province are identified as areas where crime is also high. Masitsa (2011) notes schools in Free State lack safety and security, and perpetrators carry out violence within and outside the schools. Additionally, not much research about cyberbullying has been conducted in the Free State province (Odora and Matoti, 2015), especially the eastern region, which poses a high risk when such rural schools are ignored. Also, Odora and Matoti (2015) found a higher Internet usage among learners in Free State's township schools. This observation means increased exposure to smartphones and Internet, in turn leads to cyberbullying (Odora and Matoti 2015). Hence the researcher chose the Eastern Free State region for conducting the current study.

Furthermore, the Eastern Free State Region of South Africa was selected as the setting of the proposed study. Burton (2016) notes existing data in South Africa indicates that learners aged between the ages of 15 and 17 reported being cyberbullied over a period of one year. Also, Trends in International Mathematics and Science Study (TIMSS) found 17% of grade 9 learners in South Africa had experienced some form of bullying nearly weekly (Mullis, Martin, Foy and Hooper, 2016). Therefore, the schools that enrol both male and female pupils who are 14 years and older were selected for this study (Ttofi and Farrington, 2011), and in schools that are already interacting with law enforcement agents. Participation of teachers and pupils who own or have access to smartphones was solicited in this study.

4.6.2 Sampling technique

The sample for the proposed study was purposefully sourced from the social crime prevention officers of the South African Police Services, who are responsible for social crime prevention in schools (Prinsloo, 2005). Also, Neuman (2013) notes in qualitative studies, participant selection is based on their relevance to the research objectives. Cresswell and Plano Clark (2011) suggest a sample should be selected on the basis of their experiences in the domain. Hence, the choice of the purposeful technique is informed by the prevalence of cyberbullying in schools, and the officers' existing relationship with schools, and their experience on social crime issues (Smit, 2015; Prinsloo, 2005; Badenhorst, 2011). Malterud, Siersma and Guassora (2016: 1757) suggest "the larger information power the sample holds, the lower N (sample size) is needed, and vice versa". That is, a larger sample size is not necessary if a sample can provide information that aids a study.

As a result, this study employed the non-probability sampling technique to facilitate collection of appropriate data (Saunders, 2012). Trust is increased between participants and the researcher when the same groups should be used in both EFG and CFG (Hoover and Morrow, 2015; Tremblay *et al.*, 2010). Therefore the police participants were asked to remain available for the duration of the study.

4.6.3 Sample characterisation

In order to validate participants' contribution to the current study, the researcher used digital divide to characterise participants. The factors that contribute to digital divide include age, gender, physical disability, and racial segregation (Chetty *et al.*, 2017; Singh, 2017). Studies show that persons who are aged 45 to 54 rarely used Internet – at least once a month, while those who are aged 15 to 24 used Internet daily (Singh, 2017). Digital divide is characterised by high costs of connectivity, lack of telecommunication infrastructures, and limited digital literacy (Chetty, *et al.*, 2017; Singh, 2017). Digital literacy includes ability to write, read, and share information in online environments such as smart mobile devices (Chia, Choo, and Fehrenbacher, 2017). Generally in South Africa, Chetty *et al.* (2017) note a five-year timespan from getting access to digital tools and becoming proficient users of those tools. With respect to age, persons who are 45 and older are referred to as "digital immigrants" as these people grew up in an era when smart mobile device technologies were not available or still developing (Chia *et al.*, 2017). Smith (2013) notes some of the digital immigrants resist having to learn new system, while others welcome the new system and almost match digital natives' (persons who grew up surrounded with technology and regard it as part of life) level of proficiency.

Ginsburg *et al.* (2017) note youth are the major age demographic in Facebook usage, however adults over 50 are consistently the fastest rising age group.

Ginsburg *et al.* (2017) note older adults (age 50 plus) do need more time to learn using social network sites, "in part validating the age stereotype".

In a study titled "Who Are the Internet Users, Mobile Internet Users, and Mobile-Mostly Internet Users?: Demographic Differences across Internet-Use Subgroups in the U.S." Antoun (2015: 105) in their data analysis used "age (18–24 versus 25, 34, 35–44, 45–54, 55–64, or 65 and older)". Similarly, in this current study, participants were grouped by demographics. Furthermore, participants are grouped as minors (ages 14-17), young adults (ages 18-35), and middle-aged adults (ages 35-55) and older adults (age 55 and older). Using the identified digital divide characterising information, participants' demographics were collected including age, gender, and frequency of social media use, familiarity with mobile bully-victim phenomenon.

Toepoel and Funke (2018) suggest a measure of specific usage frequency on surveys helps to predicts respondents' satisfaction. Also, frequency may be an indication of acquaintance with social media. Hence, participants demographic included a measure of social media usage frequency (Tezci and İçen, 2017).

According to Tremblay, Hevner, and Berndt, (2010) focus group discussions in Design Science data collection should have at least six participants. Therefore, the researcher aimed for at least six participants in each focus group discussions using purposeful sampling. The police personnel, who are designated for social crime prevention in schools, particularly intermediate and high schools, were invited to participate in the study.

As noted earlier (see Chapter 3), this study's procedure is guided by the Design Science Research methodology, which involves an iterative process of design-build-evaluate until the artefact meets the designated requirements (Baskerville *et al.*, 2009). Therefore, the chosen samples changed between the police, teachers and learners in each of iterations of this study in order to accommodate varied roles (learners as reporters of mobile bully-victims and adults as interveners) in the use of the proposed artefact in schools of the Eastern part of the Free State province in South Africa. However, the researcher preserved the identified key characteristics of the samples throughout this study. These key characteristics included the police who were responsible for social crime preventions, and are already interacting with schools. The learner participants had to be enrolled in high schools, be between the ages of 14 and 18, and own a mobile phone or have mobile phone access, and could be of any ethnicity, gender, religion, and tribe.

4.7   Ethical considerations

Conducting research ethically can ensure the integrity of any study. Morgan (2007) notes axiology is a good way of considering values parallel to ontology, epistemology, and methodology issues. Epistemic practices are inherently ethical practices (Simon, 2015). As such, the importance of both ethical issues and values is generally undeniable in any social science research. The following sub-sections present accounts for gaining access to research field (participants recruitments)

4.7.1   *Participants recruitment*

Gaining and maintaining access to police organisations for research can be a difficult task because of their operational sensitivity and organisational culture (Cunliffe and Alcadipani, 2016). Also, the common challenges to gaining access to police as participants involve concerns of viewing the researcher as being planted (Oscar, Ola, Robert and Markus, 2018). Hence, workshops were convened with the police to provide an account to recruit the police participants (Bower *et al.*, 2014; Beskow *et al.*, 2012). The workshop provided a detailed description of the research objectives, the expected role of participants. Also, the definition of the mobile bully-victims phenomenon, as well as identified challenges from literature review that are faced in addressing this behaviour were provided (Beskow *et al.*, 2012). It is worth noting that the police participants indicated that they were not aware of the mobile bullying phenomenon, particularly mobile bully-victims behaviour, prior to the workshops. During the workshops participants were assured about anonymity and confidentiality of collected data, that any information that could identify them would not be disclosed.

4.7.2   *Confidentiality and anonymity*

In South Africa, the Protection of Personal Information Act (POPI) (Act 4 of 2013) addresses confidentiality and anonymity issues (Knight 2019). Confidentiality relates to the researcher's' responsibility to treat as confidential the information attained in the study (POPI Act 4 of 2013), while anonymity relates to ensuring that informant information is not disclosed (Shinde, Shukla and Chitre, 2013; Grunspan, et al, 2014). As such, anonymity was also ensured for participants, with regard to the use of the artefact, anonymity implies that nominees will not know who nominated them as bullies (Shinde *et al.*, 2013; Grunspan *et al.*, 2014). Knight (2019) notes ensuring privacy is easy in data collected through interviews, focus groups, and questionnaires using existing the guidelines such as POPI Act 4. Using codes to make anonymous the collected data in both in artefact's reports and respondent information ensured confidentiality. That is, participant details from interviews and the app reports were replaced with codes, in order to protect participants' identity. Codes merely link data with respondents (Bryant, 2017).

Additionally, in order to reduce the risk of disclosing pupils' names to police while the artefact is merely being tested, teachers in the identified schools were requested to play the role of police. At the end of the study the app will be introduced to police for use according to their regulations. As such, consents were solicited from police and school officials, and teachers, pupils and their parents as well.

4.7.3   *Ethical clearance*

In order to ensure that the current study would be conduct in a responsible and ethically accountable manner, informed institutional permissions were obtained. After the correction of the proposal according to the Department of Information Systems reviewers' suggestion, they accepted and signed off the proposal. Then the research clearance was also applied for and obtained from the University of Cape Town Research Ethics Review Committee. Finally, research permissions were also granted from participants' officials including the Department of Basic Education and Department of South African Police Service, both nationally and provincially.

The researcher ensured utmost responsibility in keeping with ethical research conduct, including ensuring all participants privacy, and adhering to the Universities values.

4.7.4   *Consent forms*

Before the study commenced, informed consents were obtained from the police, teachers, and learners and their parents. The consent forms provided the description of the study including indication of parts (design and development, and artefact testing) of the study participants chose to be involved in, the mobile bully-victim phenomenon and foreseeable risks.

4.7.5   *Rapport and feedback*

The researcher was also responsible for data collection, which helped to create rapport, and in turn improved data collection (Hoover and Morrow, 2015). In order to maintain trust and keep participants interested, the researcher shared with them the information about the progression of the study, including initial results using workshops (Mfutso-Bengo, Ndebele, and Masiye, 2008). Hoover and Morrow (2015) note rapport promotes complete and rich descriptions needed for invaluable finding. Also the feedback served as reflexive member checking – validation or trustworthiness of the study, to ensure that the researcher captured participants' subjective responses accurately (Koelsch, 2013, Kornbluh, 2015). This process included the provision of the artefact to participants so they could see the incorporation of their ideas, and identify any misrepresentations. This check was conducted by providing the artefact and user manuals to the participants. Also, participants were given draft at the end of the data collection to provide feedback (Hoover and Morrow, 2015). At the end of the study a comprehensive report of the study was provided to the police and schools officials.

Chapter 5 – Design and development

5.1. Introduction

Literature and reliable studies in Southern Africa on cyberbullying are lacking with an exception of a limited data that emanated in South Africa (Burton, 2016; Juan *et al.*, 2018). Also, most studies focus on traditional forms of violence, while mobile technology is increasingly used for victimisation, which necessitated assessment of the problem in mobile context (Kyobe and Lusinga, 2018). Furthermore, social network-mediated bullying is a growing problem in South African public schools; however, the understanding of mobile bullying is still limited (Ndyane and Kyobe, 2019). As such, there is a lack of studies that seek to develop applications to mitigate cyberbullying, except for independent developers aiming to improve safety of social media users (Ashktorab, 2018). Furthermore, Kyobe and Lusinga (2018) note reporting is important in countries like South Africa where crime rate is one of the highest in the world; however, schools lack adequate reporting. This chapter serves as an entry point to the implemented Design Science framework for developing the proposed artefact. The selected framework for guiding the artefact's features (for reporting mobile bully-victims) is presented with reference to the existing cyberbullying tools and their limitations. Also, the rational for the artefact's design and development is presented with reference to the identified limitations of the existing interventions. The adopted Design Science framework for the development of the proposed artefact is presented. This chapter concludes with the discussion about participants training during the design and evaluation of the artefact.

Rural secondary schools are also experiencing violence, and so far research has focused on fewer rural areas in South Africa, such as Eastern Cape, Mpumalanga and Limpopo (Juan *et al.*, 2018) but Free State particularly the Eastern part, has not received much focus. Kyobe, Mimbi, Nembandona and Mtshazi (2018) note a high ownership of mobile phones and high youth crime, which may equally imply predominance of mobile bullying in rural area schools.

5.2. Framework for mobile bully-victim mitigation tool

The focus of design science is the innovative creation and evaluation of artefacts to offer a solution to real world problems (Hevner *et al.*, 2004; Peffers *et al.*, 2007). A suitable framework is required in order to position intervention and guide the implementation of the proposed artefact.

There are proposed frameworks for dealing with children and adolescent's safety online, especially cyberbullying. Wisniewski, Ghosh, Xu, Rosson and Carroll (2017) surveyed available and free mobile applications that are designed to help mitigate cyberbullying by promoting adolescents online safety. Of the 75 applications that fitted their research criteria; 59% of available apps were freely available. Overall they found that apps' features that targeted teens were limited compared to those available for parents; apps that are designed just for teens were rare. Based on these findings, Wisniewski *et al.* (2017: 55) proposed "Teen Online Safety Strategies (TOSS) Conceptual Framework" as shown in Figure 5. Their framework includes parents' roles as monitors of children's online activities, and restricting time spent online and accessing risky content or activities, and engaging teens on discussion about online activities. On the other hand, adolescents are empowered to practice self-regulation, such as being aware of their motivations and actions, self-control, and managing negative incident occurrences. Clearly this TOSS advocates children development towards responsible technology users through parental control and exposure to online activities. However, TOSS does not provide ways to prevent cyberbullying incidents, but seeks to build risk coping from online activities.

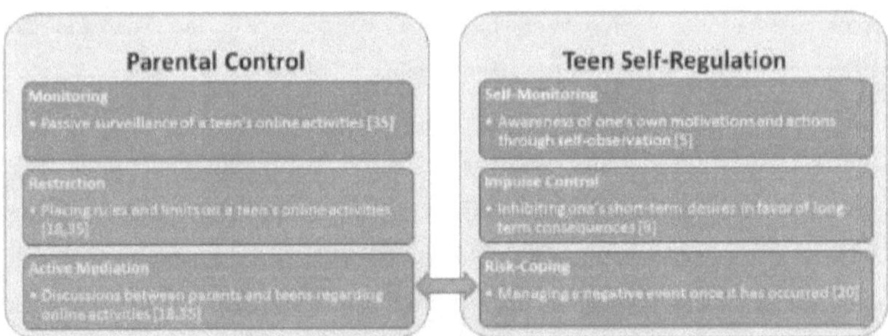

Figure 5: "Teen Online Safety Strategies (TOSS) Conceptual Framework" Wisniewski *et al.* (2017: 55)

Also, Ashktorab (2018) proposes a framework for mitigating cyberbullying at various stages of cyberbullying aggression. This framework is based on the approach outlined to identify opportunities to intervene in domestic violence prevention along the

"Continuum of Harm" (Wolfe and Jaffe, 1999). On one side of the spectrum lies gender-based jokes and vulgarity, and on the other end lie physical abuse and rape. Cyberbullying triggers the continuum, where self-esteem damages occur at one end, and formation of suicidal ideas lie on the other end (Ashktorab, 2018). The continuum is used to determine the best entry point of intervention. As in the domestic violence prevention framework, three approaches of prevention including *primary* prevention, *secondary* prevention, and *tertiary* prevention. Figure 6 presents "Cyberbullying Continuum of Harm", which "describes the different types of emotional distress that follow cyberbullying" (Ashktorab, 2016:127). The *primary* prevention focuses on deterring online users from committing cyberbullying. Online users are led to reflect upon the consequences of their meditated actions, and reconsidering their motivation and values (Fan, Yu, and Bowler, 2016; Lieberman *et al.*, 2011). The *secondary* prevention seeks to decrease the identified cyberbullying problem, by filtering cyberbullying contents for recipients. In particular, secondary intervention provides control of cyberbullying for victims. The *tertiary* prevention, focus on providing support for harmed victims that are suicide inclined and depressed victims after the occurrence of cyberbullying, by providing support to. However, the "Cyberbullying Continuum of Harm" framework provides a generic intervention that focuses on supporting victims, and does not provide mechanism for direct reporting and identification of culprits so that they can account for their behaviour. Particularly, the framework does not cater for bully-victims that inhabit the characteristics of both pure victims and pure bullies (Olweus, 2001, Juan *et al.*, 2018).

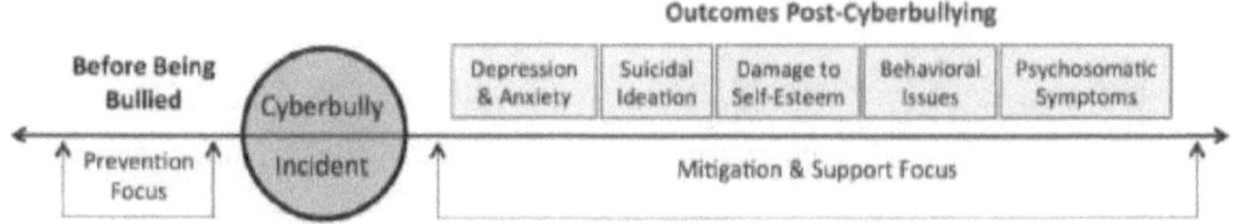

Figure 6: "Cyberbullying Continuum of Harm" (Ashktorab, 2016:127)

Ashktorab and Vitak (2016) note there are existing applications such as "You are valued" that aim to boost users' self-esteem and confidence from cyberbullying effects. However, their design or evaluation over looked the involvement of adolescent's perspectives. Studies on the design of technological solutions for cyberbullying are limited; however, there are independent developers focusing on the well-being of social media users (Ashktorab and Vitak, 2016). There are mobile applications developed to address cyberbullying behaviour in schools. Public Safety Canada (2018) provides descriptions of mobile applications (apps) that are designed to mitigate cyberbullying, including ReThink and STOPit. ReThink is an Android based app that deters users from sending inappropriate content, by detecting harmful language or messages before sending. However, ReThink does not enable reporting and solving existing mobile bullying incidents, which is a limitation because often victims face challenges in report mobile bullying incidents (Perren *et al.*, 2012; Paullet and Pinchot, 2019; Troop-Gordon, 2017).

On the other hand, STOPit is based on both Android and Apple platforms, and provides instant and anonymous reporting of general inappropriate behaviour, including cyberbullying, in school context. The STOPit uses a generalised approach addressing inappropriate behaviour that might not be life-threatening, such as bullying, especially cyberbullying. However, there is evidence that incidents of bullying can have devastating impact on victims. Notably, a single incident of bullying such as posting embarrassing information online can harm victims, and in other instances victims have committed suicide as a result (Olweus, 2013; Volk, Dane and Marini, 2014). Hence, STOPit may not be effective in addressing mobile bully-victims behaviour. In light of the Cyberbullying Continuum of Harm (Ashktorab, 2016), ReThink focus on primary prevention, while STOPit focus on secondary prevention.

The researcher deemed the "Cyberbullying Continuum of Harm" framework a suitable guide for the implementation for the proposed artefact. School classes have a major influence in predicting addressing cyberbullying (DeSmet *et al.*, 2015). Hence, the aim of the proposed artefact is aid police to diagnose to diagnose mobile bully-victims behaviour in school classrooms. Table 8 presents an overview of a sample app's features in relation to "Cyberbullying Continuum of Harm", and their limitations. Notably, none of the apps in the sample address specific types of cyberbullying (victims, bullies, and bully-victims), or diagnose behaviour in order to provide tailored interventions for the identified victims or bullies.

Table 8: Sample app's features in relation to "Cyberbullying Continuum of Harm"

Name	Applicable framework	Features	Limitations
Stronger than Bullying (Ouellet-Morin and Robitaille, 2018)	Primary and tertiary prevention	Provides information about bullying and helps youth to better understand their experiences and learning coping strategies when facing cyberbullying.	General approach. Only awareness. No reporting.
ReThink (Public Safety Canada, 2018)	Primary prevention	Discourage users from sending inappropriate content, by detecting harmful language or messages before sending.	General approach. Does not address existing incidents.
STOPit (Public Safety Canada, 2018)	Secondary prevention	Provides instant reporting of general inappropriate behaviour, including cyberbullying, in school context.	General approach.
Feelbook (Fan, Yu, and Bowler, 2016)	Primary and tertiary prevention	Aims at preventing and mitigating mean and cruel online behaviour. Provides coping strategies for victims. Provide connection to trusted adults for reporting and support help.	General approach. No impact assessment.
KnowBullying (Shieh, 2016)	Primary and tertiary prevention	Enables parents and caregivers to raise awareness about and prevent cyberbullying in classroom, and recognising warning signs of victimisation on children.	General approach. No reporting. No impact assessment.
Cybersafe (Shieh, 2016)	Primary prevention	Game based app that provides practical guidance and skills on how to address cyberbullying.	General approach No reporting. No impact assessment.
CyberBully Hotline (Shieh, 2016)	Secondary prevention	Enables anonymous reporting of bullying and other problems in school.	General approach. No impact assessment.
Put an End to Cyberbullying (Shieh, 2016)	Secondary prevention	Provides resource for children, educators and parents to identify, stop and prevent cyberbullying.	General approach. No impact assessment.
BullyBlocker (Shieh, 2016)	Secondary prevention	Provides components to block messages and reporting cyberbullies, recording bullies in action for evidence.	General approach. No impact assessment.
The BullyBØx	Secondary prevention	Provide anonymous platform for learners to report bullying.	General approach. No impact assessment.
KiVa (Salmivalli and Poskiparta, 2012)	Primary, secondary, and tertiary prevention	Provide virtual learning about bullying based on computer games, and informed targeted intervention through adults in schools.	General approach.

The identified sample apps are either geared for children's or caregivers' usage; however, none are designed to aid or from law enforcement perspectives. None of the identified applications focused on bullying perpetrators or bully-victims, possibly as an attempt to avoid learner labelling, as also noted by (Tłuściak-Deliowska, 2018). While the cited apps empower children against bullying, they employ a general approach and focus on victims only, without attention to mobile bully-victims who are more at risk (Rodkin *et al.*, 2015; Schwartz, 2000). Also, literature shows that bully-victims face higher risks of poor conduct, academic, and peer relationship problems, as well as substance abuse compared to bullies (Juvonen and Graham, 2014; Protogerou and Flisher, 2012; Sangalang, Tran, Ayers, and Marsiglia, 2016). Since bully-victims characteristics include victims and bullies' behaviour (Gámez-Guadix, Gini, and Calvete, 2015; Pouwels *et al.*, 2016), *they may not be inclined to report incidents, seek help or even finding applications that can help them realise their unacceptable behaviour, or intentionally seek guidance to change their behaviour* (Tłuściak-Deliowska, 2018). This could be as a result of their involvement in bullying others and lack of safe platforms. The aim of the proposed artefact is to enable both victims and bully-victims to report incidents. In order to make the proposed artefact a better intervention the design of the artefact aimed to enhance the following qualities: (1) mitigating fear, (2) empower the marginalised, and (3) provide control, and (4) addressing effects of cyberbullying on learners.

Mitigate fear: Perren *et al.* (2012) note that children feel that their parents are not accustomed to cyberspace, as such they may not be able to help against cyberbullying. Up until now the lack of reporting bullying still persists, as noted by Troop-Gordon (2017), often children do not report bullying experiences. For fear of further bullying, victims are unlikely to report incidents to adults (Kraft and Wang, 2009; Crothers and Kolbert, 2008). Lereya *et al.*, (2015) notes being bullied lead to conditioned fear response, such that children tend to have heightened expectations of threat and danger. Also, bully-victims' sheer fear of punitive consequences for their actions (Walgrave, 2013) may discourage reporting. As such, learners need to be assured of their safety so they can report bullying incidents. One of the ways to alleviate the lack of reporting may be the use of voting – peer- and self-report, to identify bully-victims without risks of further victimisation to learners. Asking learners to nominate their victims, provide information from the bullies' perspective, while asking learners, about *who* bullies them provides victims' perspective. The proportions of this information lead to peer- and self-report on bullying and victimisation (Volk, Veenstra and Espelage, 2017). Perren *et al.* (2012) suggest children who are aware of cyberbullying as aggressive behaviour, were more likely to report incidents to trusted adults. Furthermore, awareness initiatives about cyberbullying and its risks should be directed to all stakeholders (teachers, children, parents, and the police), which could create a trusting context for victims regarding adult authorities (Perren *et al.*, 2012). The design artefact will help to provide surveillance against mobile bully-victim.

Empower the marginalised: Bukowski and Sippola (2001) argue that victimisation is a process of ostracising individuals who may impede a group from attaining its goals. The design of the artefact seeks to provide mobile bully-victims, who are often marginalised by teachers and peers because of their impulsive and provocative behaviour (Popovac and Leoschut, 2012; Yang and Salmivalli, 2015), a reporting platform to seek help without further victimisation. The telegraphic nature of online communications often makes proving a definite meaning or intention to harm difficult for authorities, though bullies and victims may understand the meaning (Fraser *et al.*, 2013: 32-33). Since bullies may conceal their behaviour, which weakens evidence, the proposed artefact in this study enables polling, which identifies bullies through multiple victims, as an alternative evidence to ascertain reports that could otherwise be indecisive. In turn, learners will be empowered to report incidents as an attempt to address mobile bully-victims behaviour.

Providing control: Most reported cases of cyberbullying fail to bring a deserved justice for victims due to lack of convincing evidence (Fraser *et al.*, 2013), which may leave learners helpless against the perpetrators. Hence, providing learners with an opportunity to identify their perpetrators and application of restorative justice may help learners to gain a sense of control against cyberbullying, especially mobile bully-victims behaviour. Also, providing learners with definition and descriptive nuances may help to empower learners to recognise mobile bully-victims behaviour.

Addressing effects of cyberbullying on learners: While the proposed artefact enables reporting of cyberbullies and gaining control over incidents, the assessment feature, as informed by the Cool School Programme (2001), addresses the effects of the identified behaviour on learners. The artefact suggests remedial actions based on the degree of impact on each learner.

5.3. Conceptual framework operationalization

As already mentioned, the researcher deemed Ashktorab's (2016:127) "Cyberbullying Continuum of Harm" framework suitable for guiding the development of the artefact that is informed by the conceptual framework emanating from literature review in this study. The conceptual framework provided constructs to aid the *police's effectiveness in combating mobile bully-victims behaviour in schools*. These constructs were discussed in section 2.9 (Theoretical integration), this section discusses the mapping of the primary, secondary, and tertiary interventions of the "Cyberbullying Continuum of Harm" framework to the proposed framework constructs, which are:

- Diagnose mobile bully-victim behaviour
- Enable safe mobile bully-victim disclosure
- Raise awareness of mobile bully-victim behaviour
- Severity assessment of mobile bully-victim behaviour
- Resolving mobile bully-victim behaviour incidents
- Instil trust on mobile bully-victims

In order to inform the design of the artefact, the constructs of the proposed frameworks were map to the "Cyberbullying Continuum of Harm" as follows:

Primary intervention: The artefact should be designed to provide a reporting function that *enables safe mobile bully-victim disclosure (reporting), in order for the police to *identify or diagnose mobile bully-victim behaviour* among learners in schools. The result of the reports must enable the police to *resolve mobile bully-victim behaviour incidents*.

Secondary intervention: The identification of mobile bully-victims in turn should *raise awareness of mobile bully-victim behaviour*, which enables reduction thereof. That is, the results of reports as evidence must enable the police to address and discourage the identified mobile bully-victims, and foster reflection on offenders about their unacceptable behaviour.

Since mobile bullying behaviour leaves insurmountable effects on victims, the **tertiary intervention** will help to assess the degree if effects on learners in order to provide informed intervention. As such, the artefact must be designed to provide *severity assessment of mobile bully-victim behaviour.* In turn, the use of the artefact including anonymous reporting, confidentiality of the report results, and application of well-informed intervention, must aid the police to address victims and offenders. This way will *instil trust on mobile bully-victims.*

The resulting artefact should operationalise the proposed conceptual framework in this study. Therefore, the design of the artefact must be guided by the primary intervention theme to provide reporting feature in order to enable identification of mobile bully-victims. Then, according to the secondary prevention theme, the artefact must be designed to produce results of reports that will enable mobile bully-victims reduction. Also, the tertiary prevention theme must be applied in the design to provide an assessment feature and the results thereof must aid the police to support mobile bully-victims.

5.4. Rationale for proposed artefact

Mobile bully-victim behaviour adversely affects learners with long- and short-term psychological effects. The effects of bully-victims' behaviour include risks of poor conduct, substance abuse, low academic performance, depression and suicidal ideation (Juvonen and Graham, 2014; Protogerou and Flisher, 2012; Sangalang *et al.*, 2016). Although there is a significant advance in interventions for traditional bullying, few resources to date are available for cyberbullying and largely focus on reporting, monitoring, and restricting adolescents' online activities (Shieh, 2016). These resources focus on protecting adolescents by blocking profane contents, and enabling parental control (Ashktorab, 2016; Wisniewski *et al.*, 2017). Generally lacking identifications of learners' roles (victims, bullies, and bully-victims) and severity assessments, which could assist in providing tailored interventions. Although online interventions are easy to access and seen as less stigmatising compared to traditional methods and face-to-face meetings, however, they do note help to change learners attitude about cyberbullying, and therefore require support of others (Tłuściak-Deliowska, 2018), such as moderated intervention to enable following through the desired change.

Design-based projects use theories as prior knowledge referred to as theoretical framework (Wieringa, 2014). In this study, the literature review integrated reference theories (Patas, Milicevic and Goeken, 2011), to form the developed theoretical framework. This framework argues the need for a mobile bully-victim behaviour reporting platform tailored to aid law enforcement agents (police) as the main aim of this study. The constructs of the theoretical framework provide factors that can aid the law enforcement's role in the fight against mobile bully-victims behaviour. These factors include diagnosing mobile bully-victim behaviour, identifying central role players among mobile bully-victims and assessing its severity. The rationale for identifying central mobile bully-victims is similar to KiVa programme reasoning by Salmivalli and Poskiparta (2012), which focuses target intervention on popular classmates that can influence a positive change in support of victims (Smith, 2016). However, providing support for mobile bully-victims can be challenging because of their dual behaviour as bullies and victims (Olweus, 2001, Juan *et al.*, 2018). Hence, the identification of influential bully-victims that have high centrality through PageRank, or that categorised as propagators or retaliators could aid the police attempts to curb this problem through targeted intervention. In turn, the proposed constructs seek to enable resolving mobile bully-victim incidents, enable safe reporting platform, instil trust of police, and raise awareness about the behaviour.

The researcher adopted the Design Science Research (DSR) methodology in order to operationalize the identified constructs and guide the development of an intervention tool. The suitability of the chosen design approach is based on its focus on developing solutions to important problems (Vaishnavi and Kuechler, 2015). Also, the DSR framework allows iterative design and evaluation of a solution, which helps to create an artefact that fits the needs of stakeholders (Koppenhagen *et al.* (2012).

5.5. Design Science approach (Artefact design and development)

This chapter presents the main aim of this study, which is **to develop a mobile app to aid the law enforcement in diagnosing and curbing mobile bully-victim behaviour in schools**. The methodology followed in the design and development of the artefact is Design Science. The Design Science framework guides the development of artefacts for solving important problems. Brandtner, Helfert, Auinger and Gaubinger (2015) note the main focus of Design Science is the development of theoretically grounded (rigorous knowledge base) artefacts, and justification (relevance) of artefact towards its designated environment. Also the building, evaluation and improvement of artefacts can be done through experimental, observational, testing, descriptive and action research methods (Brandtner *et al.*, 2015). As also shown in this study, the evaluation and refinement of the system employed usability testing, and observational methods. During the design phase the artefact' interaction effects were investigated through a technical action research method (Wieringa, 2014). Design Science couples the development and evaluation iteratively until the completion of the artefact. The design-evaluation phase consisted of a number of loops in a naturalistic environment (Venable, Pries-Heje and Baskerville, 2012), involving police, schoolteachers and school learners.

The approach that was followed to develop the artefact is known as design-evaluation pattern, which emphasises a continuous evaluation approach to building artefacts (Sonnenberg and vom Brocke, 2012; Sturm and Sunyaev, 2019). This approach helps to avoid building insignificant artefacts by emphasising assessment of the design artefacts and design decisions throughout the research project (Sturm and Sunyaev, 2019). Providing evidence that the artefact works and created knowledge is useful requires rigorous evaluation (Venable and Baskerville, 2012). Hence, to instantiate the proposed conceptual framework, the researcher chose the design-evaluate approach. In order to ensure fit-for-purpose of the artefact, the development of the artefact had to be carefully implemented and the designs thoroughly evaluated since design-evaluate framework emphasises evaluation while developing the artefact (Sturm and Sunyaev, 2019). The adapted design-evaluate approach is suited for the development of the artefact according to the proposed conceptual framework.

Mobile application development has always faced "small screen and interface usability issues" (Varshney, 2012: 150). Hence, Neilsen (2001) suggests the true purpose of the usability test is to guide the direction of design, not simply generating reports and presentation. In addition, he suggests that usability test should involve frequent small test, instead of few large tests. Testing enables design refinement, and testing again to see if the fix solved the problem. Hence, iterative system evaluations were imperative, including testing functional utility and technical characteristics as well. During the development of the artefact, researcher tested the artefact prototypes with school learners and teachers. The *formative evaluation* of the artefact and design process was conducted during the design cycles of the chosen approach. Formative evaluation was employed in order to iteratively improve the characteristics and performance of the artefact on the basis of empirically based interpretations and decision (Venable *et al.*, 2016).

Figure 7 presents the adapted design-evaluate approach, with layout of activities and evaluations (Sturm and Sunyaev, 2019). The design-evaluation pattern comprises problem identification, design, construction, and use activities, which are linked through evaluations. Evaluation in design science is tightly coupled with design itself (Venable, Pries-Heje and Baskerville, 2016). In this study, the purposes of evaluations relate to assessment of the identified problem meaningfulness (Evaluation 1), identifying and ascertaining requirements for building the artefact towards the identified problem's solution (Evaluation 2), assessment of the artefact's performance as expected (Evaluation 3), as well as its utility within naturalistic settings (Evaluation 4). The iterative nature of the design science frameworks enables looping back to problem identification for requirements refinement and new constraints identification, which can be introduced in the design of the artefact (Koppenhagen, Katz, Maedche, and Müller, 2011).

The problem understanding and insight gained through *Evaluation 1* (literature review) informed the refinement of the initial set of requirements and specifications of the prototype as a solution to the identified problem. Since distinguishing different stakeholder groups when gathering requirements is important for designing a suitable artefact to meet target users' needs (Chorbev *et al.*, 2017). The aim of this study was to develop a mobile bully-victim diagnosis system for use between two groups of users, the police and high school learners. Hence, understanding user requirements from both learners and the police was important for designing and developing a suitable system for both groups of users. Evaluation 2 involved police and teachers who have better understanding of interacting with learners.

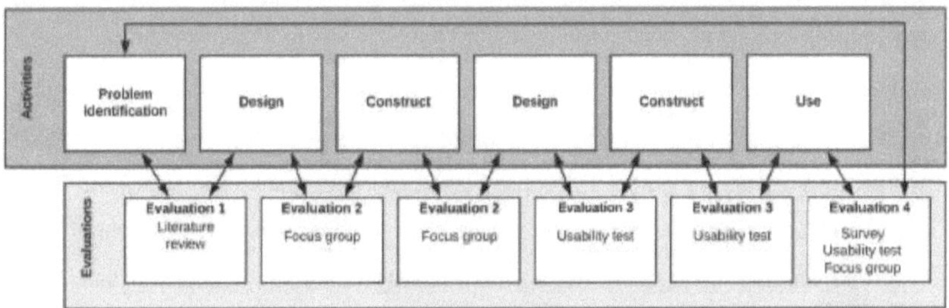

Figure 7: Adapted design-evaluate approach (Sturm and Sunyaev, 2019)

Evaluation 3 included learners from two schools and teachers. The last iteration of Evaluation 2 included police, and the final Evaluation (4), involving learners, teachers and police. The data collected during Evaluation 2 and 3 include usability tests that focused on success rates, number and types of errors (Bastien, 2010), and participants' comments about the prototype. The outcomes of activities and evaluations comprise meta-requirements and prescriptive design principles (Sturm and Sunyaev, 2019).

The usefulness of the initial design to the stated problem was assessed (*Evaluation 2)* through focus groups. As such, Evaluation 2 helped to ascertain the proposed solution requirements, leading to the initial design and instantiation (Construct) of the prototype.

The *second evaluation iteration* was conducted on the initial prototype. The initial prototype was assessed (*Evaluation 2*) using a focus group discussion with the police only. While the results of the initial evaluations helped to derive the first set of design principles, the second evaluation (*Evaluation 2)* helped to identify user interface features that could help to improve the prototype's usability. The evaluation was conducted on the artefact's user interface through a focus group consisting of 5 police officers. The results of the evaluation were incorporated into the initial set of design principles. Also, the prototype was assessed using usability testing and observation with schoolteachers in order to reveal technical and methodical issues of the design (*Evaluation 3*). The aim of usability test is to improve of an artefact's usable quality by focusing on learnability and utility of a product in achieving its goal at reasonably satisfying level (Cheng, 2016). The results of second evaluation iterations (*Evaluation 2)* and *Evolution 3* helped to identify technical feasibility of the design, as well as design issues that required additional refinements. The main issues centred on *safe usage* and *confidentiality, diagnosis coverage* – such that a learner whose bullies or victims are not in the same class can be diagnosed as well, and *time-consuming* assessment feature. Researchers have used peer nomination and/or self-report to assess bullying and victimisation among children via questionnaires (van Dijk, Poorthuis and Malti, 2017; Gutiérrez *et al.*, 2016), which automatically provide safety. However, there is a lack of usable model for mobile bully-victims identification system, and therefore the study proceeded to the second design iteration.

The goal of the *second design iteration* was to refine the prototype based on identified issues in order to improve the artefact's utility in diagnosing mobile bully-victims. Subsequently the prototype was refined by instantiating (Construct) the derived design principles.

The *third evaluation iteration*, also involved usability testing (Evaluation 3) of the prototype with the learners in school classrooms. The results thereof supported the system release for use and evaluations through surveys, focus groups in order to show its utility in aiding the police in diagnosing and curbing mobile bully-victim behaviour in schools. The results of Evaluation 4 are presented and discussed in the Chapter 8 and 9. Also, to enable the system evaluation, teachers, police and learners were provided training on the use of the system, which is presented in the next sub-section (see section 5.6 – Training).

5.6. Training

A measure threat to research questions answers is that developers can use artefacts implicitly in ways that other users cannot (Wieringa and Moralı, 2012). Hence, training other users to perform the artefact functions can mitigate this threat. Also, in order to understand end-user environment and identify optimal features for identifying mobile bully-victims, familiarity with the prototype is needed for participants for effective use (Kaplan-Mor, Glezer and Zviran, 2011; Schnall *et al.*, 2014). End user training deals with equipping participants with skills to effectively user a system (Kaplan-Mor, Glezer and Zviran, 2011). Hence, the researcher provided training and demonstrations on the use of the prototype, in order to enable the use of the prototype for evaluation purpose. The participants consisted of police, schoolteachers and learners. The researcher provided demonstrations of the prototype uses to the police. Also, schoolteachers who were to use the prototype for testing purpose were first trained on how to use the prototype before Evaluation 2 and 3 commenced. The screen captures of the prototype user interface are included in Evaluation 3 section of this chapter. On the other hand, the demonstration involved explanation of the mobile bully-victim diagnosis process that is enabled by the mobile bully-victims response system (M-BRS). Also, the screen mock-ups of user interfaces (see examples in Evaluation 2: Focus group) were provided in order to stimulate participants' creativity.

Ethics: In a research study, ethical questions arise about the research procedure including clarity about which information will or will not be reported, and who will interpret findings (Auerbach and Silverstein, 2003). As such, the current studies procedures, including the artefact's diagnosis process, were reviewed and approved by the ethical review committee of the University of Cape Town, Department of Education, and South African Police Service Commissioners at provincial and national levels (see UCT ethical clearance form in Appendix 10).

The artefact's diagnosis process involves the use of participants' details (names and gender). As such, participants were reassured that the artefact's diagnosis process enables anonymous polling, that is participant would not know which of their peers nominated them. Also, participants were also reassured about the confidentiality of the results, and that the researcher would not divulge participants' personal details in the results.

A day before the test all participants who owned mobile phones were asked to take part in the study by signing consent forms, and learners were also asked to obtain consent from their parents who also signed consent forms. The signed consent forms could be returned the following day. The consent forms provided the details of the study, including descriptions of the diagnosis procedure and risks thereof, as well as the contact details of the researcher, the supervisor, and the ethical review committee.

Participants were also informed that participation in the study is voluntary, and that they could withdraw at any time, if they wished to do so.

Participants were informed that the system enabled anonymous polling (nominations) of mobile bully-victims and the system's reports would be kept confidential. The confidentiality feature was only realised in the second designed prototype). As such, users would not know who nominated them (anonymity), and other participants would not know participant's nomination results (confidentiality), except for the police official using the server application. Also, participants were informed that they could opt not to do nomination, if the felt they had not been bullied or they had not bullied any of their peers. As such, they could not complete the assessment as well.

Training approach: The researcher adopted the Gupta, Bostrom, and Huber (2010) suggested training approach to teach participants in the use of the prototype. This approach involves three phases, *initiation, formal training and learning,* and *post-training* phases. The training starts with the *initiation* phase, which pertains to the development of training material sets and activities to impart knowledge to participants. As such, the researcher developed user manuals for the server and client applications that explained in detail each activity of the system's functions. Kaplan-Mor *et al.,* (2011) note novices learned easily with user manuals. Figure 8 presents a sample user manual for the polling activity of the system; complete user manuals are presented in Appendices 4 and 5. In the *formal training and learning* phase, the participants are taken through the system activities with the aid of user manuals. The researcher used the hands-on approach to train (face to face) participants on the use of the target system with the aid of the developed user manuals (Kaplan-Mor, Glezer and Zviran, 2011). Finally the *post-training* phase involved the evaluation of the *formal training and learning* phase, in which participants demonstrate acquired skills using the system. In this phase the researcher deemed suitable to evaluate the system's functions with the participants in order to identify optimal features of the system for diagnosing mobile bully-victims.

The system consists of the server and client applications. The client application provides a mobile bully-victim definition, to enable pupils to identify their bullies and victims accordingly. On the other hand, the server application receives nominations of learners who are perceived as mobile bully-victims. The diagnosis process consists of three steps, which are registration, polling and assessment.

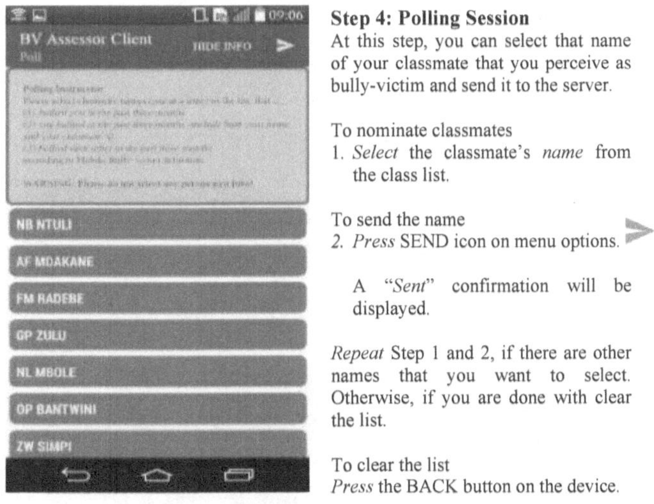

Step 4: Polling Session
At this step, you can select that name of your classmate that you perceive as bully-victim and send it to the server.

To nominate classmates
1. *Select* the classmate's *name* from the class list.

To send the name
2. *Press* SEND icon on menu options.

A *"Sent"* confirmation will be displayed.

Repeat Step 1 and 2, if there are other names that you want to select. Otherwise, if you are done with clear the list.

To clear the list
Press the BACK button on the device.

Figure 8: Sample client user manual

The system's diagnosis process involves using participants' details, including initials and surname, age and gender. The process starts by allowing learners to register on the system and obtain identification codes for authentication on the system. During registration, the system creates an identification (ID) code to enable learners to participate in the polling and assessment sessions. The ID consists of a combination of two alphabetical letters (A to Z) and three numbers (starting from 001 up to 999), which result in the code XX000. The purpose of the ID is to enable the system to track learners' nominations, which is essential for addressing learners behaviour and creating sociograms (graphs that represent nomination). The use of IDs was also to enable anonymity, which is crucial for the participants in the study. Then the official verified the number of registered learners in the class list on the server against the number of learners present. Following the registration, participants were asked to complete the poll and the assessment processes using the prototype's functions.

Registration: During training learners and teachers used their names for registering in the app. Participants were informed that the registration process required their name, gender and age. In order to complete the registration, participants were asked to insert initials and surname in the name field, following the format XX SSSSS (Initials-space-Surname). They were also informed that they should not insert punctuations or special characters in their names of which the system would not allow registration. In the gender field they were to select male or female, or if the preferred not to indicate gender, they could select "other" option. The age field required the learners to insert age from numeric soft-keys. Upon a successful registration, the system created identification code for each participant. The ID feature was only realised after the second design iteration, in order to enable learners to share a limited number of client devices. Participants were asked to note and safely keep their IDs, which will be required for authentication in the completion of nomination and assessment functions.

Poll (mobile bully-victims identification): Participants were informed that a list of names would be sent to each client device for nominations. Then participants had to first read the definition of mobile bully-victim on the client app. Also, they were asked to read the instructions and shown how to select a name on the client application and send the selected name to the server. On the server device, the system showed nomination progress for each learner. The researcher also explained that each learner could nominate a particular learner only once, and that the nominated name is removed from the list in order to prevent duplicate nominations.

According to the initial design, participants had to select a name (one at a time) in the list and tap the send button on the client app in order to successfully nominate bullies, and the confirmation would be sent back by the server app as an indication of a successful nomination. However, the refined prototype allowed multiple nominations of bullies in the first step, and victims as well in the second step.

Confirmation and severity assessments: Participants were shown how to complete the *confirmation* assessment, by selecting their response *("yes", "not sure" or "no")* to the question: *"You have been nominated as a mobile bully-victim. Do you agree?"* The confirmation includes one question, while the severity assessment consists of three questions regarding *"Impact"*, *"Content obscenity"*, and *"Frequency"*. For the severity assessment, they could select between *"Moderate"*, *"Major"* or *"Sever"* answer options in order to indicate: *Impact* (level of support needed), *frequency* (count of bullying incidents), *and content obscenity* of mobile bully-victim behaviour. Explanation of the predefined answer options was given, that *"Moderate"* means minor, and *"Major"* means serious, while *"Sever"* means critical.

The initial prototype design enables only those who have been nominated during the poll session to complete the assessment. Therefore participants had to select their names from the list of identified learners and complete the confirmation and severity assessments. Also, participants were asked to type *"None"* in the notes field, if they felt they had nothing to say when completing the assessment. Most importantly, participants were informed that the app does not allow submission of assessment information if confirmation or one of severity assessment questions is not completed.

Results: At the end of the polling or assessment, the official using the server device can create reports that provide details of the number of participants who completed the polling or assessments, which helps to decide progression to the next step of addressing mobile bully-victims behaviour, or giving an opportunity to those who did not complete a step.

Submission success: Most importantly, participants were asked to note receipt proof notifications from the server app after sending information in each function. They were also requested to seek help from the researcher if they encountered problems, or if no notification was received for each transaction while using the system. This would enable the researcher to note failure or success rates of the system's functions.

The design and development of the artefact consisted of three components (Ponelis, Renaud, Venter and de la Harpe, 2015), (1) conceptual design as a general solution – a conceptual framework emanating from literature review, (2) architectural design, (3) design and development of the solution regarding functionality of the artefact. The conceptual model served as a representation of the mobile bully-victim diagnosis domain for the police, and is an important step towards an artefact development (Vom Brocke and Buddendick, 2006).

5.7. Reliability and validity

Reliability and validity are two important characteristics of any quantitative measurement. On the other hand, the manner of ensuring trustworthiness of the analysis and authenticity of data in qualitative studies is "similar to ways of ensuring validity and reliability" in quantitative studies (Sargeant, 2012:2), and essentially have the same meaning irrespective of study methods (Long and Johnson, 2000). Another important aspect to ensuring validity and reliability, as well as authenticity and trustworthiness of the observed results is triangulation. Triangulation is the combination of methods to help overcome their inherent biases, thus reducing a validity risk (Gilad, 2019). Also, the goal of triangulation is to enhance validity of overall findings through complementarity (Tonkin-Crine *et al.*, 2015). This study employed methodological triangulation, using more than one data collection technique, and data triangulations, using multiple sources of data (Tonkin-Crine *et al.*, 2015). The collected data included the M-BRS diagnosis results, specifically nomination and assessment, and survey, usability test, focus group discussions.

5.6.1 Validity

The validity of an instrument is closely associated with its reliability. That is, an instrument's validity is dependent on its reliability, however reliability is independent of its validity (Tavakol and Dennick, 2011). While reliability of an instrument is concerned with consistent measurement, validity focuses on the extent to which an instrument accurately measures the phenomenon. Validity can be ensured by first testing internal consistency using alpha in a reliability rest. In turn, alpha adds validity and accuracy to the interpretation of data (Tavakol and Dennick, 2011). Furthermore, validity of an instrument can be assessed against existing gold standard scales (Williams, 2003). As such, this study used an adapted and well-established IBM PSSUQ questionnaire (Sauro, 2019; Tullis and Stetson, 2004). The survey items were validated through the literature review, including the framing of questions using similar studies as a guide, and the bullying expert also evaluated the clarity, readability and completeness of the items (Yaghmale, 2009).

Additionally, the experimentation method was employed in this study for validation, to ensure external and internal validity of the observation made about the use of the artefact (Vaishnavi and Kuechler, 2015). Validation in experimentation involves the assurance of external and internal validity of the observations emanating from the constructed artefact. The following are criteria that influence the confidence of the results established by an experiment, classified according to (Vaishnavi and Kuechler, 2015; Wohlin *et al.*, 2010):

Construct Validity: surrogates can be used where participants are cannot be readily observed in the experiment, sample must be a valid substitute in the measurement of constructs. In essence, the developed artefact in this study is for use between the police and school learners. However, due to logistical issues, learners were not available during the test of the artefact. Hence, only the police were involved in the validation of the artefact with the researcher, whereas, learners also participated in testing of the artefact with the researcher only (please see Evaluation 4 in section 9.2.1). Construct validity is mainly essential for practical purposes, not predictive, whereas predictive validity can be examined experimentally (Eikeland, 2006). Vaishnavi and Kuechler (2015) suggest that external validity is met if research outcomes are valid for the phenomenon to which the outcomes apply. This implies that the actual phenomenon should be used, and if not possible surrogates can replace elements of the phenomenon as long as the surrogates are approximate of the actual elements. In the current study, the researcher conducted experiments with either the police or school learners. Rigour is necessary so that the results of the artefact testing can be used to judge the validity of the design theory (Vaishnavi and Kuechler, 2015). In approximation of a naturalistic of the M-BRS, the nature of subjects and procedure helped to strengthen the external validity of the experiment (Vaishnavi and Kuechler, 2015).

Internal Validity: Ensuring that no other constructs will influence the observed behaviour except for those that are part of research question. That is the outcomes of the experiments should not be as a result of manipulated independent constructs. Also, subject experience of in the experiment tasks is a threat to internal validity. This threat was eliminated since the subjects did not have any experience related with mobile bully-victims diagnosis using the M-BRS.

External Validity: If the purpose of the experiment results is to generalise findings, but are extracted in a simulated limited environment. An argument should be presented to show the applicability of results to generalisation. The subjects were not familiar with mobile bully-victim diagnosis process until before training during the experiment, so the threat to the duration of the experiment time could be ruled out. Regarding the representative of the results, the experiment was conducted in a simulated context with subjects that had no prior experience of tasks of the experiment. Therefore the results express novice assessors' perceptions without prior experience in mobile bully-victims diagnosis using the M-BRS.

Validity conclusion: The main thread of the experiment related to the applied statistical test. As a result of a small sample size in this experiment, no statistical tests were applied to answer the research question. However, the results that were obtained through the confirmatory focus group and observations were considered. *Reliability* requires that the experiment should be repeatable in a similar setting. The reliability of the questionnaire instrument is also discussed in Section 9.2.1 (Reliability test) of Chapter 9.

Chapter 6 – First cycle

6.1   Introduction

This chapter presents the first cycle of design and development, beginning with evaluations of the conceptual model stemming from the literature review (see Chapter 2) and confirmation of the requirement. It then concludes with the design and implementation of the initial functional prototype is designed.

6.2   Evaluation 1 – Problem identification and suggestion

The literature review in this study helped to identify the research problem and developing a conceptual model (see Chapter 2 – Theoretical integration), henceforth simply referred to as "conceptual model". Evaluation 1 focused on identifying requirements of the envisioned solution for aiding police in diagnosing and curbing mobile bully-victims behaviour in schools. Explanatory design theory provides functional details that support the need for designs and artefacts to have specific attributes and features, and encourages design goals decomposition into solid requirements that must be fulfilled by artefacts' components (Patas *et al.*, 2011). The design and implementation activity involves deciding on desired functionality of an artefact and its architecture and then producing the real artefact (Peffers, Tuunanen, Rothenberger and Chatterjee, 2007). In the initial development cycle, constructs in the conceptual model enabled the creation of the initial design principles list. As also noted by Wieringa (2014), conceptual model constructs can also be used as design specifications of an artefact. According to Wieringa (2014) constructs uses include:

- Defining the architectural structure of an artefact and its context,
- Describing a phenomenon in the artefact and context,
- Creating questions about the phenomenon, and
- Stating generalizations.

The conceptual framework, stemming from the literature review in this study, presented constructs or aspects that are deemed influential to law enforcement's efforts against mobile bully-victims behaviour in schools. Artefacts include constructs, models, methods, or instantiations (Peffers *et al.*, 2007), which can be transformed into a process or a product such as software (Gregor and Hevner, 2013). Instantiation relates to operationalization of empirical finding about a problem

(Koppenhagen, Katz, Maedche and Müller, 2010), as well as constructs, models and methods (Vaishnavi and Kuechler, 2015). Gregor and Hevner (2013:341) posit, "many IT artefacts have some degree of abstraction but can be readily converted to a material existence; for example, an algorithm can be converted to operational software". Also operationalising constructs enables their measurement for validity (Wieringa, 2014). In order to enhance the effectiveness of law enforcement in curbing mobile bully-victim behaviour, six depended constructs of the conceptual model were transformed into functions or requirements and components of the artefact. Table 9 presents the mapping of the conceptual model constructs (developed through literature review) to initial set of requirements. The "Resolve mobile bully-victim behaviour" and "Instil trust on mobile bully-victims" constructs were not transformable, but they are seen as outcomes of the artefact application. These are non-functional requirements in the design of the artefact (Cysneiros, do Prado Leite and Neto, 2001).

Table 9: Mapping construct on requirements

Constructs	Artefact functions/requirements
Diagnose mobile bully-victim behaviour	• Learners registration • Mobile bully-victims diagnosis
Assess impact of mobile bully-victim	• Measurement of mobile bully-victim effects
Enable safe mobile bully-victim behaviour disclosure	• Ensure informant safety
Raise mobile bully-victim behaviour awareness	• Educate learners about mobile bully-victims behaviour
Resolve mobile bully-victim behaviour	
Instil trust on mobile bully-victims	

The requirements were confirmed by eliciting users perceptions of the identified problem. The Evolution 2 provides the confirmation of the requirements through focus group discussions, which led to initial set op requirement in the design and instantiation of the artefact prototype.

6.3   Evaluation 2 – Ascertaining requirements

The aim of the Evaluation 2 was to identify and ascertain requirements for the artefact towards the identified problem's solution. The researcher deemed focus group discussions a suitable method for eliciting these requirements.

6.3.1 *Focus groups*

The problem conceptualisation was established through a framework model that emanated from literature review. Kenny, Dooley and Fitzgerald (2016) note human-computer interaction research emphasises that the design of technology-based interventions should first start with understanding user needs. In order to substantiate the perceived problem, and discover the underlying causes of the perceived problem, the researcher conducted exploratory focus group discussions with stakeholders. Focus group discussions were chosen for their ability to generate data that helps in gaining insight into peoples lived experience (Tremblay, Hevner and Berndt, 2010). Thematic analysis was employed to gain deeper understand of the stated problem from participants perspectives. The researcher investigated the subject matter from police, who are responsible for crime prevention in schools, and schoolteachers. This approach was necessary because of the limited number of police who are designated to social crime prevention in schools. Altogether, the researcher gathered detailed domain and problem descriptions from eighteen participants. Ndyane and Kyobe (2019) note bully-victim is one type of bullying that has received limited research focus in South Africa. As such mobile bully-victim is not a widely known phenomenon, thus on average focus group discussions lasted for 30 minutes.

In order to gather participants' first-hand experience and in-depth knowledge on mobile bully-victim behaviour, this study employed a qualitative and explorative approach (Neuman, 2013). According to Patton and Cochran (2002:3) "qualitative research is characterised by its aims, which relate to understanding some aspects of social life, and its methods which (in general) generate words, rather than numbers, as data for analysis". Thus the application of qualitative and exploratory approach merited participants to share their real-life and lived experiences to inform the research as well as responding to research questions of this study. Also, Merriam (2009) explains that qualitative research is a process, understanding and meaning-oriented which makes the research the primary instrument of data collection and analysis.

Focus group interviews enable the understanding of end-users' environment (Hove and Anda, 2005; Schnall *et al.*, 2014; Tremblay, Hevner and Berndt, 2010). The purpose of the focus group was twofold. Firstly, to uncover challenges faced by the police in addressing mobile bully-victim behaviour by in school. Secondly, to confirm the conceptual model proposition, stemming from the literature review in this study – henceforth referred to simply as conceptual model, as a solution, as well as identifying the artefact's utility risks. A semi-structured approach was adopted to seek expected information using specific questions, as well as unexpected information through open-ended questions as guides (Hove and Anda, 2005; Kallio, Pietilä, Johnson and Kangasniemi, 2016). Kallio *et al.* (2016) note semi-structured interviews are appropriate to use when respondents are not well aware of a subject or phenomenon. At the beginning of the study, a workshop was conducted to provide participants with an overview of mobile bully-victim phenomenon. The workshop discussions also helped to reveal that the level of participants' knowledge about the phenomenon was minimal. As a result, eight guiding questions informed by the conceptual model constructs and research questions were formulated (Gibson and Arnott, 2007). The types of questions included experience and knowledge probes (Hove and Anda, 2005). Experience questions were used to solicit description of actions and behaviour from participants. This allowed participants to describe how they deal with mobile bully-victim cases in schools. The use of knowledge questions was to elicit factual information regarding mobile bully-victim behaviour.

Neuman (2013) notes in qualitative studies, participant selection is based on their relevance to the research objectives. Hence, in the context of this study, subjects were chosen based on specific characterisation given the nature of the subject matter. Thus the researcher used a non-probability method to select participants. Through convenient sampling, participants were selected based on their characterisation of being educators in Intermediate and High Schools, and social crime prevention officers in the South African Police Services (SAPS) within the study areas, Harrismith and Phuthaditjhaba.

Four exploratory focus group interviews were administered on a sample of 15 participants in the Eastern region of the Free State Province in South Africa. Participants were categorised as police and schoolteachers within groups, to enable homogeneity and differences in opinions (Gibson and Arnott, 2007). The SAPS personnel included two focus group sessions, in the first with two and the second consisted of three participants. The researcher is aware that Tremblay *et al.* (2010) suggest that a minimum number of participants in a focus group should be four, however, the unforeseen circumstances of the three members from the first session being on leave and two members not availing themselves for the second session was noted as the main challenge faced in this study. Coupled with the fact that within the SAPS, a limited number of staff is deployed solely to focus on social crime prevention in schools. For the selected region, the Harrismith sector consists only of five officers, and six officers in the Phuthaditjhaba sector. Based on the above justification, if a topic required group discussions, where potential participants' pool is too small, or hard to reach, a mini focus group can be conducted (Nyumba, Wilson, Derrick and Mukherjee, 2017).

Table 10: Participants' profile

ID	Gender	Age group	Rank/ Occupation	Experience (in years)	Knowledge level of mobile bully-victim behaviour	Dealing with mobile bully-victim behaviour	Social media usage
HP1	Male	36-50	Warrant officer	31	Adequate	Rarely	Frequently
HP2	Male	36-50	Sergeant	16	Minimal	Rarely	Never
PP1	Female	36-50	Captain	35	Adequate	Frequently	Rarely
PP2	Male	36-50	Warrant officer	29	Minimal	Frequently	Frequently
PP3	Male	36-50	Warrant officer	24	Minimal	Rarely	Frequently
PP4	Male	50+	Sergeant	30	None	Rarely	Rarely
PP5	Female	20-35	Sergeant	9	Minimal	Rarely	Frequently
PP6	Female	20-35	Sergeant	11	Minimal	Rarely	Frequently
LTT1	Male	20-35	Teacher	7	Minimal	Rarely	Frequently
LTT2	Male	20-35	Teacher	9	Minimal	Rarely	Frequently
LTT3	Female	20-35	Teacher (SBST)	6	Adequate	Frequently	Frequently
LTT4	Male	36-50	Teacher	20	None	Never	Rarely
IIT1	Female	20-35	Teacher	6	Minimal	Rarely	Frequently
IIT2	Female	20-35	Teacher (SBST)	8	Adequate	Frequently	Frequently
IIT3	Male	36-50	Teacher	23	Minimal	Rarely	Rarely
IIT4	Female	36-50	Teacher	20	None	Rarely	Frequently
IIT5	Male	20-35	Teacher	7	Minimal	Frequently	Frequently

Data analysis was done in Nvivo 12 to create themes that emerged from focus groups discussions. A deductive coding approach was used and informed by a   provisional list of codes from the conceptual framework (Miles, Huberman, Saldaña, 2014). Data excerpts were split into small codable moments (Saldaña, 2013). Themes were derived through jotting and analytic memos (Saldaña, 2013). The following subsections discuss results from exploratory focus groups.

Discussion procedure:
The researcher began with brief introductions in all five focus group sessions. Followed by a request to capture an audio recording with the intention to complement note taking. Which was advantageous as the researcher was going to be able to maintain direct contact, observe or notice the physical reaction and attitude of the subjects during the focus groups. All participants welcomed the request. The issue of confidentiality was addressed, and the participants were assured that the report would capture the correct and accurate reflection of their responses, especially during transcribing and data analysis stage in their absence.

Participants were addressed in a language that they understood, and they were informed that even though questions were in English form, the researcher could explain in their language should need be for better understand. The participants were taken through the prepared questions in detail. The importance of honesty was highlighted as participants were informed that it would be much appreciated if they can be truthful, give factual answers and not answers that they think are socially accepted, or that would sound correct to the researcher. This assisted in addressing the issue of trustworthiness of the collected data. Participants were informed that yes, there are no wrong and right answers, but it would be appreciated if subjects can stick to facts. The rationale behind using semi-structured questions was explained by informing participants that their responses can open room for further questions, which will be advantageous in relation to obtaining in-depth information. Participants were taken through the informed consent, informed that this is purely an academic study, and no remuneration would be received for their participation. Also, should they feel the need to stop participating at any time during the focus group session they could do so.

Table 11: Data themes and code formulation

Research question	Themes	Identified elements/codes under themes
Have you had a report about mobile bullying-victim brought to you as police?	Reporting mobile bully-victim behaviour	Role-players ignorance Inexistence VS under reporting
Have you had children in class report bullying incidents to you as teachers, especially mobile bullying?	Reporting mobile bully-victim behaviour	Role-players ignorance Inexistence VS under reporting
If you were to verify the complaint and a student come to you and say I've been bullied by one of my classmates how would you be handling that?	Verifying bully-victims reports	Misunderstanding Limitation of interventions
How are mobile bullying victim complains resolved among pupils?	Resolving mobile bully-victims Justice miscarriage	Flawed system Non-protective system Policy and legislative neglect Self-justice
Is there a way of measuring the impact of mobile bully-victim behaviour on reporters?	Measuring the impact of mobile bully-victim	Flawed system Differentiation
How do you measure if the person needs professional help?	Measuring the impact of mobile bully-victim	Systematic flaw Differentiation
Is there education or awareness on mobile bully-victim behaviour done in school?	Mobile bully-victim awareness	Capacity enhancement
As police, in your programs when visiting schools do you maybe talk about mobile bullying or bully victim?	Mobile bully-victim awareness	Capacity enhancement
Do you think the children trust the police to resolve their problems?	Pupils' trust on police	Generalisation
As teachers, do you think students can trust you with their issues such as mobile bullying?	Pupils' trust on teachers	Generalisation
How are emotional distressed pupils helped?	Helping emotionally distressed pupils	Misunderstanding of victimisation
Using names and pupil's recollections of bullying experiences are possible risks of participating in this study. Can you identify any other risks?	Possible risks of using this application	Safety assurance
What can be done to encourage learners to come forward and report mobile bully-victim behaviour	Hindrances to investigation of mobile bully-victim incidents	Cyberbullying extends to traditional bullying

Interpretation and reporting of the qualitative data and findings:

This section presents analysis, interpretation and report of the qualitative data and findings. Table 10 provides the summary of participants' profile. Respondents were assigned identification number (ID) to enable anonymous reporting. The police IDs were composed of a first letter of their location and first letter of their occupation, and a number in the respondent list. Similarly, teacher IDs were composed with abbreviation a school name and a number in the respondent list. That is, HP1 up to HPn and PP1 up to PPn as IDs for police in two respective stations. Schoolteachers' IDs were IIT1 up to IITn and LTT1 up to LTTn for respective schools. The n is a decimal numbering of respondent names in the list, starting from 1 (one).

Themes and code formulation from focus group transcripts are presented Table 11. In order to keep respondents anonymous while providing a verifiable report, participants' work-role and profile are presented, but their names are withheld. The participants' work-roles were either police officers or teachers.

Reporting mobile bully-victim behaviour

Identified across all participants' responses when asked whether they have received mobile bully-victim reports was a limited number of or no reports at all. On both sides of the policeman and teachers, there was no definitive 'yes' answer or experience with an existing or old mobile bully-victim case. This observation is in accordance with Troop-Gordon (2017) that often children do not report bullying experiences. Noticeably, all participants seem to lack knowledge about mobile bully-victim behaviour and its characterisation, making the researcher believe that there might have been cases of mobile bully-victim behaviour, but the police and teachers might have viewed them as harassment, conventional bullying or pupil feuds. This is based on one of teacher's response that stated that they do get *"reports that there are some learners who are bullying them through Facebook. They are talking bad things about their parents and bad things about their lives"* (IIT1).

The above response indicates that there is a high possibility that learners, teachers and even police officers are unaware of the forms of bullying or their characterisations. Also, as shown in one of the police's statement, *"it was raised by some of them [learners] that there is mobile bullying in schools, they did not know what the name is for it, but they described bullying by cell phones and WhatsApp, and I said, it is called mobile bullying"* (HP1). Seemingly, if there were mobile bully-victim incidents, it would be challenging to encourage learners to come forward and report. This led the researcher to conclude that even though there is no on-record report of bully-victim behaviour, in reality, this form of bullying goes unnoticed and unreported at best.

Seemingly, teachers were uncertain if mobile bullying is a criminal offence. This is because the South African law is also ambiguous about cyberbullying offence, relying on civil and criminal law responses (Badenhorst, 2011). This could be one of the main hindrances to reporting instances to police. It can also be argued that upon coming forward and reporting a mobile bullying incident, there is no direct line of corrective or punitive approaches, which may make perpetrators accountable, and the victims to feel that justice has taken place. This argument is drawn from the responses from both teachers and police participants who made mention of cases being reported to the school principals or bringing the parties involved together to address the matters. Explaining a particular school-reported incident of posting offensive material on a Facebook wall, one of the law enforcement participants stated, *"Most of the children of the school were not aware of these cybercrimes. They are using the computer and cell phones. So we managed to get that culprit on Tuesday, and try to show him that this is a not okay, but we informed the principal that we will bring someone to address all schoolchildren"* (PP2). When asked on how would the police handle a reported mobile-bully victim behaviour case, responses from law enforcement participants were limited to mediation and getting both sides of the story from the victim and perpetrator. *"I will call the victim and the perpetrator, sit them down and show them the consequences of cyberbullying"* (HP2).

Taking a look at these statements, it can be argued that the impact of such an aggressive or humiliating practice on the victim has not been taken into account, which directly speaks to the need of a proper response mechanisms or approaches that will not only be just, but make the perpetrator accountable and rehabilitated in order for them to take responsibility and be aware of the implication that accompanies cyberbullying, especially when the view of the police takes an approach that *"in actual fact, they are minors we cannot do anything harsh on them"* (PP1). *This observation indicates the need to involve the parents in attempt to curb mobile bully-victim behaviour.*

These comments provide evidence that a proactive intervention is necessary for three reasons. Firstly, teachers and police are unaware of the forms of bullying or their characterisations. Secondly, teachers and learners are not aware of the law's responses to mobile bullying, especially mobile bully-victim behaviour. Lastly, learners may be concealing occurrences of mobile bullying or even mobile bully-victim, until they break into physical fights.

Verifying bully-victims reports

The interaction with participants revealed that all participants had different views on how they would go about verifying mobile bully-victim reports or complaints. These were based on current approaches each participant uses or follow when addressing reported complaints. The teachers' responses were limited to taking the matter to the deputy principal or principal's office. This lack of adequate, direct and first-hand initiative or procedure towards verifying bully-victim reports for personnel who are at the forefront and possibly the go-to people for learners in distress is a cry for concern. Clearly the school environment is not friendly or well equipped to identify, monitor or even support learners who are mobile bully-victims. The researcher then questions the extent to which high schools can prevent or deal with mobile bully-victim or any other form of bullying.

Police officers, on the other hand, spoke of gathering evidence and opening a case if there was enough evidence to establish criminal doing. These responses indicated that there are limited direct procedures in place to verify bully-victim reports besides evidence-based backing, which determines whether or not reports are attended to. However, Fraser *et al.* (2013) note that cyberbullies may use a figurative speech or telegraphic slang when attacking others, which makes it difficult to draw definitive meaning and intentions to harm from evidence. Also, the quality of evidence is important for investigation (Gabbert, Hope and Fisher, 2009). There is a need for better channels or platforms that will be learner-centred and be driven by the need to address distress, threats and all challenges associated with mobile bully-victim behaviour. Such interventions may address the psychological and social wellbeing of learners in response to mobile bully-victims behaviour.

Teachers' responses on verifying reports were contradictory. One teacher stated that they rely on sincerity, *"...whether the person is willing to apologise and explain what they meant about what they said"* (LTT3). However, another teacher (IIT1) felt that "there is no honesty" in learners when dealing with incidents. Seemingly, some of the mobile bullying reports are dismissed due to lack of sincerity or honesty. This observation implies that there is a need for a tailor-made verification process, such as the proposed artefact.

Additionally, teachers' comments indicated that providing evidence on reports of cyberbullying incidents is hard. This is because teachers do not check pupils' phones, but rely on learners' sincerity, or reporting the matters to the deputy principal. Also, the anonymity affordance and impersonation (Fraser *et al.*, 2013; Hoff and Mitchell, 2009) of social network platforms makes it hard for officials to link bullying incidents to perpetrators. One teacher participant shared an example of an unfruitful investigation of incidents that involved Facebook, "*the educators were talking to learners, where they actually did not get to a solution or to even say who did it*" (LTT3). Similarly, another teacher participant commented, "*I decided to talk to them privately and say to them you know what you do not have full evidence*" (IIT2). These observations indicate that teachers are reluctant to report mobile bullying incidents to the police unless they are certain of the evidence. One can then question what happens to the victim in this process, especially those that came forward and reported being victimised.

To make a case permissible in the court of law, the police "*rely on witnesses and maybe on injuries if it was physical bullying, but if it was cyberbullying they can maybe show you the message on the phone so that you can read it for yourself*" (HP1). However, concealed or fake identities on social network accounts also make it close to impossible to link evidence with perpetrators, which could result in case dismissal from courts. In such instances the police may inform complainants that nothing can be done (Kwan and Skoric, 2013). This observation may imply that complainants succumb to helplessness of the verification process, while perpetrators may continue their behaviour, or might seek vengeance in alternative ways such as confrontations.

These observations strongly suggest that besides evidence gathering, an alternative way to verify reports is needed. An approach is needed to aid the police in addressing mobile bully-victim behaviour, by empowering all learners to safely and anonymously disclose their mobile bully-victim experiences. Possibly, through elicitation of personal experience, and observed experience as well (Phillips and Cornell, 2012). Hence a possible strategy would be to employ peer- and self-reporting, as proposed by the researcher, a mobile bully-victim identification and confirmation mechanism.

Resolving mobile bully-victim reports

Similar to the above responses on verification of mobile bully-victim reports, the participants indicated reliance on evidence and inquiry-based methods to resolve reports. Unlike any other form of aggression or physical and tangible threats, cyberbullying has a component of anonymity and telegraphic slang, making it difficult to identify perpetrators and meaning of their actions (Fraser *et al.*, 2013). This observation indicates a need for developing effective systems, approaches or methods to deal with mobile bully-victim or even cyberbullying as a whole in the school environment. However, the police participant (HP1) indicated that cyberbullying cases tend to be addressed through the Protection from Harassment Act, 2011 (Act 17 of 2011). The noted absence of learner-centred approaches of reporting, verifying and resolving mobile bully-victim reports should be addressed at the central or national policy-making level. The researcher recommends that the Department of Basic Education's relevant policymakers relook at the National Safe Schools Framework and make amendments inclusive of information about all forms of bullying and direct procedures of its prevention, reporting and resolving such cases in a learner-centred manner.

While punitive measures such as sanctions may be preferable, as they do not only curb misbehaviour, but also serve as a warning to other potential bullies (Rigby, Smith and Pepler, 2004). Such measures may not be applied consistently as a result of different forms of bullying (Rigby *et al.*, 2004). Also, Corss *et al.* (2015) posit cyberbullying as a teenage behaviour that needs to be addressed restoratively instead of being treated as discipline problem only. Evident in police's responses is the use of Restorative Practice (RP), particularly, the victim-offender mediation (Walgrave, 2013), when resolving bullying incidents, *"we will call both pupils and address them, and also show the other party the results of bullying others. For me I think that one has helped a lot in our area"* (HP2). The suitability of restorative justice is made evident in Walgrave (2013) noting punishments in juvenile justice seem unfruitful, but restorative justice enables a constructive response to children crime and to better address legal requirements.

Also, the comment from one of the police stated that *"sometimes for these children it is difficult to accept that they are doing wrong, so that is why we involve the Social Workers"* (HP2). That is, at other times other learners do not see their actions as offensive. Hence using RP helps learners to reflect on their unacceptable behaviour and experience a sense of remorse, and enable restoration of a damaged relationship. This approach also helps to address negative effects of bullying on learners (Duncan, 2011).

The structure for resolving reports in schools starts with SBT and the principal and then moves to social workers. *"If there is no way of solving it [the incident] then we let them [learners] sign the referral forms, and we refer them to our Social Workers"* said one of the teacher participants (IIT2). However one teacher who is part of the SBST commented, *"We can start by talking to a child to find out what is wrong. Then we have to fill in the forms, we also don't like filling the forms, but we have to, so that there is evidence that this is what happened"* (LTT3). Seemingly, when trying to resolve learners' complaints, teachers find the process of acquiring social workers' help unpleasant. Similarly, time is of essence when trying to resolve incidents, which is shown in teachers' desperate statements, *"even when it comes to referrals themselves [they] can take forever, ..."* (LTT3); *"it takes a long time"* (IIT3). Both schools' teachers shared same sentiments about unduly delays to get the needed help through counsellors, as also noted by Phillips and Cornell (2012). However the stage at which parents are involved is not precise for schools. On the other hand the police involve social workers and parents. The police comments indicated they involve parents, such as *"when the issue cannot be resolved parents are called in"* (HP1). Another police commented, *"but when parents come, they [parents] would like to know who did this to my child. Since they are minors"* (PP2). This observation is in accordance with Popovac and Leoschut (2012) suggestions to use a whole school approach in trying to address mobile cyberbullying or bully-victim behaviour.

Evident in this observation is the need for the Department of Basic Education together with the South African Police Services to devise a clear structure for reporting and resolving incidents. Firstly, the lack of consistent structure for resolving reports by schoolteachers and the police is a concern. Secondly, while social workers' assistance is readily available through the police, the same is not true through schoolteachers, but it is plagued with delays and a cumbersome process. Lastly, the stage of parents' involvement is unclear.

Measuring the impact of mobile bully-victim

Central in key responses of participants was the subjectivity of impact assessment, as cases and situations may differ from one learner to another. That is, it would be difficult to measure the impact of mobile bully-victim on learners. Also, to determine the impact on pupils, responses pointed that learners are referred to either a social worker or psychologist through the School-Based Support Team (SBST) for emotional and psychological support. However, as also noted on the resolving mobile bully-victim reports section, processes for acquiring social workers' help for learners take too long, and sometimes never materialize. As shown in one of teachers' responses, *"even when it comes to referrals themselves, they can take forever, but it's only so much that they can do"* (LTT3). One can argue that all responses from the participants indicated that there is currently no way of measuring impact of mobile bully-victim within schools. Also, this observation implies that the social worker services may be overloaded with cases that could have been resolved within schools. Impact assessment is essential for measuring the state of the reporters, and to filter referrals based on impact levels because counsellors availability is confined by lack of time (Phillips and Cornell, 2012). This observation led the researcher to conclude that there is a need for an impact assessment on mobile bully-victims, which directly links to the appropriate remedial actions.

Mobile bully-victim awareness

What can be drawn as a noteworthy theme from participants' responses is the need for the Department of Basic Education as well as the South African Police Services to train and capacitate personnel on mobile bully-victim. The training should begin with overall specifications and breakdown of cyberbullying. Although bullying awareness is normally raised by teachers personally or through the Life Orientation subject, and the police in schools. All teacher participants and police in this study indicated that there is no direct awareness on mobile bully-victim. Also, teachers mentioned that their schools work with the police, which provide a platform for police officers to support awareness initiatives in schools. However, there is no common and adequate technique to raise mobile bully-victim awareness, instead police use various scare tactics. This was observed in one of the police's comments, *"As for now we just use [scare] tactics to say this and that will be done on the perpetrators [to discourage their behaviour]. However it is going to be a difficult thing at some stage, because we don't have full equipment for that. We just tackle it with fear"* (PP1). The existing police and schools partnership could help to address the concern arising from inconsistent structures of resolving reports in schools. This observation reiterates the need to capacitate the police and teachers about mobile bully-victim knowledge. In return, the police and teachers can cascade their knowledge to pupils through various awareness initiatives in schools. As also noted in one of the police comments *"we need to go to more schools and present this mobile bullying, so they can know more about it. In that way they will be able to come to the police station and report it [mobile bullying], if it is happening to them. So they need to get more knowledge about this mobile bullying"* (PP5). The researcher highly recommends this action given the fact that mobile bully-victim is not a commonly known social phenomenon. Therefore, increasing knowledge base for teachers and police officers may be the first step towards developing effective strategies to fight against mobile bully-victim behaviour. Additionally, these observations support a need for a tool that can be used regularly to raise awareness for learners in schools.

Pupils' trust on police and teachers

Given that the first question addressing the reporting mobile bully-victim cases resulted in all participants indicating no official record of any reports brought forward, the question of pupils' trust on police and teachers to report mobile bully-victim had generalised responses. Teachers mentioned that *"sometimes learners cannot talk to their parents, but they find it easy to talk to us [teachers]"* (IIT3), and let them in when they face challenges such as quarrels and fights in general, but not mobile bully-victim behaviour precisely. This observation is also affirmed by Pepler *et al.'s* (2008) report, which states learners who have low parental monitoring also lack parental trust. Also, the responses from one police officer highlighted the likelihood of younger learners having more trust in the police compared to teenagers. Additionally, the police suggested that *"children below grade 6 are not such a big problem but once they start from grade 6, 7, 8 they start to have doubts about adults"* (HP1). This observation is in accordance with Rigby's (2010: 49) view, pointing out that older learners are generally more distrustful of institutional authority than younger ones. Also, learners may not trust teachers and parents' understanding of cyberbullying to resolve incidents without aggravating the situation (Popovac and Leoschut, 2012). These observations indicate the need for an intervention in schools that facilitates reporting of cyberbullying instances such as mobile bully-victims. Possibly these responses draw attention back to the recommendation of equipping teachers and police with knowledge on mobile bully-victim behaviour, accompanied by proper structures of how schools should go about handling complaints and providing support for learners. In this way, gaining pupils' trust would be easier, so that in a case of mobile bully-victim problems they can report to teachers or police because the system and procedures to aid and resolve such incidents are in place. Also, Perren *et al.* (2012) propose raising awareness about cyberbullying and its risks to learners, teachers and parents could facilitate a context for trust on victims regarding adult authorities. These arguments once again reiterate the importance and need for developing effective interventions to address mobile bully-victim behaviour.

Helping emotionally distressed pupils

According to teacher's responses, the school system of assisting emotionally distressed learners involves teachers taking the responsibility of counselling and talking to the pupils and involving the parents. Adding to this, one of the informants stated that, *"depending on how great is the harm. Lots of our learners who show signs of problems are referred to SBST, which comprises Life Orientation subject teachers as well as the head. In that they try to assist the learners themselves, and should they not be able to. They fill forms and refer the issue to the district, and when learners are referred to the district, they are assisted whichever way they need"* (LTT3). This response indicates a lack of urgency in attending to the emotional ill-being of pupils. This raises a concern because effects of emotional distress in youngsters can result in risky situations and at times can be life-threatening (Volk, Dane and Marini, 2014). This demands a more holistic and easily accessible emotional support structures for learners in schools. On the other hand, responses from the police shows that for social services that they offer to pupils, there is always a designated social worker as part of the team. This observation reiterates the need for joint forces between the Department of Basic Education and Department of Social Services at the local level for the purposes of availing accessible and less time-consuming referral methods in order to assist emotionally distressed pupils.

Justice miscarriage

"Mam, they wrote about my mom, I'm so angry, and if I find them, those two girls, I'm going to fight them because they spoke about my parent" (IIT2) stated by one of the teacher participants, citing two aggravated boys who come forward about addressing a social media incident. Drawing from this example, one may argue that in cases where learners feel that when they face mobile bullying, reporting to the teachers may not result in perpetrators receiving a well-deserved punishment for their actions. Instead, these learners may opt to take matters into their own hands as a venture to seek self-administered justice. It also touches on the learners' trust on teachers as well as current processes used to resolve mobile bully-victim incidents in a satisfactory manner. However, authorities rely on good evidence to investigate incidents, and lack thereof may result in justice miscarriage (Gabbert *et al.,* 2009). This observation reiterates the researcher's argument, pointing out the need for improved approaches that will be learner-centred and effective when dealing with mobile bully-victim behaviour. Ncontsa and Shumba (2013) also cite a public concern of safety in schools across the country that has even gained publicity on social media. Amongst these safety issues is cyberbullying (Unesco, 2017: 8). One may argue that issues of lack of trust and clear processes for resolving cyberbullying incidents may be fanning school violence, as a result of unreported and unresolved cyberbullying incidents.

Possible risks of using this application

In all five focus group sessions, the researcher detailed that the application works by facilitating peer-nominations (Smith, 2016). That is, an informant learner is asked to nominate him or herself or classmates who are or perceived as mobile bully-victims. The researcher explained that learners' names would be used for nomination of menaces using the app. However, the nominees would not know their nominators. Then the participants were asked if they foresee any potential risks. Responses ranged from not seeing any possible risk to the concern of involving parents once victims or mobile bully-victims have been identified. The police felt that the use of the app would be safe, as noted in one of the following participant's comment in response to the possible risk question: *"I like the idea and agree with you 100%, because it is a closed system, no one will know except for us [police], when we assess to say, okay ten of the pupil identified one person, meaning that person is a suspect. We can say this person is the culprit"* (PP1). However, an informative contribution advised on the potential risks of using the app spitefully by pupils. That is learners could use the app falsely, as a way to get even with their peers. It was an eye-opener and taken into consideration that there must be a verification process after the nomination of names as there can be naughty pupils who would pick their peers for mockery or further bullying. This then brings the issue of reliability, which the researcher will consider as a possible risk moving forward.

Enabling safe mobile bully-victim behaviour disclosure

Teacher participants' responses indicated that their schools have no formal way for pupils to report mobile bully-victim incidents. As such teachers learn about incidents by chance or rumours. This is evident in participant's comments, that *"we just heard the rumours that these [learners] did that"* (IIT1), *"you hear somebody else saying these [learners] are fighting because this one wrote such and such* [on Facebook] *about the other"* (LTT3). Further comments by teachers indicated that school policies play a crucial role in dealing with mobile bully-victim reports. Their policies forbid phone usage in school premises, which helps maintain a suitable learning environment. However, these policies may be ineffective against cyberbullying. The ineffectiveness of these policies is seen in participants' comments such as *"there is a school policy, we don't allow phones at school, but you know the learners"* (IIT3). Also teachers implore to learners, *"don't come with the phone to class leave your phone at home,* but they are still coming with their phones" (IIT1). As such learners are exposed to mobile bully-victim behaviour even in school premises, while they cannot report incidents.

The lack of reported incidents could be attributed to school policies that prohibit learners from bringing and using mobile phones in school. These policies may be creating a context that hinders learners from reporting mobile bully-victim behaviour. As such learners may not seek help about mobile bully-victim incidents that take place inside and outside of school premises. Also, learners may not report mobile bully-victim incidents for fear of getting into trouble for violating the school policy by bringing their phones in schools. Also, Perren *et al.* (2012) noted that children fear that their mobile phones will be confiscated if they reported mobile bullying. One can argue that the presence of such policies indicates a lack of will and preparedness on school part to deal with cyberbullying behaviour.

The observed lack of reporting in schools and to the police needs a way to proactively diagnose cyberbullying behaviour, instead of waiting for reports. This confirms the need for developing an artefact to proactively diagnosis learners' involvement in mobile bully-victim behaviour in schools. Another persisting challenge of cyberbullying is the difficulty to positively identify menaces, due to anonymity afforded by technology use. Even worst, the swinging nature of bully-victim traits, between pure bullies and pure victims, makes it difficult to identify menaces. Therefore identification methods using self- and peer nomination measures could help to address mobile bully-victims (Phillips and Cornell, 2012; Volk *et al.*, 2017).

Questioning the law enforcement participants on what can be done to encourage learners to come forward and report mobile bully-victim behaviour, responses spoke to the need of emphasizing mobile bully-victim behaviour awareness. *"It [encouraging learners to report incidents] might be the problem, because some of the learners. They are shy, so they are afraid to come forward to report that crime"* (PP2). The participants further suggested initiatives like a radio announcement on cyberbullying and making the community aware as the best ways to encourage disclosure and reporting.

Hindrances to investigation of mobile bully-victim incidents

In their response about what can be done to encourage learners to come forward and report mobile bully-victim behaviour, the police cited learners' fear of their cyberbullying perpetrators. One police respondent stated, *"I think if we can cut [stop] gangsters at schools. Some of them [learners] are being bullied, and afterwards there are gangsters maybe that are controlling other learners, maybe they are afraid to report this mobile bullying"* (PP4). Another police respondent also reported on the investigation in one of the schools, where insults to teachers were posted on a Facebook account: *"Let us take for instance this one [investigation] of today, we come from the class now. That guy [learner] is afraid of those people who have created the account (Facebook account) on his name*" (PP1). It seems that learners are afraid to report incidents because they think the perpetrators would know who reported them. This observation reiterates the need for a mechanism to facilitate safe disclosure.

Learners know their perpetrators, but they are afraid to report them. The police further explained that "*they [perpetrators] are bullies from the class itself, it's a threat to him [suspect or victim]. He [suspect or victim] knows that when he reports. When he comes back those people are going to do whatever they want to him. It's a fear*" (PP1). These observations reaffirm the need for an investigation mechanism that does not threaten learner's safety, such as developing a mobile bully-victim diagnosis artefact.

Conclusion

The overall picture drawn from the focus group sessions is that little is known about mobile bully-victim behaviour amongst the police and teachers. The existing investigation techniques are inadequate for mobile bully-victim, and the same can be said for processes employed to resolve incidents. There is still a great need for awareness on this form of bullying and central to this knowledge base are teachers, police, pupils and parents. Adding to the knowledge creation is the noted challenge with the lack processes for enabling safe reporting of mobile bully-victim incidents, and handling and resolving reports. On a larger scale, there is a need for effective and efficient initiatives to address mobile bully-victim behaviour in high schools. These will bring schools one-step closer to the preparedness to deal with mobile bully-victim phenomenon. Meaning, initiatives should focus on prevention, intervention and mitigation. These results from focus groups support the need to develop an artefact designed to diagnose mobile bully-victims primarily to enable (1) a safe reporting environment, (2) behavioural effects assessment to inform remedial actions, (3) raise awareness about the phenomenon, (4) instil pupils' trust on police, so that (5) pupils can report incidents to police.

The evaluation of the design with the participants revealed additional insight to the design of the artefact. The issues raised included a possible misuse of the system to spite other learners, a suitable method for resolving incidents, and the need to involve parents. The concepts emanating from this evaluation include:

i.   Confirmation of nominees to avoid false diagnosis and accusations

ii. Using restorative justice to resolve mobile bully-victims behaviour

iii. Involving parents when resolving bullying incidents

The first requirement is functional and reiterated the need to *"ensure informant safety"*, and provided insight for validating nominations. The last two additional requirements are non-functional, but provide application methods for the initial requirement, "resolve mobile bully-victim behaviour".

These outcomes informed the instantiation of the first prototype mobile bully-victims response system (Construct), with a user interface.

6.4   Design (first cycle)

Instantiation is necessary in order to show that a solution for the research problem is feasible, while evaluation helps to demonstrate a solution's validity (Vaishnavi and Kuechler, 2015). Design is the proposition of a specific artefact resulting from related components that can produce a desired utility (Patas, Milicevic and Goeken, 2011). A design principles list can be derived from the literature review and represents user requirements (Gass and Maedche, 2011).

6.4.1   Requirements

In Design Science (DS), the research problem can be transformed into artefact's objectives through requirements analysis (Peffers *et al.*, 2007). Conceptual models that are derived from sound theories help with documentation of requirements for further design processes (Vom Brocke and Buddendick, 2006). The artefact was constructed by operationalising design theories (Patas, Milicevic and Goeken, 2011). "The design goal can be based on reference theories in order to motivate and reason the construction of the artefact based on empirical research" (Patas *et al.*, 2011:37). Components are viewed as means while requirements are viewed as ends of design goals (Patas *et al.*, 2011). Requirements are made practical through components. The components are legitimised by definition of requirements (Patas, Milicevic and Goeken, 2011).

A set of user requirements can be derived from kernel theory (Baskerville and Pries-Heje, 2010). Reference theories help to explain how and why things are with regards to causes and effects in natural phenomena (Patas, Milicevic and Goeken, 2011). These theories are empirically tested hypotheses and evidence, which provide insight into phenomena. Consequently, DS researchers try to bring positive change into natural phenomena by constructing artefacts. The design action helps to form the component's feature and attributes (Patas, Milicevic and Goeken, 2011). Baskerville and Pries-Heje (2010) note requirements, as documented representation of capabilities needed to solve problem or achieve an objective for users. In IS, requirements are defined as statements about physical and functional needs that can be fulfilled by a specific product or service (Koppenhagen, *et al*, 2012). "It is a statement that identifies a necessary attribute, capability, characteristic, or quality of a system for it to have value and utility to a user" (Koppenhagen, *et al*, 2012: 7). In the design and development phase, the artefact's features relating to desired functionality and architecture are determined, and then the actual artefact is created (Peffers, Tuunanen, Rothenberger and Chatterjee, 2007).

The conceptual model, in the literature review of this study, presented constructs that could help address mobile bully-victim behaviour in schools. The use of the prototype was to identify optimal features of the artefact. In this study, the researcher also combined existing studies and research results into requirements, which later were aggregated and abstracted into design principles in the subsequent section. The following list presents the identified key requirements:

i.   The system must enable registration of learners for participation

ii.   The system must enable peer nomination in order to identify mobile bully-victims

iii. The system must enable informant safety (anonymity)

iv.   The system must enable assessment of mobile bully-victim severity

v.   The system must raise awareness about mobile bully-victims behaviour

vi.   The system must enable confirmation of nominees to avoid false diagnosis and accusations

vii. The police must involve parents when resolving bullying incidents

viii. The system must create the diagnosis report

The inclusion of requirement viii can enable the police to use the results of the system to address the identified non-functional requirements:

i.   The system must enable resolving mobile bully-victims reports

ii.   The police must use restorative justice to resolve bullying incidents.

iii.   The system must instil trust of police on mobile bully-victims.

The requirements were transformed into design principles in the following section, in order to enable instantiation of the prototype. Design theory is upper-level type of artefact, of which design requirements and design are principles are central. While design requirements are seen as special type of model, design principles also known as guidelines form part of methods (Prat, Comyn-Wattiau and Akoka, 2014).

6.4.2   Design principles

Design principles can be derived from literature review and empirical studies results. Gass and Maedche (2011) relied on literature review for creating design principles. Then they employed conceptual modelling techniques to transform the design principles into detailed solution design. On the other hand, in their study titled "How do procurement networks become social?" Koppenhagen, Katz, Maedche, and Müller, (2011) compiled requirements by combining the literature review and their exploratory study results. Then the requirements were further aggregated and abstracted into design principles.

Table 12: Mapping design principles to requirements

Code	Design principles (DP)	Key requirements
DP1	Enable registering learners	i
DP2	Enable anonymous mobile bully-victims identification	ii, iii and vi
DP3	Enable confirmation of nomination	vi
DP4	Enable seamless severity assessment of mobile bully-victims	iv and v,
DP5	Enable creation of reports	vii, and viii
DP6	Enable raising awareness about mobile bully-victims	v

The design decisions for the artefact were deducted from design principles stemming from a list of requirement descriptions (Koppenhagen, Katz, Maedche, and Müller, 2011). In order to generate an innovative approach to the solution, the key requirements were aggregated and abstracted into design principles (Koppenhagen *et al*, 2012). The design principles are outcomes of the problem conceptualisation, which include requirements documentation. Table 12 presents the initials design principles to address the identified key requirements.

DP1 provides the system with a function to register learners. Registration creates learners nomination list that is used in DP2 in order to enable police to safely diagnose mobile bully-victims. Anonymity implies that the nominees will not know which of their peers nominated (reported) them in order to ensure informant safety. Also, for police to complete the diagnosis, definitions and descriptions of the mobile bully-victim behaviour should be provided. DP3 enables nominated learners to confirmation or refuse nomination, in order to avoid false accusations. DP4 provides the system with a function to enable police to measure the severity of mobile bully-victim behaviour on identified learners, in order to inform required remedial actions in addressing the behaviour. DP5 provides the system with ability to enable police to create reports, in order to inform remedial actions against the behaviour. In turn, DP6 provides the use of the system (reading the definition before nominations) and its reports to facilitate educating learners about the mobile bully-victims behaviour.

6.5   Construct (First cycle)

The initial features of the prototype were created using the information that emerged from literature review and focus group discussions. The critical aspect during mobile application design is providing authentic usage context for a user, that is, users need to see and interact with realistic applications (Kangas and Kinnunen, 2005). Since a conceptual framework of a solution was devised from the literature review to inform the design and development of the initial prototype. Prototyping enables users to visualise intended functions of an application, and creation of semi-functional mock-up that can be turned into the finished product (Lowdermilk, 2013).

The design decisions specifying the prototype features were deducted from design principles in the first design iteration. This section presents the instantiation of initial prototype design including system architecture. Instantiation is described as "a real system implementation of conceptual IT meta-artefact" to produce diagrams or prototypes (Iivari, 2015:110) or creating operational software (Gregor and Hevner,

2013). System architecture involves context, structure and design decisions (Ahmed, Ganti and Kyhlbäck, 2010). Context represents the defined interfaces to the external entities, while structure is the element of the system. Design decisions represent rules, and constraints of the system design.

6.5.1   *Architectural design*

Architectures are part of useful structuring instruments for design such as when creating artefacts (Wieringa, 2014: 78). In design, architecture helps to segment a large design problem into manageable sub problems, solve sub problems, and create the whole system using solutions to sub problems. This study adopted an architectural structure as the bases for developing the artefact as a system of mobile applications. The artefact's behaviour will be such that when a stimulus is applied on the systems, a response will be produced according to a pattern of components interaction (Wieringa, 2014). This function is referred to as mechanism, and software and hardware mechanisms are deterministic. Therefore a system is a collection of component interactions and forming a whole. While an interaction refers to an actions that agents performs on a unit such as a system's function (Bækgaard, 2015). Also Prat, Comyn-Wattiau and Akoka (2014) view a system as related parts that are organised to forming a whole with designated purposes, which yield emergent properties. Additionally, "five fundamental dimensions: goal, environment, structure, activity, and evolution" characterise systems (Prat, Comyn-Wattiau and Akoka, 2014: 25).

A client-server system consists of client processes and server processes. A client process sends a service request to the server process. Clients provide front-end applications, while servers execute transactions and manage data in order to provide services to clients (Yakubu, Ngene, and Gambo, 2017). The communication between the client and the server is based on Wi-Fi Direct technology, which allows peer-to-peer connection between devices (Conti, Delmastro, Minutiello and Paris, 2013).

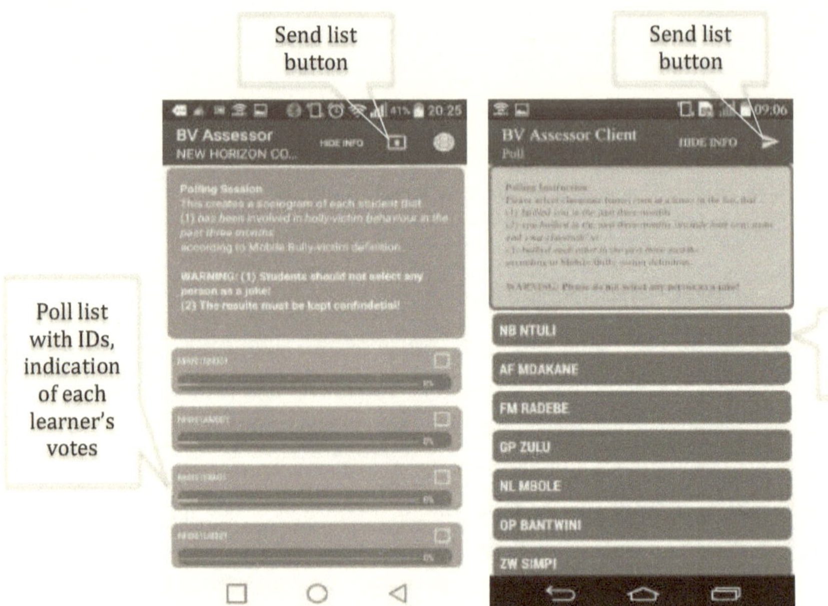

Figure 9: Server's poll screen   Figure 10: Client's poll screen

Figure 9 and 10 present the client and server's interfaces of the prototype system that was designed to diagnose mobile bully-victims behaviour in schools. The client application consists of a responsive user interface, which facilitates nomination, confirmation and severity assessment of mobile bully-victim using learners list sent from the server. The learners can make selection of names in the poll list and send back to the server. The server services clients by making queries and updates against the database, and sends to and receives information from clients. Both server and client's interfaces and applications are written in XML and JAVA following the model-view-control (MVC) architectural pattern using Android platform. All application data provided by user or collected from clients is stored in an SQLite database. The SQLite database does not need a separate server process and is stored in a single cross-platform disk file, and it is embedded in the applications (Mutti, Bacis, Paraboschi, 2015).

6.5.2 Technological platform

In the South African rural areas, the ownership of mobile phones among youth is the highest (MyBroadband, 2013). Also, Internet usage among learners in Free State's township schools is high (Odora and Matoti, 2015). According to Statistics South

Africa's General Household Survey (2017) mobile access to Internet was 39.6% and the most common in rural areas than in urban and metros. These observations also imply a higher exposure to mobile bullying (Odora and Matoti, 2015). Since children learn novel mobile application easily (Hietajärvi *et al.*, 2020), that is enabled by their immersion on mobile technology daily (Singh, 2017), the researcher chose to develop the artefact in mobile platform in order to enable using the familiar platform for learners.

6.5.3 *Software technologies*

This section provides an overview of software technologies that were used to design and implementation of the mobile artefact. Koppenhagen *et al.* (2012) suggest building an artefact already in its technical target platform and architecture, enables overall utility evaluation including platform and architecture elements. The central architecture of the artefact is based on a client-server model. Both the client and server applications were developed based on the model-view-control (MVC). The interface for both client and server application was created in Extensible Mark-up Language (XML), while their functions were coded using JAVA language. SQLite database was used for persistent storage of user data on the server.

The technologies that were used in the implementation of the prototype include open-source Android Studio development platform, and Wi-Fi Direct API, GraphStream API version 2 for android, and MPAndroidChart version 2.2.4 graphical application programming interface (API). Nowadays mobile smart phones are popular among teenagers, which they see as an important element of daily life (Xie, Zhao, Xie and Lei, 2016). Among different brands, Google's Android Operating system is an open source and has the largest market share – 83% (Mugagga and Winberg, 2015; Wisniewski, Ghosh, Xu, Rosson and Carroll (2017). Hence, the researcher sought to take advantage of the widely used platform in mobile technologies by developing the artefact for Android smartphones. The choice of the connection between the server and clients was informed by the fact that Wi-Fi is embedded on the devices, making it free of charge with no need for extra intermediary devices in between (Conti *et al.*, 2013). Specifically, Wi-Fi direct API was used to enable connection and exchange of data between client applications and the server during mobile bully-victims diagnosis. Wi-Fi direct is easier to set up than Wi-Fi ad-hoc mode (Conti *et al.*, 2013).

In order to enable data visualisation, understanding and discover patterns of mobile bully-victims behaviour from diagnosis reports of the system, representations of network graphs and charts were developed on the system (Wang, Perez-Riverol, Hermjakob and Vizcaíno, 2015). The graphical representation of the diagnosis results was implemented the GraphStream dynamic graph library in Java (Dutot, Guinand, Olivier and Pigné, 2007; GraphStream Team, 2018). GraphStream provides a framework to visually present social network interactions between users using nodes and edges, and evaluations such as user prominence on the network (Lightenberg, Pei, Fletcher, and Pechenizkiy, 2018). Similarly, MPAndroidChart API was used to visually present summaries of diagnosis results using pie charts (Malhotra, and Bahl, 2017; Wang *et al.*, 2015).

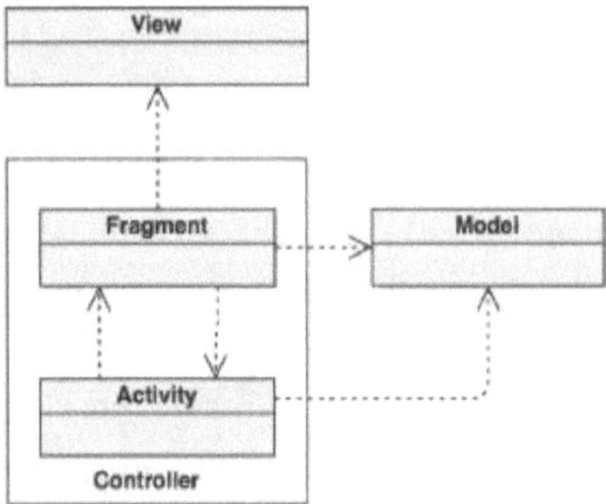

Figure 11: Android MVC

Android native applications are designed based on Model-View-Controller (MVC) architecture (Phillips, Steward, Hardy and Marsicano, 2015). Figure 11 presents MVC Android implementation UML class diagram. The *model* object holds of the business logic, and models main functions the product is designated for. As such the *model* component consists of complex object classes that store and retrieve data from containers. The *view* object provides graphical user interface to enable users to interact with the application. The *controller* links the view and model objects together, and contain application logic. As such controller object respond to events triggered in the *view* object and also manage data flow between *model* and *view* objects. The View objects draw themselves on the screen using XML and respond to user input such as touch (Phillips *et al.*, 2015). Also, the server stores the system's data on an open source database relational database called SQLite. The reports from database are created as plain text in the CSV file format.

6.5.4   Instantiation

The implementation of an artefact instantiation also motivates learning (Iivari, 2015). As such, the researcher's understanding of the problem may be demonstrated in the ability to develop a prototype as the solution. Artefacts as outcome of Design Science Research (DSR) strategies include (1) creation of real system to address particular problems of clients, (2) conceptual IT models as DSR contribution and (3) instantiation of those models (Iivari, 2015). Information system practitioners try to understand how IT artefacts ideas are formed, constructed, and implemented (Benbasat, Zmud, 2003). The design decisions were drawn from design principles to provide the following server and client functions.

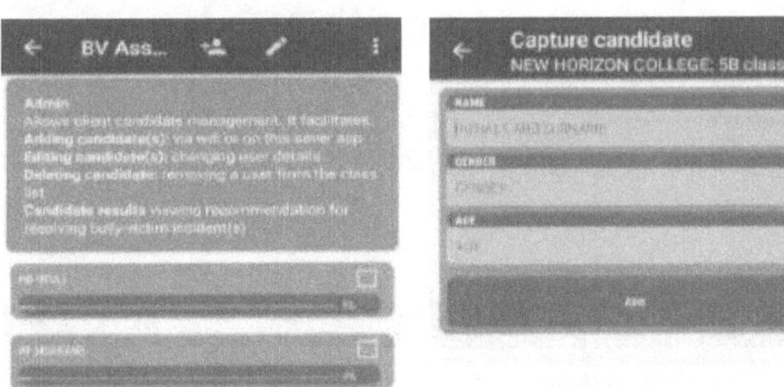

Figure 12: User administration screen   Figure 13: Registration interface

DP1 is implemented to enable police to register and update learners' details. The interface of the registration function is shown in Figure 12 and 13.

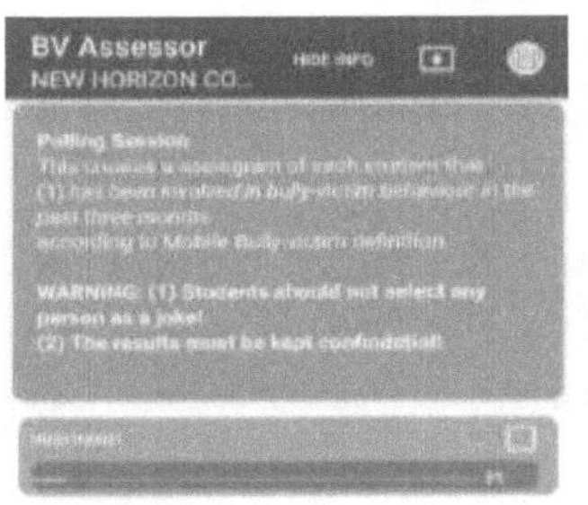
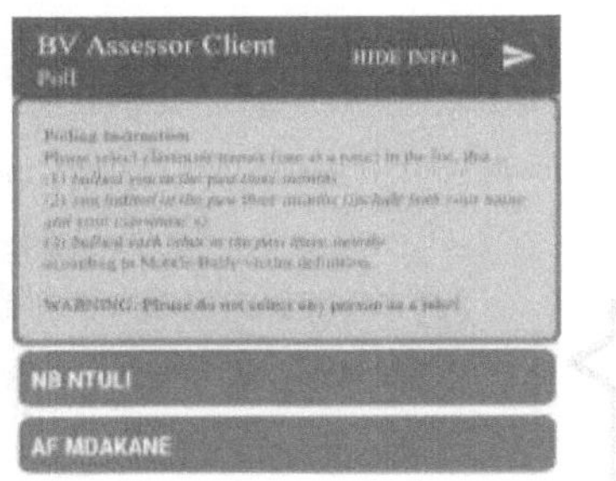

Figure 14: Nomination (Server)   Figure 15: Nomination interface (Client)

Anonymous mobile bully-victims identification (DP2) is implemented by creating nomination functions. Figure 14 presents the user interface of the server's monitoring function with an indication of nomination percent for each learner in the list. Also, Figure 15 shows the user interface of the client's nomination function with instructions and a list of names that can be selected by learners. During diagnosis, the police send the list of names to client devices so that learners can anonymously select their bullies and victims, then send back nominations.

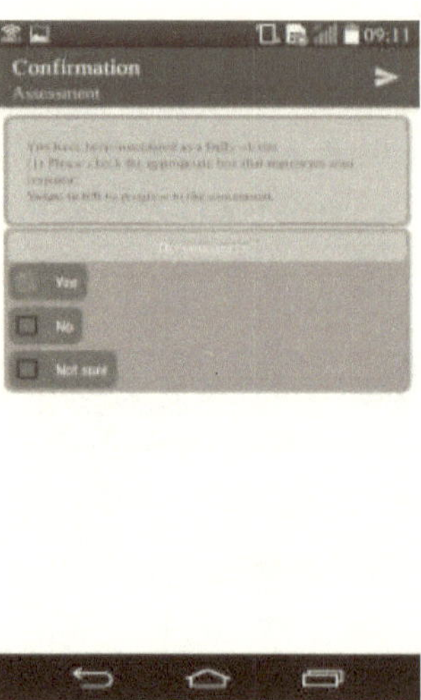

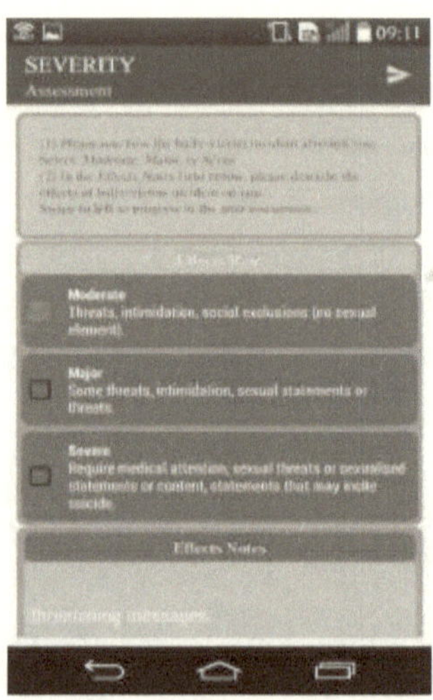

Figure 16: Confirmation (Client)　　　Figure 17: Severity Assessment (Client)

Figure 16 displays the initial client's user interface with the instantiation of DP3 for confirming of nominations. DP4 implementation user interface is displayed in Figure 17 showing severity assessment function (initial user interface design).

Figure 18 and 19 show the instantiation of DP5, which helps in addressing mobile bully-victim behaviour by providing nomination and assessment reports, and remedial actions. Also the reports that are created include text file that indicate the number of nominations that each learner received, and whether a learner is identified as a mobile bully, bully-victim or victim and recommendation of remedial action to address the behaviour.

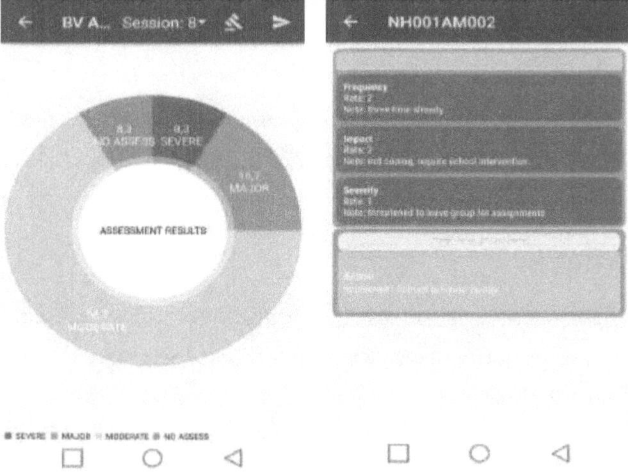

Figure 18: Assessment stats (Server)   Figure 19: Assessment results (Client)

Chapter 7 – Second cycle

7.1   Introduction

This chapter presents the second cycle of the design and development of the artefact, starting with second iteration of Evaluation 2, and the first iteration of Evaluation 3. Then the outcomes of the evaluations are implemented to refine the artefact design.

7.2   Evaluation 2

In order to gain understanding of about the limitations of the design, the researcher employed a task analysis of the system with teachers. This evaluation consisted of one focus group discussion.

7.2.1   Focus group

In Information Systems, the use of focus group methods to evaluate and refine artefacts began recently (Tremblay *et al.*, 2010). The suitability of focus group stems from its flexibility to enable a range of techniques to support the full design process, starting with (1) conceptualisation of user needs during the initial stage of the project, (2) prototype testing in the design stage, and concluding with (3) final artefact evaluation (O'Raghallaigh *et al.*, 2012). In the study titled "Use of Design Science for Informing the Development of a Mobile App for Persons Living with HIV", Schnall *et al.* (2014) used focus group discussions to elicit functional requirements and understanding end-user environment. In Schnall *et al.* (2014), some of the participants had never used apps on a smartphone, therefore to stimulate discussions they used existing apps' pictures, screen mock-ups, and probing questions (Schnall *et al.*, 2014), The researcher in current study followed Schnall *et al.* (2014) focus group procedure and used printed screen captures to stimulate discussion and creative ideas. The discussion procedure included explanation of the artefact's design motivation, usage scenarios, and evaluation tasks (Tremblay *et al.*, 2010).

The aim of the focus group was to collect target participants' views to inform the system design that can aid the police in addressing mobile bullying in schools. In qualitative research participants are selected based on their relevance to the aims of the study (Neuman, 2013; Cresswell and Plano Clark, 2011). Hence participants in the current study were selected for their experience of social crime prevention in schools. Table 13 presents participants' profiles, a group of five police officers, which are responsible for social crime prevention, participated in the focus group for designing the app system. South African labour force includes persons from 18 - 54 old. The participants' group included four males and one female, and their age ranged between 36 and 50. Only one of the participants did not use social media.

The key challenges in developing mobile technology interventions include harmonising user preferences, and feasibility, design and development constraints (Kenny, Dooley and Fitzgerald, 2016). After the prototype was created that was informed by conceptual model's constructs, a focus group was conducted with target users.

Table 13:Participants profile

ID	Gender	Age group	Education	Rank	Experience (in years)	Social media usage
HP1	Male	36-50	Diploma	Warrant officer	31	Frequently
HP2	Male	36-50	Diploma	Sergeant	10	Never
HP3	Female	51+	Grade 12	Captain	36	Rarely
HP4	Male	51+	Grade 12	Warrant officer	36	Frequently
HP5	Male	36-50	Grade 12	Warrant officer	29	Rarely

Thematic analysis was applied on the collected data, in order to obtain richly detailed description of data set and generate insight into participants' perspectives regarding the topic (Braun and Clarke, 2006; O'Raghallaigh, Sammon and Murphy, 2012). Following this method, a master coding-frame of themes was developed as presented in Table 14. Themes are subjects relevant to the research question that come as response patterns out of data set (Braun and Clarke, 2006). In this study, themes were considered to be any subject that was discussed by participants during focus groups (Kenny, Dooley and Fitzgerald, 2016).

Figure 20: Overall result screen mock-up

Figure 21: Nomination results screen mock-up

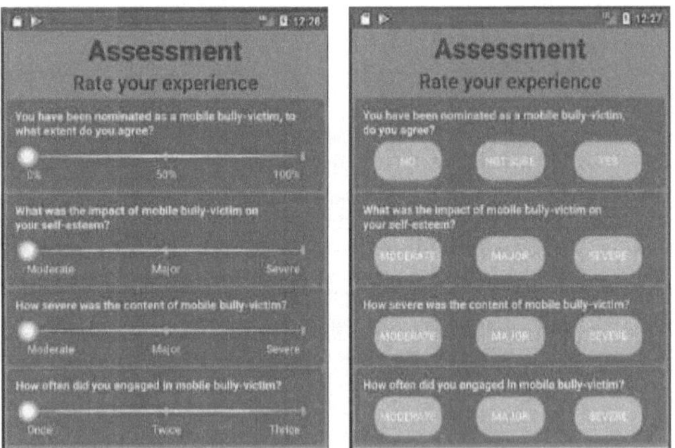

Figure 22: Assessment screen mock-ups

The researcher noted that the volume of transcribed data did not necessarily require in depth analysis. Hence, data analysis from design focus group discussions was done in the form of short report as a summary of the prevailing mood in the group, and colourful quotes are used as illustrations (O'Raghallaigh, Sammon and Murphy, 2012). In this way the researcher identified "for common themes and variations within the transcripts that provide rich descriptions of participants' reactions to design features" (O'Raghallaigh *et al.*, 2012: 257). Also, tabulating results helped in displaying a summary of supporting or counter-evidence of the artefact's utility or participants' views (O'Raghallaigh *et al.*, 2012). In this design cycle, the results are tabulated to present participants perspectives regarding the design of the artefact. Table 14 presents five themes and 10 subthemes. Overall, participants highlighted safety, confidentiality, credibility, simplicity, clarity, and understandability as main issues during the second evaluation iteration, as also noted by Kenny, Dooley and Fitzgerald (2016). There was one subtheme that overlapped between safety and credibility.

Credibility: The police had been informed about using learners' names in a peer nomination procedure for identifying mobile bully-victims. As shown with a sample nomination list in Figure 15, learners' are represented with initials and surname in the name list. Then the police were asked what other information would they need to identify mobile bully-victims. The police's responses indicated that using a list of learner's names would be appropriate. However, police were concerned about the credibility of the results, citing the possibility of false nomination due to name similarities. Also learners would not recognise perpetrators name, if they know their peers by *nicknames* instead of official names. As a result, learners might not be able to distinguish between peers who *share names*, resulting in wrong peer nomination. On the contrary, participant believed that learners in sequential grades (where learners move together from one grade to another) should know their peers by name. Also teachers address learners by their official names. Therefore *nicknames* should not be used because other learners may feel bullied.

Safety: Participants' views showed concerns about learners' safety, if *nicknames* are used, and nominator (informant) *confidentiality*. The police understood that the use of the app supports informants' confidentiality, which can only be broken by police themselves.

Table 14: Sample responses from police across themes

Themes	Response
Credibility	
Official names	*"The name list as in the screen is fine for nominations, but other learners know their classmates by nicknames" (HP1).*
	"But in schools the teachers use learners' official names to address them [learners]" (HP2).
Shared identity	*"If learners share a surname and [or] initials are the same, learners will not know which is which" (HP4).*
Safety	
Confidentiality	*"Can the nomination be done privately, so that other learners will not know who nominated them?" (HP3)*
	"Polling is conducted in a way that learners will not know or see their classmates' nominations" (HP2).
	"Only the police can break the confidentiality, otherwise other learners will never know who nominated them" (HP2).
Nicknames	*"Using nicknames, other learners do not like it – that may be embarrassing, and may be another form of bullying" (HP5).*
Ambiguity	
Answer options	*"What is 0%, 50% and 100%? The learner can only choose two options only; they cannot choose 25% or so?" (HP1)*
Questions	*"The confirmation question is not clear about what the percentages indicate. That could be made clearer" (HP4).*
	"Using scales only would be better" (LT2).
	"I think if we use scales with radio buttons, like 1 to 10 range to obtain how children feel about their nomination" (HP1).
	"The nomination question is not clear about what percentages indicate" (HP4).
	"The assessment questions look alike, and it does not make sense to have similar questions assessing different issues" (LT3).
Results	
Organisation	*"Maybe we could have a summary list that indicates identified learners in an ordered manner. So that bullies are put next to each other, and other identified learners in the same way" (HP1).*
	"the list can be sorted by their [identified learners'] behaviour, so that it will be easy to read or find learners in that list" (HP2).
Completeness	*"The percentage in the screen shows the number of identified learners as bullies, so that we know how many children we need to address" (HP2)*
Colour coding	*"The screen looks okay. The frequency rate can be there, maybe we could use colours bars to differentiate effect scores, say lime, orange, and red for impact rate and severity" (HP1).*
Understandability	
Visualisation	*"Children are visual; maybe we should use images, like smile faces (with smile, and sad faces) to indicate how severe were affects on them" (HP1).*
	"The frequency rate can be there, maybe we could use colours bars to differentiate effect scores, say lime, orange, and red for impact rate and severity" (HP1).
	"Children can choose how they feel about this bullying" (HP3).
	"Polling is conducted in a way that learners will not know or see their classmates' nominations" (HP2).
Intuitiveness	*"I can see clearly which learners were identified as mobile bully-victims from this sociogram" (HP1).*

Clearly, participants understood the risk of wrong accusation if the names in nomination lists are not distinguishable, as well as protecting learners from victimisation. Also, this observation shows participant's need for assurance about learners' safety when using the app.

Results: The discussion about presenting polls results was stimulated by reference to the prototype screen that represents a directed network graph (sociogram). Figure 21 presents the graph indicating which learner nominated the other learner by using arrows (arcs) and nodes. Nodes represent learners, arrows represent a nomination, and the arrowhead at the end of the arc indicates that the destination node is a nominee (bully). All participants could intuitively identify mobile bully-victims, bullies and victims from the network graph. However, participants suggested that using colours could help differentiate the assessed categories (impact, frequency, and content obscenity) could be improved the presentation of results. A probe for additional thoughts about poll results in Figure 20 also revealed that results should be presented in a sorted list according to identified behaviour. The participants felt that the overall report for diagnosis was informative, including a pie chart that shows the number of identified bully-victims, bullies, and victims.

Understandability: The participants seemed to understand how the app works, conducting polls (peer nomination) to identify behaviour, and giving learners an opportunity to assent to or deny nominations. Figure 22 presents screen mock-ups to enable confirmation and severity assessment. However, participants felt that the confirmation answer options were confusing. Similarly, the questions and answer options for severity assessment were found to be vague and restrictive. The illuminating suggestion to these concerns was about reinforcing learner's understanding of questions and their answer options through visualisation of answer options.

Ambiguity: Similar to understandability, participants felt that the confirmation and assessment interfaces lacked details about how the questions should be answered. Also the three assessment questions were indistinguishable from each other. Therefore, participants suggested that using scales as answers options and phrasing questions succinctly to their purposes could make the app use simpler. The researcher also conducted a usability test order to gain a deeper understanding of the technical challenges of the system, as shown in the next section.

7.3   Evaluation 3

7.3.1   *Usability test with teachers*

The goal of this test was to identify and address major technical and usability limitations of the M-BRS. The user interfaces for nomination (polling) and severity assessment processes of the M-BRS are presented in Figures 23 and 24. The evaluation session lasted for one hour and involved five teachers from one of the selected high schools. Three of the participants had taken part in the one focus group in Evaluation 2, so they were familiar with focus group discussion and the purpose of the study.

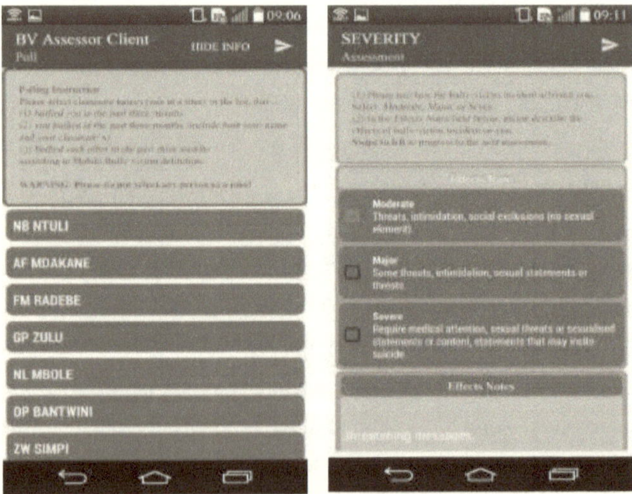

Figure 23: Nomination screen mock-up

Figure 24: Severity assessment screen mock-up

Table 15 presents participants profile, which includes three male and two female teachers whose ages ranged between 20 and 50 years. All the participants owned smartphones. Participants were informed that they were going to use a prototype for evaluation purposes, and were encouraged to ask questions or comment about the application features.

Table 15: Participants profile

ID	Gender	Age group	Education	Occupation	Experience (in years)	Social media usage
LTT1	Male	20-35	Bachelors	Teacher	7	Frequently
LTT2	Male	20-35	Diploma	Teacher	9	Frequently
LTT3	Female	20-35	Bachelors	Teacher (SBST)	6	Frequently
LTT4	Male	36-50	Diploma	Teacher	20	Rarely
LTT5	Female	20-35	Bachelors	Teacher	7	Frequently

Having designed the artefact's prototype through the first design-evaluation iteration. Tremblay *et al.* (2010) suggested the following procedure to facilitate evaluation and design revision of an existing artefact through group discussions:

i.   Begin with explanation of motivation behind the design of the artefact.

ii. Follow up by broad explanation of scenarios on where and how the artefact could be used, a description of the details of the design of the artefact, and

iii. Finish with a task where participants are asked to use and evaluate the artefact.

The usability test focused on application installation on participants' devices, and connection between server and client applications, and completion of the system's functions. The main tasks included using the system to diagnose mobile bully-victims and assessing nomination confirmation and severity.

The system's connection was tested between six smart phones (including the researcher's device), which were of four different brands (Huawei, Hisense, LG and Samsung). Each brand was tested as clients by installing the client application of M-BRS. The devices tried to establish Wi-Fi Direct connections with server device. *However, at least one client could not connect to the server, and kept sending a connection requests. Another client also dropped connection to the server shortly after establishing the connection.* Since the system is designed for use with a number of learners in classrooms, which could lead to large number of varied devices, the server application would be bogged down by continuous requests for connections. The continuous request for connection resembled a Denial-of-Service attack (Tan *et al.* 2013). The connection failure was as a result of different models and brands that implement varied Wi-Fi Direct networking securities. As also noted by Dobre *et al.* (2016: 13) the Wi-Fi Direct standard is "implemented differently by various phone manufacturers, making phone-to-phone communication rather difficult to achieve across-vendors".

The natures of paired-user testing enables a normal interaction style and collaboratively learn how to interact with the system, and yields more comments than think-aloud (Bastien, 2010; Mazzone, Xu and Read, 2007). The system's functions consist of four main tasks, each with at least 1 to 2 subtasks:

i.   The first function establishes connection with the server (searching for and select server, 2 tasks);

ii.   The second function enables registration on the system (typing name, gender, and age, and send: 2 tasks);

iii. The third function facilitates peer nominations (selecting name and sending the selections: 2 tasks); and

iv.   The last function enables assessment of identified mobile bully-victims (answering confirmation and severity questions: 2 tasks).

Of the five client devices, only three managed to keep the connection long enough to test the system. As such the researcher opted to continue the testing, and asked participants whose devices maintained the connection to share their devices with those whose devices could not. Ultimately, four participants formed two dyads using one device, which is known as paired-user testing (Bastien, 2010), and only one participant worked alone.

The researcher explained that the system enables the identification of mobile bully-victims, through the number of nominations made and received by a participant. The researcher provided details of the system's functions and guided participants on how to complete the registration, nomination, and assessments. Demonstrating how to complete each function includes (1) registering on the system; (2) selecting a name on the list and sending the selection to the server (nomination); (3) completing the assessment which consists of confirmation and the three severity questions. Selecting an applicable pre-set answer option, and providing additional information on notes fields complete the assessment. Participants were asked to type "none" if they felt they had nothing to say in the notes fields, so that the system would allow them to submit their assessment information.

The researcher also explained that participants, who are identified as mobile bully-victims, would be required to complete the assessment using the systems' function. In the assessment function, the confirmation required participants to agree or disagree with nominations, and selecting answers to assessment quizzes regarding impact, frequency and content obscenity of mobile bullying. The researcher clarified that assessment results helped to recommend a suitable remedial action for the identified bully-victim.

Table 16: Sample responses from teachers across themes

Themes	Comments
Safety	
Confidentiality	*"Will all pupils receive the same list of names"? (LT#)*
	"The appearance of all names exposes those who have been identified as mobile bully-victims to others, this may cause problems for victims, such as further victimisation" (LT#)
	"The app could send the full names in the class list, including those who were not selected in the poll session, to avoid a possibility of exposing pupils" (LT#)
Ambiguity	
Questions	*"The assessment questions looked alike, and it does not make sense to have similar questions assessing different issues" (LT#)*
Credibility	
Diagnosis coverage	*"What happens if pupils who have been bullying others are not in the list?" (LT#)*
	"Allowing all learners to complete assessment might provide those who could not report their bullies an opportunity, and extend investigations in other classes, even if they have no nomination scores" (LT#)
Ease of use	*"The exercise of typing notes using mobile phone's soft keyboard was cumbersome" (LT#)*
	"Using scales only would be better, as the student might not like to type information during the assessment" (LT#)
	"I wished I could select many names and send only once, than to select one name a time!" (LT#)
Ambiguity	
Questions	*"The assessment questions looked alike, and it does not make sense to have similar questions assessing different issues" (LT#)*
Credibility	
Diagnosis coverage	*"What happens if pupils who have been bullying others are not in the list?" (LT#)*

During the test session, the researcher used the server app, while the participants used the client app. The researcher requested participants to complete the registration, nomination, and assessment functions, while their interactions with the system were observed. The participants were encouraged to ask questions about the system's use, and the researcher scribbled participants' comments and actions while completing tasks.

Focus group analysis can be a simple and short report about prevailing participants reactions, and using colourful quotes for illustration (O'Raghallaigh, Sammon and Murphy, 2012). This is due to unstructured nature of groups making detail analysis difficult and time consuming. Therefore notes-based analysis was employed to infer participant views about the system's usability. Notes-based analysis is rapid and adequate for pilot testing, such as "when the purpose of the study is narrowly defined" (Krueger and Casey, 2015: 347). Similarly the researcher observed in workshops that conducted to kick-start the research project with the police that the phenomenon of mobile bully-victim seemed obscured. The researcher requested participants' availability on the phone for clarification when notes were later expanded into a report. The report was created the same day after the session. Then participants' comments were analysed to identify additional design aspects that could be added or refined. O'Raghallaigh *et al.* (2012: 7) suggest "summary tables can be very helpful, displaying both evidence and counter-evidence of the utility of the solution by focus group". Table 16 presents the prevailing themes from analysis of the usability test.

Ambiguity: The participants felt that all severity assessment questions were *indistinguishable* from each other. Also, the participants' comments revealed that using scales only as answers options and rephrasing questions succinctly to their purposes could make assessment simpler.

Confidentiality: The requirement to complete the assessment was that learners should have been nominated, and the system sent the name list of nominees to all client devices. Since the system assessed nominated learners only, participants raised a concern about the *confidentiality* of nomination results. A further probe for clarity revealed that learners should not know which other learners were identified as mobile bully-victims, to avoid breaking *confidentiality*. The participants were also concern was the appearance of all names exposes those who have been identified as mobile bully-victims to others, which may cause problems for victims, such as further victimisation. These comments suggested that the app should not expose learners who have been identified as bully-victims to others. The alternative was that "the app could send the full name list, including those who were not selected in the poll session, to avoid a possibility of exposing pupils.

Ease of use: The ease of use challenge was noted when participants nominated their bullies and victims, and completed the assessment matrix component of the artefact. Participants wished to complete the nomination by selecting multiple names in each category of bullies and victims. Participants were reluctant to take time and type information on the note field, as most participants simply typed "none", while other participant left the field empty. When asked why they did not type information other than "none"? Most participants felt that typing notes on a mobile phone's soft keyboard was cumbersome, and suggested that using scales only would be better, as the student might not like to type information during the assessment. Also Kowatsch *et al.* (2017) note one of requirements to answer Likert-scale type questions on mobile devices is to enable users to select pre-defined answer sets for efficient and error free interaction. As a result of the observed participants' actions and comments, the decision to remove the notes field was made, as it also seem to take more time to complete the assessment feature.

Diagnosis coverage and Accessibility: Participants felt that if other pupils are not participating in the study or in the same class as their victims. Other learners who are involved bullies or victims could miss the opportunity of being diagnosed. As such, participants suggested that learners should be able to indicate that their bullies or victims are not in the same class and be able to complete the assessment. Also the participant felt that this method could automatically extend diagnosis to other classes in a school.

The system must enable all participants to use the system. Perhaps provide standard devices of the same make for use during the app tests in schools. In this way, all participants would take turns using provided devices to complete nominations and assessments. This change required updating the nomination and assessment processes of the system so that students could first identify themselves by using unique identification (ID) codes before they continue. Using IDs, the system will be able to keep track of user nominations and assessments.

7.4   Design (Second cycle) refinements

7.4.1   Requirements

The requirements for the artefact development were collected through User-Centred Design (UCD) method and participatory action research method to inform the artefact design (Brandtner *et al.,* 2015). UCD "emerged from HCI and is a software design methodology for developers and designers" (Lowdermilk, 2013:6). The purpose of UCD is to create applications that meet users' needs. UCD helps with the production of application through active engagement of users. The designer makes decisions about the product by listening and observing to users instead of personal preferences (Lowdermilk, 2013). UCD also helps to examine application's effectiveness in achieving its purpose. The initial design of the artefact was derived from requirements that were drawn from literature review. The design included three levels of granularity: polling, effects assessments and producing reports.

The insight gained through participants' comments during the usability test led to the refinement of the existing and addition of new requirement. The following list provides categorise of refined and additional requirements (R):

Registration:
(R1) The system must enable registration of learners, creating unique identification code for each learner, and prevent duplicate names to enable credible results

Nomination:
(R2) Provide the system with credible ability to enable police to identify mobile bully-victims in a safe and anonymous peer nomination of learners
(R3) The system must enable sharing of devices among learners, while keeping track of their nominations, and enable multiple names nominations

Assessment:
(R4) The system must enable confirmation of nomination of learners, and confidentially assess the severity of mobile bully-victim behaviour among learners
(R5) The system must use clear questions for confirmation and severity assessment

(R6) The system must use predefined answer options for confirmation and severity assessments questions, with clear answering instructions and options

(R7) The system must use visually augmented answer options, in order to aid selecting suitable responses

Reports:

(R8) The system must create and present organised reports

(R9) The system must raise awareness about mobile bully-victims behaviour

(R10) The system reports must enable resolving mobile bully-victims reports using restorative justice, and parents' involvement

(R11) The system's use must instil trust of police on mobile bully-victims

7.4.2 *Design principles*

Five design principles were created to address the requirements of the system. The structure of the design principles is based on Chandra *et al.* (2015), which specify material system property, user action, and conditions of design application. Design principles describe the behaviour and functionality for particular requirements. Design principles are primary output of the design process. They describe the functionality of the solution through the user interface, and detail how things should work from non-technical perspective. These design principles can be regarded as both materiality – information about properties such as forms and functions, and actions enabled by the system (Chandra, Seidel and Gregor, 2015; Sturm and Sunyaev, 2019).

(PD 1 – User registration) Provide the system with the ability to enable police to register learners and create unique identification name for each learn on the database record to address R1. Learners' records must be created on the system using fore and middle names' initials, and surnames in the format (XX Ssss) without punctuations. If learners have the same names or initials and surname, learner will not be able to tell them apart during nomination. Hence, the app should be able to detect occurrences of name duplicate. The system must use learner's first name and surname, or second name and surname, or the position of the learner's name in the class list to enable unique name registration on the system. Therefore, the resulting unique name can be in the format XX Ssss1, X Xxxx Ssss, or Xxxx X Ssss. Then all learners in classroom must be informed when a particular learner's name is stored

differently. Also, in order to address R3 the system must create identification codes for each learner, which they can use to authenticate into the system. This will address the need for credible result about mobile bully-victims diagnose, and tracking learners nominations. Most importantly, each learner will have to authenticate before nominating his or her mobile bully-victims (Shinde, Shukla and Chitre, 2013; Karokola, Kowalski and Yngström, 2012).

(DP 2 – mobile bully-victim identification) Provide the system with ability to enable police to identify mobile bully-victims using a safe and anonymous peer nomination (polling) among learners, while learners share client devices. Polling includes self- and peer-nomination in order to identify learners' behaviour by using social network analysis (Clifton and Webster, 2017; Volk, Veenstra and Espelage, 2017). The police and teachers were adamant about learners' safety while using the system to identify mobile bully-victims. Hence, in order to address the R2, learners should be enabled to anonymously nominate peers for identification of mobile bully-victims. Anonymity implies that nominees will not know who nominated them as bullies (Shinde, Shukla and Chitre, 2013; Grunspan *et al,* 2014). This way, identified mobile bully-victims will not know which of their peers nominated them, which can prevent seeking revenges and calling others snitches. Also, in order to address R3 by keeping track of nominations or map nominee—nominator relationships, learners must authenticate into the system with their IDs before they nominate their peers. Learners should be able to nominate multiple names only twice (one their bullies and two their victims), hence the system must prevent duplicate nominations (Shinde, Shukla and Chitre, 2013).

(DP 3 – confirmation and severity assessments) Provide the system with the ability to enable police to confirm learners' nominations, and confidentially assess the severity of mobile bully-victim behaviour among learners. To address R4 about the possibility of false accusations, learners must be provided with an opportunity to assent or reject their nominations. Confidentiality relates to preventing access to intermediate (nomination) results during diagnosis. Shinde, Shukla and Chitre (2013) note access to intermediate result as unfairness. As such the diagnosis process must not reveal which learners were identified as mobile bully-victims.

(DP4 – instructions and answer options) Provide the system with the ability to enable learners to complete nominations, confirmation, and severity assessments using clear instructions, predefined and visually augmented answer options to address R5—7. The police were concerned about the possibility of using the system spitefully or as a joke. Therefore, in order to guard against false accusations, learners' nominations should be confirmed. As also noted by Mazzone, Xu and Read (2007: 155) images help "allow children (and not only children) to envision and visualise their ideas". The police suggested visualisations of assessment instructions in order to enable children to accurately perceive instruction in order to provide required information. As such instructions and answer options of the system must be designed to the level of the cognitive development of learners to enable effective expression of their ideas (Mazzone, Read and Beale, 2008). In order to provide visual stimulus for confirmation and assessment questions, the app will employ smiley faces.

(DP5 – system report) Provide the system with the ability enable the police to create organised reports of identified mobile bully-victims, and severity assessment to address R8—12. The organisation of reports should clearly indicate identified learners with regards to mobile bullying behaviour. The elements of diagnosis reports should indicate learner's prominence in relation to all involved learners. A suitable way to determine learners' prominence is the use of PageRank calculation. PageRank is the best centrality measure and is based on the concept of voting (Aggarwal *et al.*, 2018; Souma and Jibu, 2018). The report should include a social network (a graph with nodes and linking arrows) construction to visually mobile bully-victims, bullies, victims, and uninvolved (Volk *et al.*, 2017). The report will serve as evidence to address mobile bully-victim behaviour among learners using restorative justice, and facilitate involvement of parents (10). The availability of the statistical reports will also help to raise awareness about mobile bully-victim and bullying behaviour in school (R9). Overall, the system report will enable learners to trust the police to report mobile bully-victims incidents (R11). Overall, the system must enable hiding learners identity against unauthorised use (Shinde, Shukla and Chitre, 2013).

The major changes to the initial design included enabling (1) multiple selection of names on the clients in order to identify mobile bully-victims; (2) linking confirmation and severity assessment to the polls functions, in order to ensure confidentiality of the nomination results; (3) Including smiley faces to enable learners to visualise the meaning of questions and select predefined answers options; (4) Using authentication codes for learners when few devices are shared between learners, because of incompatibility issues of various smart phones, when using participants devices.

7.4.3   *Use-case diagram*

A use-case diagram was used to document the system, specifying users interactions with the system (Salah, Paige and Cairns, 2014). While requirements outline all of the needs and obligations that the artefact must live up to, use-cases provide description of possible actions. As also specified by Johnson and Henderson (2002) the value of the conceptual framework in this study was also to:

- create scenarios of the product such as use-cases to describe the product functions, and can be used in usability test, and
- clarify what the interface of the mobile application has to provide for the user including the look of objects and actions to be created.

The actors represent roles or users, and use cases describe interactions between the system and users. Figure 25 presents a use-case diagram of the system to diagnose mobile bully-victims. The actors in the system are police and school learners.

The *Login* use-case enables police or learners to login the system. Login is required for learners to enable the system to keep track of each learner' nominations, while the police login to protect the system against unauthorised usage. The *New user* use-case enables the police to create new user accounts, which are validated through the *Validate* use-case. On the other hand, the *Sign up* use-case enables the system to validate user's credentials through the *Validate* use-case. The *Register learners* use-case enables the police to add learners list in the system, while the *Check duplicates* use-case helps to ensure that identical names are resolved, so that each name can be uniquely identifiable. Then each learner is provided with an identification code (ID), so that they can authenticate into the system and be able to nominate (identify) mobile bully-victims. The *Setup up* use-case enables police to activate Wi-Fi Direct communication between the server and client devices, in order for learners to send nominations to the server for identification of mobile bully-victims. The *Create reports* use-case enables the police to create a list of identified learners, and statistical results of nominations and severity assessment, in order to address mobile bully-victims behaviour.

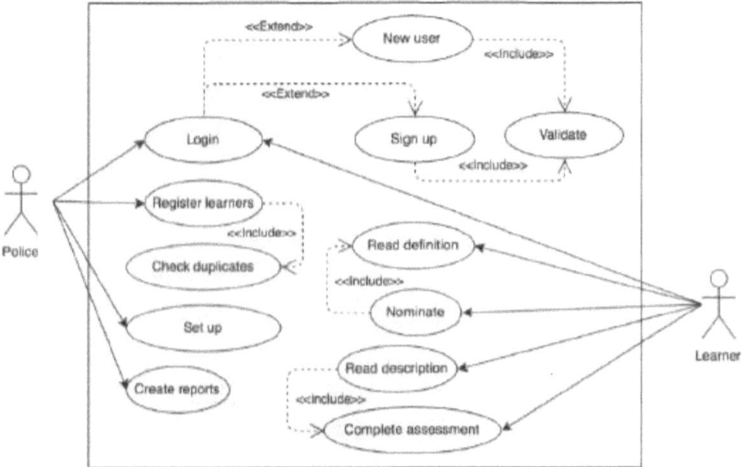

Figure 25: M-BRS use case diagram

The *Nominate* use-case enables learners to select their peers that they perceive as bullies and or victims according the definition of mobile bully-victims provided through the *Read definition* use-case. The *Read definition* use-case helps learners to familiarise themselves with mobile bully-victims. Similarly, the *Complete assessment* use-case enables learners to confirm (deny or accept) their nomination and rate the severity of mobile bully-victim behaviour on their lives. The *Read description* use case enables learners to understand the meaning of each of the severity rating (impact, frequency, and content's obscenity), in order to respond accordingly.

7.4.4 Sequence diagrams

UML sequence diagram represent interaction between objects by mapping sent messages as object functionalities. Also, Sequence diagrams can be used to represent interaction scenarios for use-case of a system during design (Campean and Yildirim, 2017). A sequence diagram represents the system behaviour by showing the sequence of activities and the conditions for organising actions. The actor and the system are represented in rectangle with dashed lines descending from the base of the rectangle.

The lines represent lifetime of the actor and the system, and are generally called lifelines. The interactions between lifelines are plotted in relation to sequence of messages exchanges, with respect to time (Campean and Yildirim, 2017). The system's functional requirements are extracted from the sequence diagrams. The functional requirements of the system were modelled using sequence diagrams to further clarify use case scenarios. They are used in designing the descriptions of system interfaces. As such, sequence diagrams describe a sequence of steps, activities and the interactions over the time.

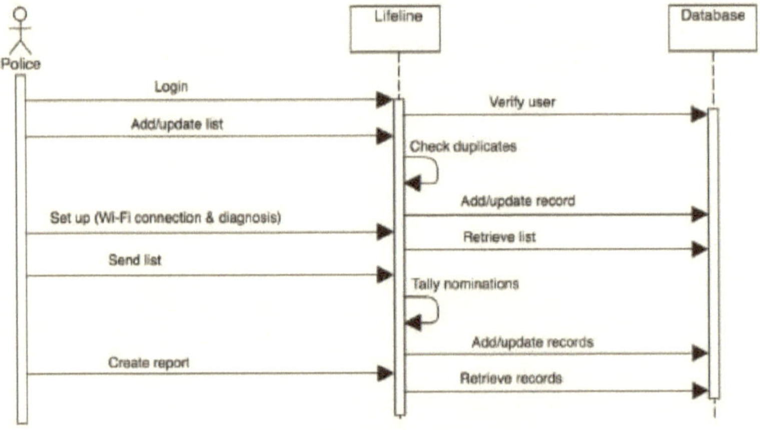

Figure 26: Sever sequence diagram

Figure 26 presents the sequence diagram for police roles in the system. The police create new admin user on the system and login. After login, the police can add new learners for a specific class. The system checks for duplicates and creates validation IDs for learners, which are given to learners prior to the diagnosis process. The police set up the system for mobile bully-victim diagnosis. The set up makes learners list available on the system to enable peer nominations. After learners finish nominating mobile bully-victims, the police create reports of the diagnosis. The report can be used to address mobile bully-victims behaviour among learners, and provides evidence when parents are involved.

156

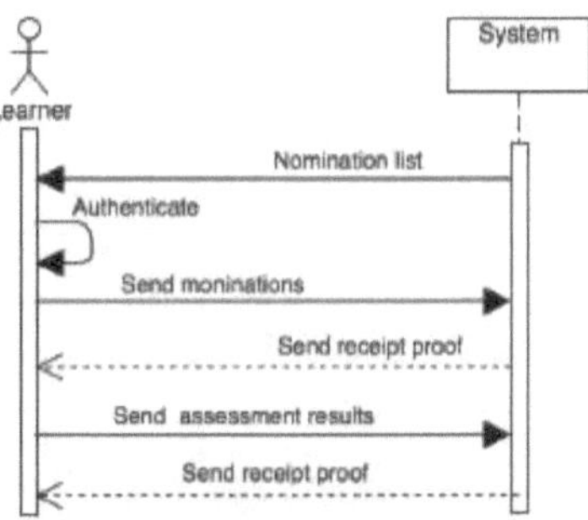

Figure 27: Client sequence diagram

Figure 27 presents the sequence diagram for learners' role in the system. Learners are given IDs for authenticating on the system in order to nominate mobile bully-victims among their peers. The learner insert ID, which the system has checks for validity. Upon validation, the system presents the list of names for each learner. Learners select their bullies and victims from the list, while the system tally each learner's nomination counts. Right after selecting their bullies and victims, learners also complete the confirmation and severity assessment, before passing the device to the next learner. Then the system adds or updates nominations and assessment results on the database.

7.5   Construct (Second cycle)

7.5.1   *Instantiation*

The five design principles were instantiated in the form of prototype designed to aid the police in diagnosing mobile bully-victims in schools. Figure 28 presents the software architecture of the M-BRS that consists of server and client applications that interact via Wi-Fi Direct connection. The system was designed as Android native app.

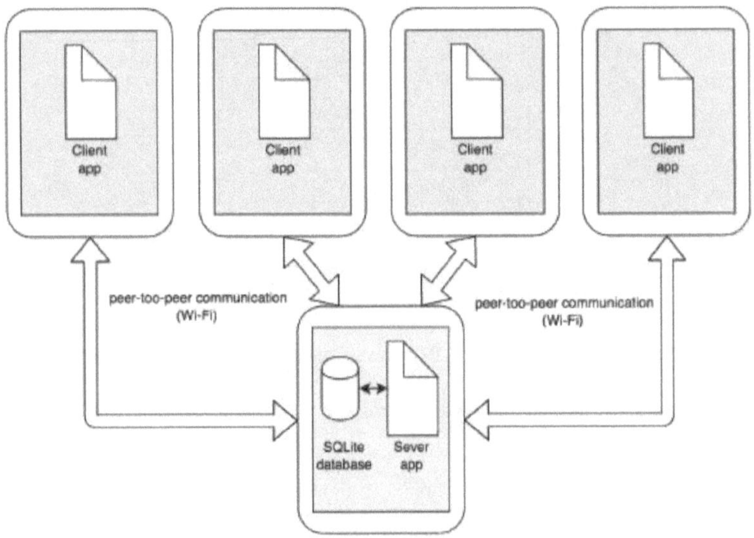

Figure 28: M-BRS client-server architecture

Figure 29 presents the M-BRS' functional architecture while Figure 30 – 32 present the system's user interfaces for the implementation of the five design principles. Learners' names are shaded in order to keep participants anonymity.

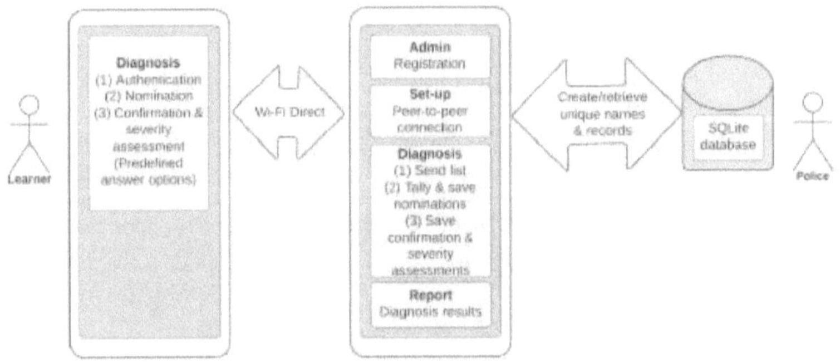

Figure 29: M-BRS architecture

Figure 30 presents the server's main user interface that provides access to four main functions of the system, *user administration, poll* and *assessment (diagnosis)*, and *report*. The *user administration* function enables the police to create a list of unique identification names and authentication code (ID) for a specific classroom (DP1), the user interface for this function are presented in Figure 12 and 13 (see section 6.5.4). Also, Figure 14 presents the list of names that can be sent to client devices during the diagnosis of mobile bully-victims, to enable learners to identify bullies and victims among their peers. On receipt of the list on client device, learners are required to authenticate before nominating their peers.

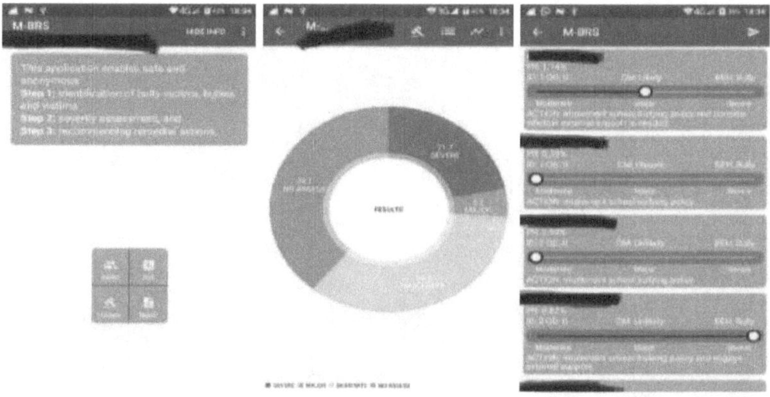

Figure 30: Main screen (Server)   Figure 31: Nominations (Server)   Figure 32: Diagnosis overview (Server)

The *poll* function is facilitated through Wi-Fi Direct connection, which enables sending the election list from the server device to client devices. At least four mobile devices are used as clients that are sequentially shared between students during diagnosis of mobile bully-victims. On each client device, learners can view and select peers' names that they perceive as bullies and or victims, and send the selection back to the server device. The server receives nominations and sends a receipt proof back to client devices so that learner may be certain their nomination was received. Then the server tallies the number of nomination for each learner as shown in Figure 32, in order to determine behaviour (DP2). Nominations are presented as in-degree (ID) and the number of incoming nominations, and out-degree (OD) and the number of outgoing nominations. Learners' behaviour is determined using scores and noting nominations patterns (Volk *et al.*, 2017), as already discussed in section 4.4.3.

Although client devices are shared, nominations were done individually and secretively in order to enable informant safety. As such learners who are identified as mobile bully-victims will not know which of their peers nominated them.

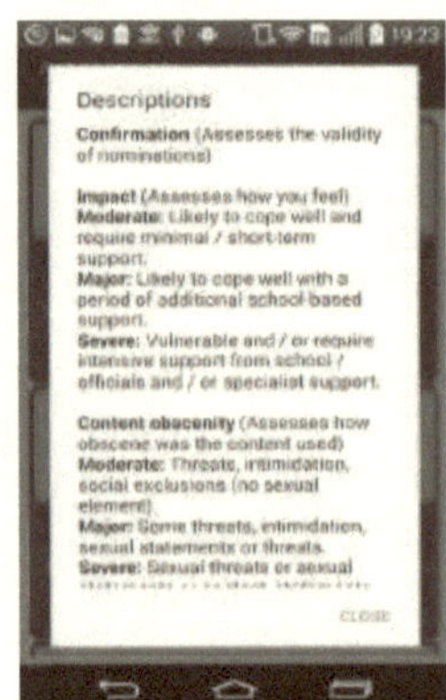

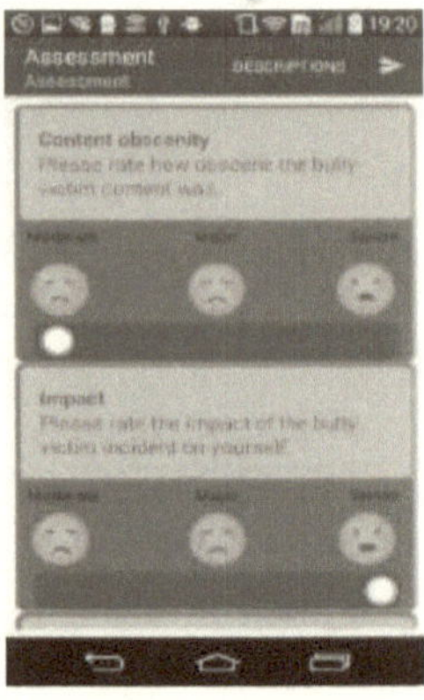

Figure 33: Assessment Descriptions (Client)	Figure 34: Assessments (Client)	Figure 35: Assessments continued (Client)

In order to enable efficient use of the system while learners interchange the limited client devices, the system links the confirmation and assessment to the poll function. Therefore, immediately after bullies and victims' nominations, learners also complete the confirmation and severity assessments and send results to the server (DP3). As a result, all learners can complete confirmation and severity assessments immediately after polling, which ensures confidentiality of nomination results, such that learners cannot guess which of their peers was identified as mobile bully-victims. Figure 33 presents user interfaces for reading descriptions of each assessment. Figures 34 and 35 show clear instructions and questions provided along with predefined answer options for the confirmation and severity assessment function (DP4), which also helps to avoid ambiguity. Learners respond to assessment questions by touching the smiley faces that are shown in Figures 34 and 35. The smiley faces resemble the predefined answers option, so that learners can visualise the meaning of assessments as well as their answers.

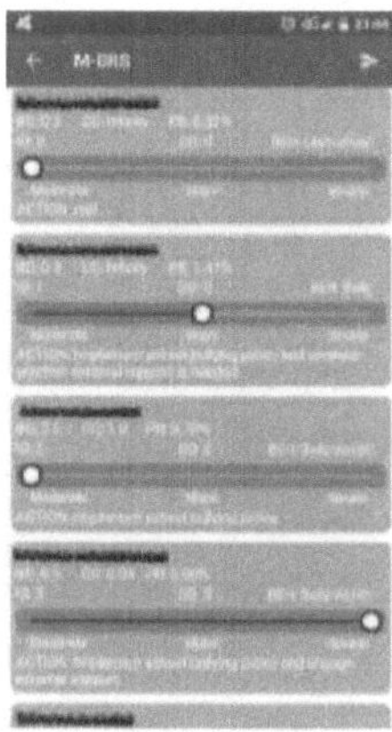 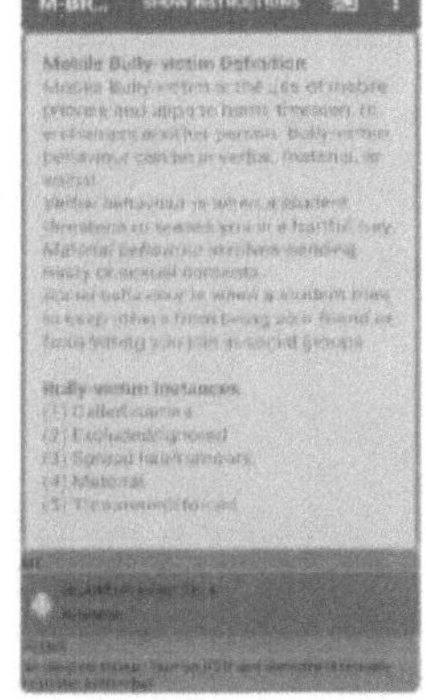 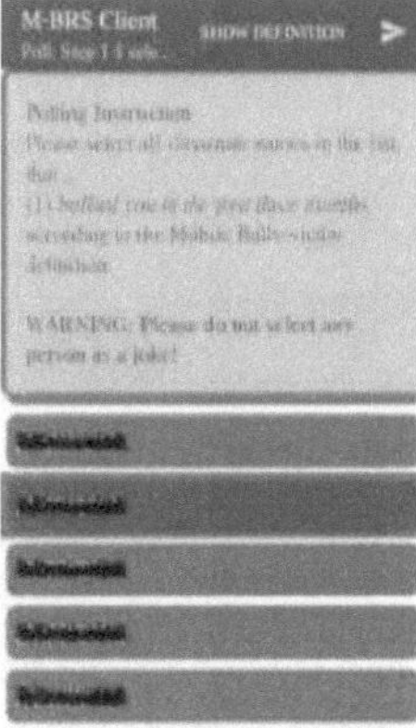

Figure 36: Diagnosis overview (Server)	Figure 37: Definition (Client)	Figure 38: Nominations (Client)

The system also allows the police to create reports about each learner diagnosis, including the identified mobile bullies, bully-victims, victims and uninvolved (DP5). Figure 36 provides a diagnosis report that can be used to address learners' behaviour in school classrooms. Figure 37 presents the definition and description of mobile bully-victim behaviour, and Figure 38 presents the nomination function with a list of names in the client application.

7.6   Evaluation 3 – usability tests

The aim of this evaluation was to identify and address the M-BRS's major usability challenges (Kowatsch *et al.*, 2017). The prototype consisting of server and client was developed based on Álvarez-Bermejo *et al.*, (2016) sociogram and the bullying assessment matrix provided by Bullying Prevention Advisory Group (2015: 8) to assess the effects of mobile bully-victim that needs a formal response. The sociogram is created by selecting names of learners in the list that are perceived as mobile bully-victims, while a participant that has a high sociogram score completed the assessment matrix. The assessment matrix seeks to measure the severity of mobile bully-victim on participants in order to inform a remedial action. The assessment results can be used to address bully-victims and bullies behaviour.

Usability testing is an acceptable strategy for improving artefact's quality. Users are observed while they complete tasks using the artefact, which provides quantitative findings (Toribio-Guzmán *et al.*, 2017). In order to improve the design and system acceptance, a usability test was conducted. Usability testing helps to ensure that interactive systems are suitable to the users, tasks, and without unfavourable usage outcomes. The naturalistic method was employed to evaluate the system. Naturalistic evaluation assesses the artefact's performance in its real setting, within the organisation (Venable *at al.*, 2012). The system's user interface, functions were assessed for their suitability to users' needs. The user-based evaluation of the system was employed in order to assess the system's effectiveness, efficiency and attitude from intended users (Meritam, Ryvlin and Beniczky, 2018). Effectiveness refers to the degree to which an artefact satisfies purpose and achieves designated benefits in practice, while efficiency is the degree to which an artefact produces intended effects narrowly, without considering conditional constrains (Venable *et al.*, 2012). Simply put, efficiency is described as the amount of resources such as time or effort required in using and completing tasks for which the system is design (Bastien, 2010).

The goal of user testing is to determine whether participants completed tasks successfully, as well as the artefact's usability and satisfaction (Toribio-Guzmán *et al.*, 2017). User testing is normally conducted in a laboratory. However, laboratory-based usability testing for native mobile application is often too costly (Ma *et al.*, 2013). The results of the system functions served as automatically captured of success rates on the server application, which complements traditional laboratory testing and support usability analysis (Ma *et al.*, 2013), such as:

ii. registration: the receipt of the details in the server app indicated success rate;

iii. nomination and assessment: the number of received responses against the number of participants indicate success rate; and

iv. the indication of the number of connected client devices to the server device indicated connection success;

v.   feedback, the system sends notification to clients on receipt of nominations or assessment information, and represents failure it not received.

As such, the researcher could investigate functions' success rates for registration, nomination and assessment, and client connections during the usability testing. Absence of feedback to clients after sending information (nomination or assessment), indicated problem. The user success rate matrix, defined as total number of correctly completed tasks by users, was used to measure usability (Nielsen, 2001). As such collected data included the system records, observation notes, and participants comments. The evaluation consisted of two usability tests with two groups of learners and teachers from two different schools.

7.6.1 *First usability test with learners*

In order to gain a deeper understanding of the challenges that were observed in the first two tests with learners, the researcher also conducted a usability test with learners. This test focused on evaluating technical aspects of the system. The teacher introduced the research and invited the researcher to take the floor. The researcher took over and explained the purpose of his visit, and explained that the purpose of the visit was to test an app. The app is designed to aid identification of mobile bully-victims among learners in a classroom. The research also described that the app consists of a server that can be used by officials, and client that will be used by learners.

The researcher explained what is mobile bullying and mobile bully-victim. Only 25 learners who owned mobile phones were invited to participate in the test. The learners were asked to sign consent forms with their parents, and informed that participation is voluntary, and they could withdraw their participation any time, if they wished to do so. Learners were asked to return signed forms the following day. Of 25 learners, only 9 students returned signed forms and they were asked to register their details on the system using the researcher's phones as client devices, and received IDs for use with the system in the polling and assessment sessions. *During the registration process, the researcher observed that the registration activity unnecessarily wasted time, as a result of sharing devices.*

After the registration learners were asked to participate on the polling session. *Other learners commented that they intend to nominate learners who were not in the list, since 16 learners on the group did not stay for the session.* The researcher explained that they could not be nominated if they have not registered on the system. However, it was important that the available learners participate for the purpose of testing the app. All nine learners successfully completed the polling session task while taking turns with the provided phones. *The researcher also observed that turn taking on the device wasted time.* In order to identify learners who were eligible to complete the assessment, the server app determined if there were mobile bully-victims in the group of participant. Learners were identified as bullies, bully-victims, victims or uninvolved.

Finally, just as in the polling task, learners were also invited to complete the assessment task, by confirming or denying their nomination and selecting scale options to answer three severity questions. No difficulties were observed for the four learners who were eligible to complete the assessment.

Table 17: Task success rates

User	Connect	Registration	Authenticate	Nominate
1	S	S	S	S
2	S	S	S	S
3	S	S	P	S
4	S	S	S	S
5	S	S	S	S
6	S	S	P	S
7	S	S	S	S
8	F	F	F	F
9	F	F	F	F

Table 17 presents success data for the use of M-BRS to diagnose mobile bully-victims in a classroom. "S" represents a complete success with a scale of 1, and "P" represents partial complete (with assistance) with a scale of 0.5, while "F" represents complete failure with a scale of 0. Then a success rate is calculated by dividing the sum of complete and partial success by a total number of attempts using their representative scales.

A total of thirty-six attempts on the system functions were observed. Of those attempts 23 (64%) attempts were successful, while five (14%) were partially completed, and eight (22%) failed. Overall, the usability of the system indicated a positive progress of 25.5 (71%) success rate towards a usable design. Of note, is that two learners needed assistance in order to complete the authentication task, as also Toribio-Guzmán *et al.* (2017) note filling form fields is challenging for users. These learners needed to be reminded of their authentication code before completing the nomination task. On the other hand, only two learners could not complete all tasks as a result of lost connection. In order to sufficiently test the utility of the system, another usability test with a larger group of learners was performed, as shown in the next section.

7.6.2   *Second usability test with learners*

Another app evaluation was conducted in a second school's classroom. The app test took place in the engineering drawing class with grade 12 learners from three classes. The teacher introduced the researcher to learners, and invited the researcher to take the floor. The researcher took over and explained the purpose of his visit, to test an app for identifying mobile bully-victims in a group. All learners (35) indicated that they owned smart phones, and were invited to take part in the study through signing consent forms together with their parents. Eight learners opted not to participate when consent forms were distributed, while 27 others returned signed forms the following day.

The app consists of a server that is used by the police official, and client that is used by learners. *Learners seemed very uneasy and uncooperative. Maybe this behaviour was related to them almost adults.* The researcher further explained that the app will be used to identify mobile bully-victims in the group, and that procedure requires learners to register their details on the system. After registration, the server, for learners to nominate mobile bully-victims, will send the names of registered learners to client phones. Emphasis was made that learners could select themselves and other learners. Also the nominations could be stored on the server app by selecting and sending one name at a time. The researcher also explained that selected learners would not be penalised in any way. The purpose of the test was merely to test the application; however, learners were asked to engage in the process honestly.

The interested learners were asked to use four of the provided phones that are known to connect and maintain connection to the server. Learners registered on the system using provided devices. Despite the demonstration provided at the start of the test. *Other learners inserted non-permissible data such as periods between initials and surname, and had do try again with the help of the research.*

Then the learners proceeded to the polling (nomination) session. Learners were reminded to insert their IDs in order continue with nominations. *Generally learners seemed excited for the polling session, others even said, "I know those I am going to select". Other learners forgot their IDs and the researcher reminded them their IDs again. Although the polling session consumed more time, since only four phones were shared between 25 learners. Learners were able to complete each nomination within one minute or lesser.* Learners took turns using the four provided phones, and most of them were able to do nominations without any difficulty. *One learner tried selecting multiple names, but could not because the system did not allow multiple selections.* Another learner asked, *"How many times can we select one name?"*

Table 18: Task success rates

User	Establish connection	Register	Login	Nominate	Maintain connection	Authenticate	Assessment
1	S	S	S	S	S	S	S
2	S	S	P	S	S	S	S
3	S	S	P	S	S	S	S
4	S	S	S	S	S	S	S
5	S	S	P	S	S	S	S
6	S	S	S	S	S	S	S
7	S	S	S	S	S	S	S
8	S	S	S	S	S	S	S
9	S	S	P	S	F	S	F
10	S	S	S	S	F	S	F
11	S	S	S	S	F	S	F

Moving to the assessment, learners were also reminded that the assessment procedure consists of confirmation so they could deny nominations if they felt wrongly accused. Also they were reminded to first read the accompanying questions and instruction in the confirmation and each of the three assessment quizzes. Also, for the assessment information to be relayed to the server when they were done, they had to tap the send button. *Almost all learners managed to authenticate (login) for assessment. One learner asked "is it necessary that we must type our codes before we use the app?"*

The researcher observed that the registration activity took a considerable time, which requires a relook. Other learners were relieved to see that their names were not in the list of those who were nominated as bully-victims. Other learners continued with the assessment, but they seemed uncomfortable, as if they felt exposed. The researcher also noted that other procedures should be revised to avoid wasting time with non-nominees. Table 18 presents the usability test's success rates.

In order to infer a success rate of assessment function, this test focused on learners who were identified as mobile bully-victims only. Seventy-seven attempts on system tasks were observed. Of those attempts, 61 (79%) were successful, while seven (9%) were partially completed and nine (12%) failed. Overall, usability success rate of 64.5 (84%) was observed, indicating a positive progress towards a usable design of the system. Although users completed most tasks successfully, only the authentication, connection maintenance by clients' device, and assessment tasks were not successful for some of users. Some of the users failed to complete the first authentication task, while they all successfully remembered their authentication code in the second attempt. As results of lost connection, on the other hand, assessments could not be submitted to sever. The loss of connection was caused by a prolonged inactivity of the client app, while learners passed devices to next other learners, which the Android operating system automatically removed from memory to preserve resources. Adjusting the client app's program code to reconnect to server, as part of the iterative design and development process, solved the problem of the prolonged idle time.

7.7   Conclusion

The instantiation of methods (abstract artefact) – design principles, is also an evaluation of abstract artefact (Prat *et al.*, 2014). As such, the instantiation of the established design principles served as evaluation thereof. Furthermore, formative and summative evaluations are conducted on artefacts in design science research (Venable *et al.*, 2016). Formative assessment was done iteratively during design and development of the artefact, in order to empirically improve and justify the artefact design – performance and characteristics. The evaluations revealed design requirements that are suited for children users, and ensuring safe and confidentiality. The artefact was evaluated for usability through user testing, notably, one of the best techniques for gaining insight into usability issues (Toribio-Guzmá, *et al.*, 2017). Overall, the results of the usability tests (Evaluation 3) showed the system is usable, which warrant proceeding to final stage (use) in order to address main research question of the study. The results of the system use are discussed in Chapter 8 and 9 (Evaluation 4).

This chapter presented two iterations of design and development of the M-BRS to the sufficient degree of usability. That is, the design enables registration of learners, authentication of learners before they do nominations and complete severity assessment. Primarily, as shown in Chapter 8, the system enables identification of mobile bully-victims through anonymous bullies and victims' nominations. Furthermore, the design helps to confidentially assess severity of mobile bully-victim effects, in order to recommend suitable remedial actions. Two minor challenges that were discovered did not require changing the system requirements and design principles. These were challenges as a result of wasted time in the registration process via client devices, and client app's prolonged idle time. In order to avoid wasting time on the registration of learners, the police can acquire learner registers from school and register them before the use of the system. Then on their visit to school, learner will be given their authentication codes. The loss of connection due to a prolonged idle time of the client app was resolved by adding code in the client app to automatically check and reset connection to the server. Despite the connection challenge the Evaluation 3 results showed that the system is highly usable. This conclusion is supported by the fact that the challenges that were encountered during usability tests were resolved without the need to change the intended design of the artefact.

The summative evaluation is conducted to empirically influence decisions of the artefact's selection for application as a solution (Venable *et al.*, 2016). In turn, evaluation enables analysis of the artefact's utility (Vom Brocke and Buddendick, 2006). Hence, in order to evaluate the usefulness of the artefact in meeting the recommended design intentions, Chapter 8 discusses how features in the design enabled reporting, reduction, and building confidence to mobile bully-victims. The system provides organised, visual reports for identification of mobile bully-victims, as stipulated in the design. As shown learners found the system easy to use, and they felt that the system enable them to have control over mobile bully-victim behaviour. Also, learners felt confident to report mobile bullies or victims, because of anonymity affordance of the system, which were intentions of the design.

Chapter 8 – Evaluation 4

8.1. Introduction

A natural research aims at explanation, discovery and justification of truth about a phenomenon, on the other hand, design science focuses on utility (vom Brocke and Buddendick, 2006). The evidence to whether an artefact, developed through Design Science Research (DSR), works or not is provided through evaluation (Venable, Pries-Heje and Baskerville, 2012). Hence, without thorough evaluation, design science conclusions are limited only to theorising design artefacts' utility, or simply claims that artefacts work without evidence (Venable *et al.*, 2016). However, DSR evaluation in Information Systems (IS) still "lacks a systematic list of evaluation criteria for artefacts and an associated set of evaluation methods" (Prat, Comyn-Wattiau and Akoka, 2014: 24; Venable *et al.*, 2016). Fortunately, the pragmatic nature of DSR allows a use of methods that are deemed suitable to achieve research goals (Hevner, 2007).

Artefact evaluation consists of two parts, namely, artificial evaluation and naturalistic evaluation (Prat, Comyn-Wattiau and Akoka, 2014; Venable, Pries-Heje and Baskerville, 2012). Artificial evaluation methods include both field and laboratory experimentation, criteria-based analysis, theoretical arguments, and mathematical proofs. A naturalistic evaluation assesses the artefact's performance in real-world context. While naturalistic evaluation provides internal validity in DSR, artificial evaluation provides more weight for scientific reliability (Venable *et al.*, 2012). Venable *et al.* (2012) note evaluation can be performed on design theories and principles before artefact instantiation including designs or models (*ex ant* evaluation), as well as on instantiated artefacts (*ex post* evaluation). In order to ensure an artefact's utility and efficacy, evaluation was first conducted during development cycles (Venable *et al.*, 2012).

The two terms that are related in testing phases are *evaluation* and *validation* (Wieringa, 2014). Evaluation focuses on investigating the artefact use in the stakeholder's field using methods such as statistical surveys, observational case studies, and special case (Wieringa, 2014). Building, intervention and evaluation of artefacts in design science can be done with reflection to action research (Wieringa and Moralı, 2012). Thus an artefact can be tested in an idealised context, and finally tested in the real-world context to demonstrate its utility. Utility refers to the use of the artefact to fulfil identified users' needs (vom Brocke and Buddendick, 2006). While under development, an artefact can be validated through a special case, and finally tested using technical action research (TAR) in the real-world context (Wieringa and Moralı, 2012). While a traditional action research starts with problem identification, as in design science, TAR starts with building an artefact and then finding organisational problems to which the artefact can be applied as an intervention (Parra, España and Panach, 2017; Wieringa and Moralı, 2012). Validation helps to demonstrate the artefact's contribution to stakeholder goals if implemented (Wieringa, 2014). Hence, validation seeks to answer effectiveness and utility questions about an artefact in real-world context (Parra *et al.*, 2017; Wieringa and Moralı, 2012). Since the artefact was tested during the development, the researcher deemed TAR suitable for last stage of artefact testing. According to Wieringa and Moralı (2012) technical action research (TAR) can be used in the last stages of an artefact testing. The testing sequence starts in an idealised context, and then scaled up to more realistic conditions, until the artefact can be finally tested using concrete clients' problems. Parra *et al.* (2017) note TAR helps to reveal artefact's (experimental construct) effects in practice (Parra *et al.*, 2017).

In DSR, evaluation is always done empirically, and may take any stance between interpretive, positivistic, and critical, and employ activities to determine "how well the artefact supports a solution to the problem" (Peffers, Tuunanen, Rothenberger and Chatterjee, 2008:56; Venable, Pries-Heje and Baskerville, 2012).

The *evaluation cycle* includes confirmatory focus group (Tremblay, Hevner and Berndt, 2010), a statistical survey, and the artefact's report using sociometric. A review of existing studies was conducted to inform the standard by which the artefact could be evaluated for its novelty and knowledge contribution of the study (Gregor and Hevner, 2013). Turber and Smiela (2014) used workshop participation and expert review to evaluate their model artefact for validity, utility, quality, and efficacy criteria, and the degree to which the artefact's requirements were met.

Additionally, M-BRS is designed to adhere to the following design objectives: validity, reliability, efficiency, and generality (Sturm, Schneider and Sunyaev, 2015). Efficacy is the level to which an artefact performs its required effects, and can be demonstrated by using the artefact in real examples (Prat *et al.*, 2014). While validity includes reliability and relates to the level to which an artefact works correctly (Prat *et al.*, 2014). On the other hand, generality implies that the artefact addresses broader goals more general. The evaluation of the artefact was based on the observational method – field study (Hevner *et al.*, 2004; Iivari, 2015). Participants were requested to complete a questionnaire in order to measure their perceptions about the artefact's utility. Wieringa and Moralı (2012) posit the implementation evaluation seeks to discover the effects of the artefact under evaluation. Primarily, the purpose of evaluating the prototype at this stage was to address the following research question in this study:

- *What is the effectiveness of the proposed app in aiding law enforcement control mobile bully-victim behaviour?*

This study does not base the analysis on generalisation of information and predicting learners' behaviour (Brink, 2018). However, the focus is on the knowledge generated from the artefact's design and usage in diagnosing learners' involvement in mobile bully-victims behaviour. This chapter presents the results of artefact's evaluation including reports that are produced by the artefact.

Evaluation and validation (see Chapter 9) had different research goals that followed different research approaches (Wieringa, 2014). The evaluation focused on the assessment of the M-BRS' utility in the field, whereas validation was conducted in order to justify the M-BRS contribution to stakeholder's goals if implemented (Wieringa, 2014). Also, the M-BRS consists of two important role players or users, the *moderator* to whom reports are sent, and *reporters* or *subjects* during the mobile bully-victims diagnosis. The *moderators* included the South African police and schoolteachers (included to fill gaps, as they spend more time with learners than the police), and school learners were *reporters*. Henceforth, these role players are referred to as such.

8.2. Utility evaluation

The sub-sections in the utility evaluation first present the action research procedure, as applied by Parra, España and Panach (2017) and specify the instruments used for the evaluation of the M-BRS. Then the rationale for a using Social Network Analysis (SNA) technique is discussed. Then the guide to aid interpretation of social network graphs in the results of the M-BRS is also presented. Afterwards, the utility of the M-BRS is evaluated with the lens of SNA method and presented. Then Participants demographics are presented, as well as Visual analysis, Nominations and Severity assessment, the integrated reports (Overview) of the M-BRS.

8.2.1 Evaluation procedure

The evaluation of the M-BRS was based on the actual use of the system in the field, as specified in the selected and adapted design-evaluate approach of Design Science framework (see Design science approach in Section 5.5 of Chapter 5). Hence, the use of the system was deployed in a school in three classes of grade 10 learners. This school was chosen based on the characteristics that are provided in Section 4.6.3 (Sample) of Chapter 4 including learners' age group, and existing interaction with the police. Also being in the rural area with a higher risk of cyberbullying due to the prevalence of and dominance of Internet access via mobile phones, and higher crime rates among youths (Africa's General Household Survey 2017; Kyobe *et al.*; 2018; Odora and Matoti, 2015), this school was deemed suitable for the current study. The data collected in these phase included app results, and survey data. This section presents the steps and instruments in Table 19 that were used in the evaluation of the M-BRS.

Table 19: Instruments definition

Instrument	Description
Interface screenprints	Screen prints to demonstrate reading instructions, performing nomination and assessments.
Usability questionnaire	Questions to obtain participants' perceptions about the M-BRS

Step 1: Before the study began, consent was solicited through signed consent form by the school principal, learners and their parents. The consent forms had accompanying letters that explained the purpose and the possible risks of participating in the study. The researcher emphasised that participation was voluntary, and the details of learners would be kept confidential at all times. Using sign up lists that were

completed during the distribution of consent forms, the researcher registered on the M-BRS only the learners that returned signed consent forms from their parents.

Step 2: The learners were asked to meet in the hall after school, where the researcher provided verbal training of usage and demonstration of screen prints of the M-BRS. The researcher provided assurance that nominations were completely confidential and the results of nomination were also anonymous such that learners would not know who nominated them. Learners were informed that in order to ensure confidentiality, the system has created identification codes for authenticating in the system before use. Learners were also informed that they will have an opportunity to see results of the nominations, and they will be requested to complete the usability questionnaire in order to learn how the experience of using the app was like for them.

Step 3: Right after the training, learners regrouped by their classes and were provided and asked to memorise their identification codes. Then they were asked to take turns with the four mobile devices as clients and complete the nomination and assessment, while the researcher used the fifth device as a server.

Step 4: In order for learners to be able to provide feedback about the use of the M-BRS, the researcher printed the nomination results with each learner's identification codes instead of names. The results were provided in a separate paper along with the usability questionnaire. Then learners were free to go home after completing the questionnaire.

8.2.2   *Diagnosis results – visual and statistical analysis rational*

Cybercrimes and bullying pose a great challenge in identify perpetrators. As a result of lack of adult supervision for children's online activities and anonymity affordance of technology, cyberbullies are unlikely to get caught and face consequences of their actions (Ioannou *et al.*, 2018). On the other hand, victims and witnesses are reluctant to come forward and report incidents, due to lack of available safe and confidential reporting platforms (Kenny, Dooley and Fitzgerald, 2016; Paullet and Pinchot, 2019). The proposed solution in current study was instantiated as a mobile app called Mobile Bully-victims Response system (M-BRS) to help the police identify culprits. Hence the use of the systems such as M-BRS could shed light about enabling informant safety and confidentiality in order to encourage reporting.

The M-BRS reports including digital trace data (see section 4.4.3) were analysed using the Social Network Analysis (SNA) technique, in order to provide both visual and mathematical analysis of social network (Saqr, Fors and Nouri, 2018). The visualisation of nominations was used to explore learners' interactions driven by mobile bully-victim behaviour and to facilitate interpretation of quantitative network analysis. Chiefly, the police were enthusiastic about using network graph (sociogram) to view nomination results. Furthermore, quantitative social network analysis was used to calculate centrality (popularity) scores of each learner, in order to show learners' popularity (Saqr, Fors and Nouri, 2018). In order to provide summaries about the diagnosis results, descriptive statistics were calculated (Mishra *et al.*, 2019). Nomination reports included learners' in-degree, out-degree, centrality (PageRank), confirmation and severity assessment.

The visual analytic and quantitative analysis capabilities of SNA facilitated studying relational dimensions, such as mobile bully-victims patterns of learners. Using visual analytics, learner-learner relations can be plotted in order to identify influential learners and group dynamics (Saqr, Fors and Nouri, 2018). To visually identify bully-victims, bullies, victims and uninvolved learners in classrooms, the police can use these results.

8.2.3   *Interpreting sociograms*

The M-BRS reports include a sociogram to help visualise results and easily identify mobile bully-victims, bullies, victims and uninvolved learners. Sociogram is an instrument that originated in sociomatry, which helps to visualise social networks on a graph (De Nooy, Mrvar and Batagelj, 2018). The elements of a graph include sets of nodes and lines (edges) that link pairs of nodes, to represent network structure (De Nooy, Mrvar and Batagelj, 2018; van Dijk *et al.*, 2017). In the results of the M-BRS, nodes represent learners, while edges represent nominations between nodes. Also, nodes are labelled with numbers to enable identification. Normally, nomination pathways (lines) are represented with arrows leading from a victim and point to the bully (Volk *et al.*, 2017). The direction of edges is shown with arrowheads to depict source nodes and target nodes.

Similar to arrowheads, cyclic sprites are embedded at the end of edges to indicate nominated nodes as victims. Learners may report being victimised, as well as being bullies themselves (Volk *et al.*, 2017). Hence, the artefact reports indicate a relation where learners selected their victims, in order to address false accusation risk that is possible when bullies only are nominated. As with arrowheads, cyclic sprites are positioned close to the nominee (target node) – indicating a bully-to-victim relationship. As such, arrowheads were used to indicate the nomination of bullies between nodes (Clifton and Webster, 2017), whereas cyclic sprites were used to represent victim nominations (GraphStream Team, 2018).

Since mobile bully-victims occupy a dual position, as victims and bullies as well (Olweus, 2001; Juan *et al.*, 2018). Their identification depends on the overlap between pure bullies and victims (Juan *et al.*, 2018). Hence, mobile bully-victims can be identified as such if they are nominated as bullies, while they also nominate other learners as bullies. One nomination of a learner by a classmate is an indication of victimisation (Huitsing and Veenstra, 2012; Volk *et al.*, 2017), similarly in this study the researcher regarded at least one nomination as an indication of bullying or a victimising behaviour. In order to enable interpretation of the nomination results, the systems' draws graphs using nodes, edges, and sprites. Arrowheads indicate that a learner (target) is nominated as a bully, and are placed close to and points towards the target node – indicating a victim-to-bully relationship. As such, nominations of bullies count as out-degrees to victims, and as in-degrees towards bullies.

M-BRS renders sociograms using force-directed layout algorithm. Force-directed layout algorithm draws each vertex according to nodes connections using physical simulation (Saqr *et al.*, 2018). Nodes are positioned close to nodes they connect to (attraction), whereas other nodes are far apart. The following lists provides descriptions of the elements of the graph (nodes and edges), which aid the interpretation of nominations:

Nodes

- The purple node represents mobile bully-victims, and must have at least one in- and out-degree.

- The green node represents mobile bullies, with at least one in-degree and no out-degrees.

- The blue node represents mobile victims with zero in-degree and at least one out-degree.

- The yellow nodes represent uninvolved learners with zero in- and out-degrees.

- A node's size corresponds to the PageRank, such that nodes with a high PageRank centrality are larger than normal sized nodes.

Edge and sprites

- A nomination between nodes is represented with an edge that has an arrowhead or cyclic sprite on one end.

- An arrowhead or cyclic sprite indicates edge directions. Hence an arrowhead or cyclic sprite on one side of the edge indicates a target node (nominee). That is, a source-target nomination. Source represents the nominator, and target represents the nominee.

- An arrowhead on the edge towards target node indicates that the source node nominated the target node as a bully. Hence the edge counts as an in-degree to the source node, and as an out-degree to the target node

- A cyclic sprite on the edge towards a target node indicates that the source node nominated the target node as a victim. As such, the source node admits of bullying the target node. Hence the edge counts as an in-degree to the source node, and an out-degree to the target node.

- If the nominations are reciprocal (Volk *et al.*, 2017), two arrowheads are positioned on both ends of an edge between two nodes. In this case, both nodes are bullies and victims of each other – victim-to-victim and bully-to-bully relations.

- Another reciprocal nominations use cyclic sprites on both ends of an edge between two nodes, indicating that both nodes admit of victimising each other – victim-to-victim and bully-to-bully relations.

Table 20 presents possible nomination relations between learners, which are represented with nodes, edges that embed arrowheads and cyclic sprites. Victims' nominations were used to differentiate bullies from bully-victims, victims and uninvolved (van Dijk *et al.*, 2017).

Table 20: Sociogram interpretation summary

Graphical representation	Nomination description	In- and out-degrees	Identified behaviour
	Node 2 nominated 1 as a bully, and the arrowhead points to the nominee.	• Node 1: 1 in-degree and 0 out-degree. Node 2: 0 in-degree and 1 out-degree.	• Node 1 represents a bully. Node 2 represents a victim.
	Node 1 and 2 nominated each other as bullies.	Node 1 and 2: 1 in-degree and 1 out-degree.	Node 1 and 2 represent bully-victims.
	Node 2 nominated 1 as a victim.	• Node 1: 1 in-degree and 0 out-degree. Node 2: 0 in-degree and 1 out-degree.	• Node 1 represents a victim. Node 2 represents bully.
	Node 1 and 2 nominated each other as victims.	• Node 1: 1 in-degree and 1 out-degree. Node 2: 1 in-degree and 1 out-degree.	Node 1 and 2 represent bullies and victims – bully-victims.
	Node 1 nominated 2 as a victim, and node 2 nominated 1 as a bully.	• Node 1: 1 in-degree and 1 out-degree. Node 2: 1 in-degree and 1 out-degree.	• Node 1 represents a bully. Node 2 represents a victim.

8.2.4 Participant demographics

The researcher was granted permission to conduct research in one of the schools in the Eastern Free State Province. As already mentioned, schools in rural areas of South Africa face higher crime rates, and mobile phone usage among learners, which means higher exposure risks to mobile bullying and the related behaviour (Africa's General Household Survey 2017; Kyobe *et al.*; 2018; Odora and Matoti, 2015). Also schools in rural areas have not received enough research attention about mobile bullying (Juan *et al.*, 2018), especially the Eastern Free State. Learners who owned or had regular access to smartphones in three classes of grade 10 were invited to take part in the study. A total of 52 learners volunteered to participate in the use of the M-BRS to diagnose mobile bully-victims behaviour. The choice of learner participants was guided by the characteristics that are discussed in section 4.6.3 of Chapter 4 in this study, including learners who are between 14 and 18 years old and own or have access to mobile phones. In this evaluation, the learners' age ranged between 15 and 19 years, and 35 (67.3%) learners were females and 17 (32.7%) males. The diagnosis results are presented using descriptive statistics including in-degree, out-degree, PageRank, confirmation and severity assessment. In-degrees indicate the number of nominations received, whereas out-degrees indicate the number of nominations directed to respective learners, whereas PageRank indicated learners' popularity.

8.2.5 *Visual analysis (sociograms)*

Using visual analytics learner-learner relations can be plotted in order to identify influential learners and group dynamics (Saqr, Fors and Nouri, 2018). The police to visually identify bully-victims, bullies, victims and uninvolved learners in classrooms can use these results for targeted interventions. The M-BRS present nomination results as sociograms to help visually identification of bully-victims, bullies, victims, and uninvolved learners. Volk *et al.* (2017) interpreted nomination to identify bully-victims, bullies, and victims on a social network by considering in- and out-degrees of nodes. Also, the number of in- and out-degrees on a node show the represented learner's centrality (popularity) based on the PageRank. Figure 39 – 41 present mobile bully-victim sociograms.

Figure 39 shows 8 bully-victims out of 23 learners. Nominations between learners 11, 5, 21, 19, and 22 are reciprocal, and were identified as mobile bully-victims. Peer nomination and self-report can be used together to identify victims of bullying (Phillips and Cornell, 2012). Hence, the system also enabled learners to nominate their victims (self-report), which could help to affirm nominations. Evidently, learner 22 admitted of bullying learner 19, and learner 11 also admitted of bullying learner 5. The graph shows that learner 20, 14 and 4 were also mobile bully-victims with at least one in-degree and one out-degree. Notably, bullying behaviour manifests as aspiration to gain popular social statuses (Oldenburg, Van Duijnand Veenstra, 2018). Hence, nodes with a high number of in-degrees represent most central or popular learners (Volk *et al.*, 2017). Also, sizes of the nodes 19, 21, and 22 were bigger, which correspond to higher PageRank and indicate learners' popularity. Clearly bullying adds to perpetrators' perceived popularity and is antecedent of cyberbullying (Wegge *et al.*, 2016).

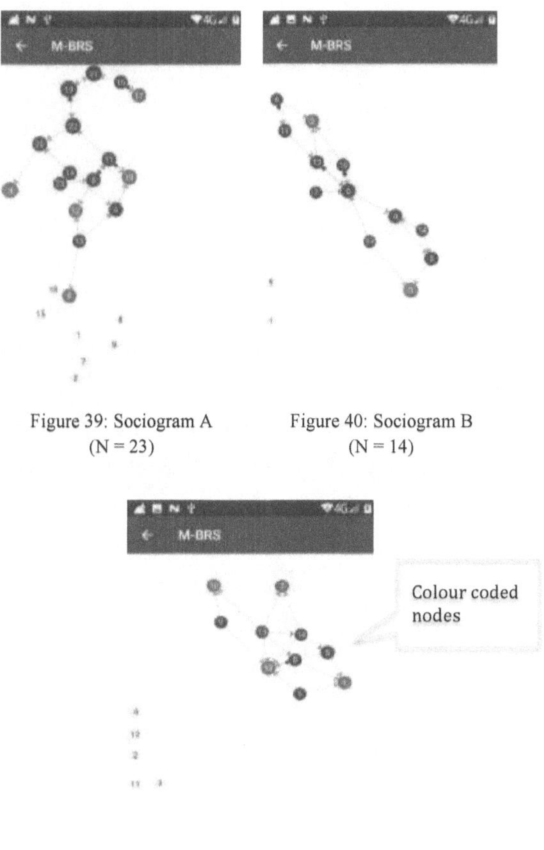

Figure 39: Sociogram A
(N = 23)

Figure 40: Sociogram B
(N = 14)

Figure 41: Sociogram C
(N = 15)

Learners 3, 6, 17, 12 and 10 were identified as mobile bullies with at least one in-degree. Learner 10 also admitted of bullying learner 11, learner 17 also admitted to bullying learner 16. Three learners – 16, 12 and 23 – were identified as mobile victims, whereas seven learners were uninvolved.

Figure 40 shows six of 14 learners who were identified as mobile bully-victims. Of six identified mobile bully-victims, two learners admitted to bullying other learners. Also, one mobile bully (learner 11) admitted to bullying learner 8 (victim). This way, M-BRS results of learners who nominated their victims are more plausible, with regard to the risk of false accusation. Learners 2 and 3 were identified as mobile bullies, and learners 7, 8, 13 and 14 were identified as mobile victims. Only two learners were not nominated nor did they nominated other learners (uninvolved).

Finally, Figure 41 shows that 10 of 15 learners were involved in mobile bullying and victimisation, while 5 were uninvolved. Three learners (5, 8, 14) were identified as mobile bully-victims, of which learner 13 admitted to bullying learner 8. Also, four learners (1, 7, 10, and 11) were identified as mobile bullies, whereas three learners (6, 9 and 15) were identified as mobile victims, and five learners were uninvolved.

Overall, these graphs represented learners' inclination to report their bullies, which also helped to identify mobile bully-victims. Victims of bullying are more inclined to self-report victimisation (Phillips and Cornell, 2012). Similarly, these graphs showed that peer nominated bullies were more likely to report themselves, which renders confirmation of nominations. This approach helped to validate nominations that could otherwise be done by counsellors if they were readily available (Phillips and Cornell, 2012). Mobile bully-victims are provocative and react aggressively to a threat or attack and sometimes target weaker victims for their bullying (Gámez-Guadix et al., 2015; Juvonen and Graham, 2014; Pouwels et al., 2016). Hence, almost all pure victims reported being bullied by bully-victims. Also bully-victims were reported for bullying other learners, as also noted in Van Dijk et al. (2017) observations that instead of resorting to avoidance or prosocial strategies, bully-victims tend to be aggressive when interacting with peers.

Additionally, mobile bully-victims, as shown in the presented graphs, bullied eight out of 10 identified victims. Also, Samara et al. (2017) observed that bully-victims target other learners who may be weaker than their bullies. Similarly, You and Lim (2016) suggest that victims of school violence (including bullying) have resentments against their bullies, which contributes to their aggressive behaviour towards online strangers instead of perpetrators themselves. Seemingly, bully-victims are motivated by revenge. In turn, bully-victims drive the bullying propagation in classrooms.

8.2.6 Nomination analysis

The nomination results were also analysed using Statistical Packages for the Social Sciences (SPSS) software, version 26. Network quantitative analysis is a mathematical technique to compute participants' prominence and the value of links in a social network (Saqr, Fors and Nouri, 2018). Mobile bully-victims, bullies, and victims can be identified using in- and out-degrees (Volk *et al.*, 2017). Links represented learners' nominations, and learners are represented with nodes.

Also, "students who fail to self-report victimisation, but are peer nominated, may have an unclear understanding of the bullying definition or may not be able to look objectively at their own situation" (Phillips and Cornell, 2012: 129). Hence self-report in this study refers to learners who identify themselves as victims or bullies, while peer report refers to learners that are nominated by other learners as bullies or victims. Furthermore, learners who are peer nominated and/or self-report as bullies and victims at the same time are identified as mobile bully-victims. The following results were group according to identified behaviour using cases in SPSS.

Table 21: Nominations summary

Degree	Bully-victims (n=17)				Bullies (n=11)		Victims (n=10)	
	In degree 1.71 (0.77)		Out-degree 1.82 (0.73)		In-degree 2.27 (1.42)		Out-degree 2.30 (1.06)	
	N	%	N	%	N	%	N	%
1	7	41.2	6	35.3	3	27.3	1	10.0
2	9	52.9	8	47.1	5	45.5	7	70.0
3	-	-	3	17.6	2	18.2	1	10.0
4	1	5.9	-	-	-	-	-	-
5	-	-	-	-	-	-	1	10.0
6	-	-	-	-	1	9.1	-	-

Table 21 presents summaries for identified mobile bully-victims, bullies, and victims respectively, including counts (in parenthesis), mean and standard deviation (in parenthesis). Seventeen (32.7%) learners were identified as mobile bully-victims with maximum in-degrees of 4 and 3 for out-degrees. Also, 11 (21.2%) learners were identified as bullies with the maximum in-degrees of 6. On the other hand, 10 (19.2%) learners were identified as victims with maximum out-degrees of 5. Interestingly, 14

(26.9%) learners were uninvolved, which are more than victims and bullies, but less than bully-victims.

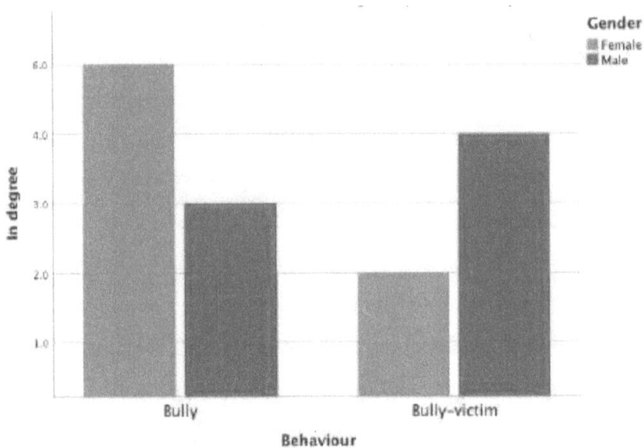

Figure 42: Clustered bar of in-degree by behaviour by gender

Figure 42 presents the clustered bar of in-degree by behaviour by gender. Female bullies received up to 6 nominations, while males had up to 3 nominations. Male bully-victims received up to 4 nominations, whereas females had maximums of 2 nominations. Nominations of female bullies were more than female bully-victims' nominations. However, nominations for male bully-victims' were higher than male bullies' nominations. Female bully-victims' nominations were lower than that of female bullies'.

Figure 43 presents clustered bar graph of out-degree by behaviour by gender. Although female are more likely to report or disclose experiences of cyberbullying than males (Burton, 2016). The system's results also show that male victims report up to five bullies whereas females nominated up to two bullies. However, both male and female bully-victims nominated up to three bullies. Overall, male victims seem more courageous than females to identify their bullies. On the other hand, both male and female bully-victims seem more inclined than female victims to identify their bullies.

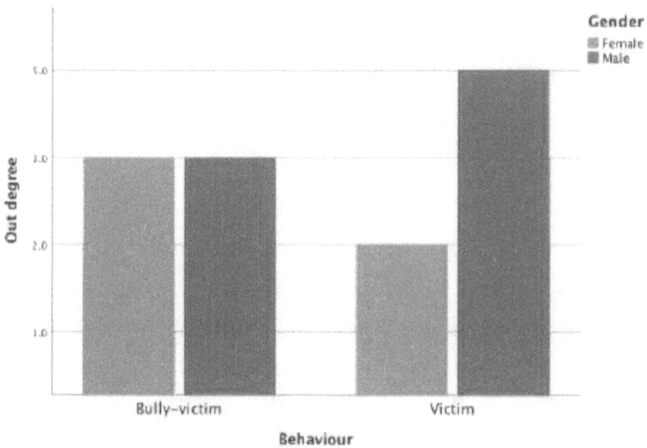

Figure 43: Clustered bar graph of out-degree by behaviour by gender

Similar to nominations of victims as discussed in section 8.2.3, in order to reduce the risk of false accusations, learners were also asked to indicate the possibility of accepting nomination, if they were nominated as bullies. The system provided predefined answer options including "Unlikely", "Unsure", "Likely".

Table 22: Confirmation

	Bully-victims (n=17)		Bullies (n=11)	
	1.82 (0.95)		1.73 (0.79)	
	N	%	N	%
Unlikely	9	52.9	5	45.5
Unsure	2	11.8	4	36.4
Likely	6	35.3	2	18.2

Table 22 presents a summary of learners' likelihood to confirm nominations. Of the 17 identified mobile bully-victims nine (52.9%) indicated they were unlikely to accept nominations, two (11%) were unsure, and six (35.3%) were likely to accept nominations. Similarly, of the 11 learners who were identified as bullies, five (45.5%) were unlikely to accept nominations, while four (36.4%) were not sure if they would accept nominations, and only two (18.2%) indicated that they were likely to accept nominations as bullies.

Table 23: PageRank summary

	Min	Max	Mean	SD
Bully-victims	0.33%	2.42%	0.96	0.57
Bullies	0.42%	1.50%	0.88	0.39
Victims	0.28%	0.39%	0.32	0.05

The number of nominations received indicates learners' centrality (popularity) with regard to their bullying behaviour (Huitsing and Veenstra, 2012; Volk *et al.*, 2017). Table 23 presents PageRank summaries for mobile bully-victims, bullies, and victims. Mobile bully-victims had the highest PageRank (2.30%) followed by bullies (1.50%), and victims (0.39%). Clearly, mobile bully-victims were most popular than bullies and victims.

Learners popularity were further analysed based on gender differences. Figure 44 presents clustered bar of PageRank by behaviour and by gender for mobile bully-victims, bullies, and victims. Uninvolved learners were not included because they do not have in- and out-degrees. Female bully-victims' PageRank was 2.42%, which is higher than female bullies (1.50%) and victims (0.39%).

Also, Females had higher PageRank than male bully-victims and bullies, contradicting Wegge *et al.*'s (2016) notion that bullying is more closely related to perceived popularity for males than females. Also, male bully-victims were more popular than male bullies and victims. Although, the revealed popularity was not based on peers' perceptions, but bullying and victimisation nominations, female bully-victims were more popular than bullies.

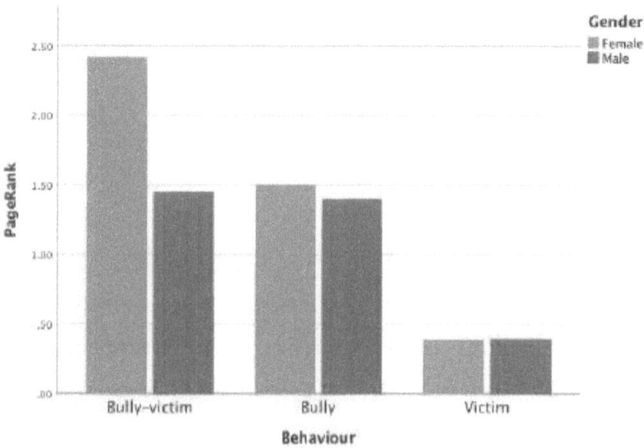

Figure 44: Mobile bully-victims' clustered bar maximum of PageRank by behaviour and by gender

8.2.7 Severity assessment analysis

Following the nomination of bullies during the mobile bully-victims diagnosis, learners also completed the severity assessment, in order to inform remedial actions (intervention) for identified bully-victims and victims. While all learners completed the nomination confirmation, only the results for learners who were identified as mobile bully-victims and victims are presented. This is because the severity assessment focuses on the bullying effects on victims and bully-victims only. The assessment evaluates the impact, frequency, and content obscenity of mobile bully-victims behaviour. Each assessment has three predefined verbal scales, including "Moderate", "Major", and "Severe".

The ratings of impact, frequency, and severity are tallied in order to indicate the degree of severity. The degree of severity helps to decide on the suitable intervention. The sum of impact, frequency, and content obscenity helps to determine the level of intervention required in order to enable resolving incidents for victims and bully-victims. Levels of interventions were determined according to the Cool School Programme (2001):

- If the sum is between 3 and 5 the first level intervention is implemented, *"Implement school bullying policy"*;
- If the sum is between 6 and 7 the second level intervention is implemented, *"Implement school bullying policy and consider whether external support is*

needed"; and

- If the sum is between 8 and 9, the third level intervention is implemented, *"Implement school bullying policy and engage external support"*.
- Additionally, the third level intervention is also implemented if any of the severity assessment (impact, frequency, and content's obscenity) is reported as severe.

Table 24 presents summary results of impact, frequency, and content obscenity in severity assessment for the identified mobile bully-victims. Similarly, seven (41.2%) learners reported a moderate impact, while eight (47.1%) learners indicated a major impact and two (11.8%) learners reported severe impact of mobile bully-victims or bullying behaviour.

Table 24: Bully-victims assessment summary

	Impact		Frequency		Obscenity	
	1.71 (0.686)		1.94 (0.827)		1.47 (0.624)	
	N	%	N	%	N	%
Moderate	7	41.2	6	35.3	10	58.8
Major	8	47.1	6	35.3	6	35.3
Severe	2	11.8	5	29.4	1	5.9

Also, six (35.3%) learners reported a moderate frequency, six (35.3%) learners reported a major frequency, and five (20%) learners had experienced severe frequency. With regard to content obscenity, 10 (58.8%) learners reported a moderate obscenity of bullying content, while six (35.3%) learners indicated a major attack with obscene content, and one (5.9%) reported a severe content obscenity.

Table 25: Victims assessment summary

	Impact		Frequency		Obscenity	
	1.40 (0.699)		1.60 (0.699)		1.80 (0.919)	
	N	%	N	%	N	%
Moderate	7	70.0	5	50.0	5	50.0
Major	2	20.0	4	40.0	2	20.0
Severe	1	10.0	1	10.0	3	30.0

Table 25 presents summary results of impact, frequency, and content obscenity in severity assessment for the identified mobile victims. The impact column indicates that seven (70%) learners experiences a moderate impact of mobile bully-victims or bullying behaviour, while two (20%) learners indicated a major impact, and only one (10%) learner report a severe impact. Similarly, five (50%) learners indicated a moderate frequency of mobile bully-victim behaviour or bullying, while four (50%) learners reported a major frequency, and only one (10%) learner reported a severe frequency. Six (50%) learners reported a moderate contents obscenity of mobile bully-victims or bullying attacks, whereas two (20%) learners reported a major content obscenity, and three (30%) learner experienced severe content obscenity.

Figure 45: Bar count of behaviour by impact

Assessment results were further analysed by comparisons between mobile bully-victims and victims. Figure 45 shows the clustered bar count of behaviour mobile bully-victims and victims by impact. Eight bully-victims indicated a major impact on their ability to cope from bullying effects, whereas only two victims experienced a major impact. Both bully-victims and victims equally reported a moderate impact of mobile bully-victim or bullying behaviour. On the other hand, two bully-victims experienced a severe impact of mobile bully-victim or bullying behaviour, while on one victim reported a severe impact.

Figure 46 presents the cluster bar count of frequency by behaviour. More mobile bully-victims (six) than victims (five) experience moderate frequency of mobile bully-victim or bullying attacks. Also, more bully-victims (six) experienced major frequencies of mobile bully-victimisation or bullying attacks than victims (four). Similarly, more bully-victims (5) reported severe frequencies of bullying attack than victims (1).

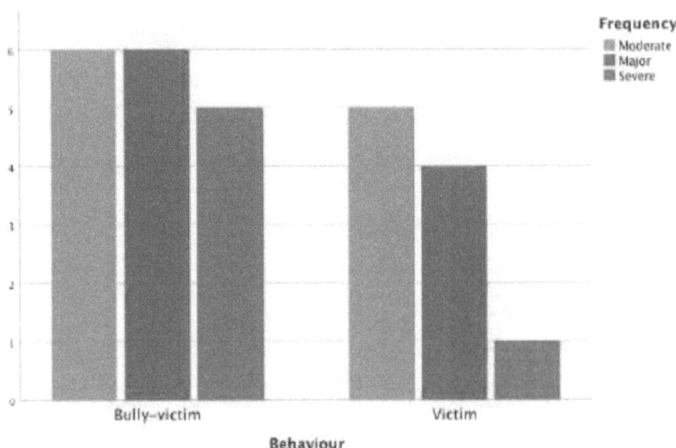

Figure 46: Count of behaviour by frequency

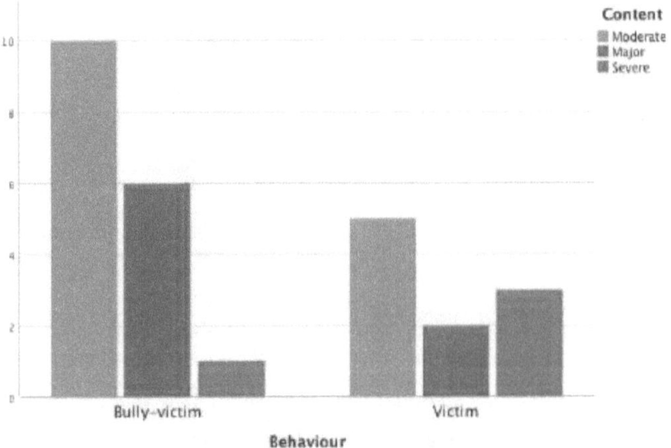

Figure 47: Count of behaviour by content obscenity

Figure 47 also shows the clustered bar count of content obscenity by behaviour. More mobile bully-victims (10) than victims (five) reported a moderate content obscenity. Similarly, more bully-victims (six) than victims (two) experienced a major content obscenity. On the other hand, more victims (three) than bully-victims (one) reported a severe content obscenity.

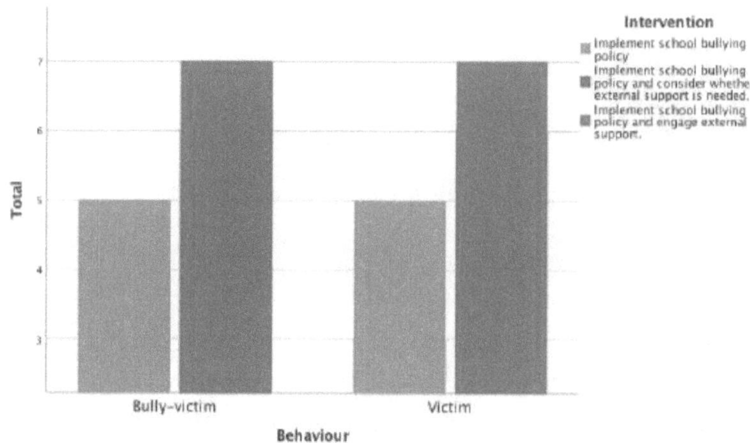

Figure 48: Total by behaviour by intervention

Totals of severity assessment for bully-victims and victims by behaviour by intervention are presented in Figure 48. Technically, none of the mobile bully-victims or victims required the level three intervention – implementing school bullying policy and engaging external support. However, as already mentioned earlier, a selection of "Severe" in any of the severity assessment scales, automatically qualifies learners for the third level intervention. Hence, both bully-victims and victims who selected the "Severe" scale, but have a total less than 8, required the level three instead of level two interventions. The level one intervention was applicable to learners who had a total between 3 and 5.

Figure 49 shows the clustered bar of severity assessment count by behaviour by intervention. Mobile bully-victims (nine) who required implementing school bullying policy were more than victims (five). Similarly, more bully-victims (eight) than victims (five) needed to be addressed by implementing school bullying policy and engaging external support.

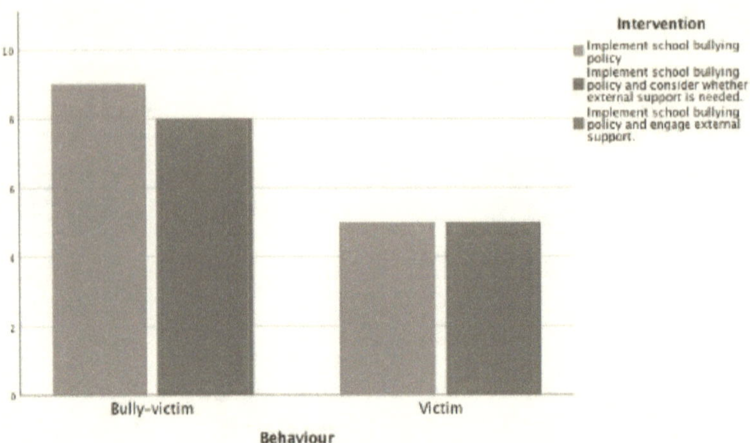

Figure 49: Count of behaviour by intervention

8.2.8 *Report overview*

The police indicated that they use restorative justice to resolve issues among school learners (see section 6.2 – Evaluation 1), and mobile bully-victims behaviour may be resolved in the same way. Paullet and Pinchot (2019) suggest providing a clear set of rules and consequences as strategy for dealing with cyberbullying in schools. At conclusion of the diagnosis processes the system created an overview report with recommendations for intervention to resolve mobile bully-victims behaviour, as shown in Figure 50. The system collated diagnosis (nomination and severity assessment) results in order to:

- enable informed remedial action and restorative justice implementation, using recommended ACTION;

- use the in- and out-degrees, and PageRank to convince identified learners of their behaviour; and

- measure behavioural change over time (not part of the current study).

In turn, the use of the report can help learners to face the consequences of their behaviour and enable constructive reflection on their behaviour.

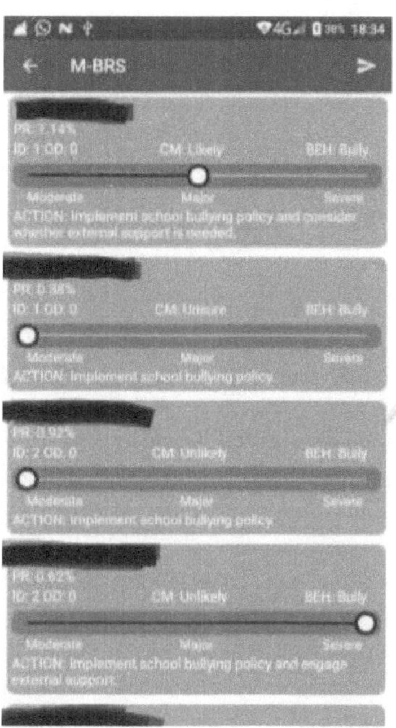

Figure 50: Overview report sample

Table 26: Identified behaviour overview

Intervention	Bully (N = 11)	Bully-victim (N = 17)	Victim (N = 10)		Uninvolved (N = 14)
First level	KB001	KS001	DM001		AM001
	KM002	MM003	KM003		DM002
	KT001	MM005	MM006		FM001
	MM002	MM010	MM013		KM001
	PM001	QQ001	NS001		MM001
	RM001	RS001			MM004
	TM001	TG001			MM007
	TM003	TM002			MM008
		TT001			MM009
Second level	NM001				NB001
Third level	KN001	EM001	DM003		NZ001
	NL001	LM001	LM002		RM002
		MG001	MM011		SM001
		MM012	TM005		TM004
		MR001	TN001		
		MS001			
		NN001			
		PK001			

Table 26 present summary of each learner's identified behaviour, including the 14 uninvolved learners that required no intervention, and the columns are divided by the chasm between the uninvolved from the rest of other columns in the table. Of 11 mobile bullies eight required the first level intervention, one learner required the second level intervention, and two learners needed level three intervention. On the other hand, nine of 17 mobile bully-victims required the first level intervention, while none of the mobile bully-victims required the second level intervention, and the other eight required the third level intervention. Similarly, five of the 10 victims required the first level intervention, while the other 5 required the third level intervention, but none of the victims required the second level intervention.

Chapter 9 – Evaluation 4

9.1. Introduction

This chapter presents the evaluation that is validation inclined. As already mentioned in Section 8.1, validation focuses on demonstrating the artefact's contribution to stakeholder goals, and answering effectiveness and utility questions about an artefact in real-world context (Parra *et al.*, 2017; Wieringa, 2014; Wieringa and Moralı, 2012). Therefore, the primary purpose of evaluating the prototype at this stage was to address the following research questions in this study:

- *What are participants' perceptions on the use of the proposed app in combating mobile bully-victim behaviour in schools?*

This chapter presents the results of artefact's validation including participants' perceptions of the artefact utility.

9.2. Survey analysis (Utility evaluation)

In order to gain insight to the finding of the utility evaluation, a questionnaire was administered at the end of the session. The goal of this quantitative analysis was to further assess the utility, ease of use, and acceptance of the M-BRS (Kowatsch *et al.*, 2017). Also, the aim of this analysis was to evaluate learners' satisfaction in using the M-BRS to report mobile bully-victims in school classrooms. The sub-sections of the Survey analyses include the discussion of the questionnaire reliability test, response rate, and data screening and preparation. Then the results of the survey are discussed.

The adapted form of IBM standardised questionnaire Post-Study System Usability Questionnaire (Lewis, 1991c) was used to assess the system in school classrooms, including closed questions, with four-point Likert scale, and open-ended questions. Additional questions were included in relation to the conceptual model constructs that emanated from the literature review. Also, the functionality and technical aspects, such as ease of use of the artefact, were considered. The use of forced-choice questionnaires effectively resists faking (Xiao, Liu and Li, 2017), thus forcing respondents to express definite opinions one way or the other. Paullet and Pinchot

(2019) also used force choice questionnaire to examine college students' perception about cyberbullying.

The questionnaire consisted of four demographic questions, 18 statements consisting of forced-choice scales (Xiao, Liu and Li, 2017), and four open-ended questions addressing usability and user satisfaction with the M-BRS. The items were categorised as follows: M-BRS use, diagnosis effectiveness, and impact of using M-BRS in diagnosing mobile bully-victims (see Evaluation questionnaire in Appendix 2). Participants were asked to grade how much they agreed or disagreed with the statements using four points Likert scale. The degree of disagreement included one ("Strongly disagree") and two ("Disagree"), while agreement included three ("Strongly disagree") and 4 ("Strongly agree"). The four open-ended questions sought to elicit understanding about frustration and general comments about the use of the M-BRS. The general comment questions were used to obtain additional responses that may have been missed. While open-ended responses can be coded into quantitative format to enable rapid analysis (Patil and Palshikar, 2013), verbatim quotes can also be used in support of studies (Williams, 2003). Hence the researcher used verbatim quotes to corroborate and supplement close-ended results by illustrating participants' opinion. Also, participants' comments are linked to their diagnosis result in section 8.2 (Evaluation). Participants' comments were corrected of spelling mistakes after transcription.

The open-ended questions were as follows:
1. What did you appreciate about the use of the M-BRS?
2. What did you find frustrating about the use of the M-BRS?
3. What do you think can be done to improve the way in which the M-BRS was used to diagnose mobile bully-victim behaviour?
4. Please provide any additional comment(s) about your experience with the use of M-BRS in diagnosing mobile bully-victims behaviour.

In order to arrange and summarise the collected data, the descriptive statistics was used including a count (percentage) of selected options, mean and standard deviation, shortened as Std. D (Divisi *et al.*, 2017; Mishra *et al.*, 2019). Likert-scales were analysed in two ways, (1) categorically by indicating counts of the selected options;

(2) as continuous set of numbers that are treated as equal points along a continuum, to enable reporting mean and standard deviation for each Likert-scale statement. The interpretation of the analysis includes tables for each construct's results.

9.2.1 *Reliability test*

Reliability of applied methods can best be established by following conventional processes and using established tools accordingly as intended (Ellis and Levy, 2010). Reliability focuses on consistent research instrument such that same results are obtained when replicated in another studies (Lameck, 2013). The widely known Cronbach alpha test was used to test the internal consistency of measures (Bonett and Wright, 2015; Cronbach, 1951; Tavakol and Dennick, 2011). The Cronbach alpha tests responses' consistency and the extent of correlation between items that measure a construct. The Alpha coefficient score ranging between 0 and 1 may be used to describe the reliability factor resulting from scales (Ursachi, Horodnic and Zait, 2015). The higher scores imply reliable scales (Santos, 1999). Scales are used to measure affective constructs, such as motivation, attitude (Bujang, Omar and Baharum, 2018). Different reports state that acceptable values of alpha range between 0.70 and 0.95 and indicate a stronger reliability (Tavakol and Dennick, 2011), meanwhile score from 0.45 to 0.98 are also acceptable (Bujang *et al.*, 2018). However, the length of the scale affects the alpha, such that low question number of questions reduces the alpha, and addition of related items that test the same concept increases the alpha (Tavakol and Dennick, 2011).

Notably, the acceptability of alpha scores, as a rule of thumb, is not always that lower alpha scores should not always be seen as indication of unsatisfactory instruments (Bujang *et al.*, 2018). In a study examining students' interest in science, Griethuijsen *et al.* (2014: 589) reported a Cronbach alpha of 0.502 in construct about "interest in school science" based on a five-item subset of a questionnaire. The authors argued that increasing the number of questions would result in an acceptable score.

Table 27: Reliability test scores

Constructs	No of items	Cronbach's alpha
Using M-BRS	6	0.705
Diagnosis	5	0.677
Impact	7	0.733

In this study the Cronbach alpha was carried out using the SPSS. For categorical data such as demographics the Cronbach alpha was not performed. Table 27 presents results of the reliability test for three applicable constructs. The "Diagnosis" reliability score was lower than generally accepted benchmark of 0.70, while the other two constructs gave acceptable scores, that is "Using the M-BRS" = 0.705 and "Impact" = 0.733. In exploratory studies, where results are not for generalisation, a score of 0.50 or 0.60 is also acceptable (Hair *et al.*, 2014). Also, the alpha score between 0.6 and 0.7 is generally acceptable and indicates reliability, while values above 0.95 may indicate redundancy of scale items (Ursachi *et al.*, 2015). Also acceptable alpha values (0.45 – 0.98) may be reported even where scale items are (1) considered difficult and can be answered correctly by few students; or (2) loosely related to each other – multidimensional (Bujang *et al.*, 2018). Similarly, the "Diagnosis" scale items in this study were multidimensional and few, which could also explain the low Cronbach's alpha in this study. Thus, the purpose of this study was to examine the use of the M-BRS in diagnosing mobile bully-victims behaviour by capturing a wider range of reactions from learners. Hence, the *diagnose mobile bully-victims behaviour* construct was identified as a key factor that could help explain the utility of the M-BRS.

9.2.2 *Response rate*

The response rate is obtained by calculating the number of responses against the number of participants (Phillips, Friedman and Durning, 2017). Although the normally accepted response rate is around 50%, researchers have little or no control over causes of nonresponse, such as participants' free will, also there is uncertainty about acceptable response rate (Johnson and Owens, 2003). Also in cases where population is fairly homogeneous and the results will not be generalised to the population, nonresponse bias may not be an issue and research resources can be conserved instead of attempting to increase response rates (Gigliotti and Fopma, 2019). The IBM PSSUQ was found effective with large sample size of 100 as well as a smaller sample size of 12 (Sauro, 2019; Tullis and Stetson, 2004). Similarly, Schulze and Krömker (2010) involved 14 participants in a usability test and concluded that the small sample size is useful to obtain important data about a product's user experience. Turner, Lewis and Nielsen (2006) note artefacts' usability problems can be identified with the first three to five participants, and additional subjects with the same test may not yield new information.

Due to the fact that the permission was given to conduct research with school learners outside schooling hours only, when learners would be rushing to find transportation to get home. In addition, cyberbullying and its types being a sensitive topic. The researcher aimed for 30% response rate of the 52 participating learners. Hence, 36.5 % response rate of 52 questionnaires was obtained at the end of evaluation session.

9.2.3   Data screening and preparation

Data collected in person through the survey questionnaire was recorded in Microsoft excel format following the coded scale values in the survey. Statistical data analysis can be done using computer programs such Microsoft excel and SPSS (Divisi, Di Leonardo, Zaccagna and Crisci, 2017). Responses to open-ended questions were coded and associated with participants IDs, using Microsoft excel. The researcher checked for missing responses that could exist in the data. Missing data can be due to absentees and choosing not to respond to sensitive questions, which can lead to different degrees of bias (Pampaka, Hutcheson and Williams, 2016). Missing data can be categorised into two, "unit" and "item" nonresponse (Heeringa, West and Berglund, 2010; Pampaka *et al.*, 2016). A unit nonresponse refers to individual or case missing as a whole, which result to selective biasness. On the other hand, item non-response is when an individual failed to give a response to some of variables. Generally, incomplete data can be analysed in three ways, including (1) analysing data as is, without accounting for missing data, (2) weighting, and (3) imputation. Weighting is suitable for unit nonresponse and can be used to compensate for nonresponse within the current sampling frame (Heeringa *et al.*, 2010). Imputation, on the other hand, may be used to address monotonic patterns of missing items and complete nonresponse (Heeringa *et al.*, 2010). Furthermore, Pampaka *et al.* (2016) suggested resolution to the challenge of missing data is to (1) report the details of missing data; (2) if possible, results can be adjusted for what is known about missing data; and (3) reporting the possible sensitivity of the results according to the missing data.

The screening of data was conducted after transcription to check for incomplete and invalid responses. None of the 19 responses were discarded, also no imputation or weighted was necessary. However, other statements were corrected for spelling errors using Microsoft Word, and then transferred into a Microsoft Excel document.

9.2.4 *Results*

Before completing the survey, each learner had an opportunity to confidentially see diagnosis results that were labelled using learner's ID code. The same ID codes that were created and used with the M-BRS to enable reporting mobile bully-victim during the utility evaluation (see section 8.2), were also used to ensure confidentiality of results. Learners were reminded their codes if they had forgotten. This was to enable learners to have a sense of the results, so that they could give informed feedback about the M-BRS use and the results thereof.

Table 28: Demographics

Class	Participant	Gender	Age	Social media frequency	Own mobile phone	Identified behaviour
First	MM001	Female	17 years	Rarely	Yes	Uninvolved
	TM001	Male	17 years	Rarely	Yes	Bully
	MS001	Female	18 years	Rarely	Yes	Bully-victim
	MM003	Female	18 years	Frequently	Yes	Bully-victim
	NS001	Female	16 years	Frequently	Yes	Victim
	TM002	Female	15 years	Rarely	No	Bully-victim
	QQ001	Female	17 years	Rarely	Yes	Bully-victim
	TM005	Female	17 years	Rarely	No	Victim
Second	MM008	FEMALE	17 years	Rarely	Yes	Uninvolved
	KM001	FEMALE	17 years	Frequently	Yes	Uninvolved
	NM001	FEMALE	17 years	Frequently	Yes	Bully
	MM010	MALE	17 years	Frequently	Yes	Bully-victim
	MM011	MALE	17 years	Rarely	Yes	Victim
	NZ001	MALE	17 years	Rarely	No	Uninvolved
	RS001	FEMALE	17 years	Frequently	Yes	Bully-victim
	MR001	FEMALE	16 years	Frequently	Yes	Bully-victim
	MM013	FEMALE	16 years	Rarely	No	Victim
Third	SM001	MALE	17 years	Frequently	Yes	Uninvolved
	LM002	FEMALE	18 years	Frequent	Yes	Victim

The teachers and learners were asked to report to the researcher any observations of psychological effects on learners that participated in the study using the M-BRS, so that counselling could be provided. The commanders in both the police stations agreed to help seek such service through their partnership with the Social Development Department (see the Letter and Consent form in Appendix 6). Fortunately, no reports or complains of psychological problems were received from learners, parents, and teachers.

Table 28 presents participants' demographics according to their classrooms. Also, each learner's behaviour is indicated according to diagnosis reports obtained through the utility evaluation (see section 8.2) in the last column. The survey was completed by nineteen learners (19) of 52 who had participated in the use of the M-BRS to report mobile bully-victim in one school. One of the reasons for a low participation was that the evaluation and survey were done after schooling hours, to avoid disruption of learning. Of the 19 participants, 14 (73.7%) were females, while 5 (26,3%) were males. The majority (57.95%) of participants were 17 years or younger, and 42.1% aged 18 years or older. Few participants (21.1%) did not own smartphones, but most (78.9%) of participants owned smartphones. While 52.6% of learners indicated that they used social media rarely, 47.4% of the learners indicated a frequently usage.

Table 29: Using M-BRS

	Response					
	SD	D	A	SA	Mean	Std. D
The M-BRS made me feel more confident to report mobile Bully-victims behaviour.	5.3	5.3	52.6	36.8	3.21	0.787
I often had difficulty in using M-BRS via mobile phone.	21.1	15.8	52.6	10.5	2.53	0.964
The use of the M-BRS in diagnosing mobile bully-victims behaviour made me feel uneasy.	15.8	47.4	21.1	15.8	2.37	0.955
If possible I would also use my personal mobile phone with M-BRS.	10.5	10.5	36.8	42.1	3.11	0.994
The M-BRS was easy to use.	0	0	42.1	57.9	3.58	0.507
The use of the M-BRS should be expanded to other classes and schools.	0	0	10.5	89.5	3.89	0.315

* Item scales codes. 1 – Strongly disagree (SD), 2 = Disagree, 3 = Agree (A), Strong agree (SA) – 4
* Standard deviation (Std. D)

Table 29 presents the usage analysis of *the M-BRS:* Learners' reports indicated a positive perception about confidence boost to report mobile bullies. Most learners (89.4%) agreed/strongly agreed that the use of the M-BRS made them feel ***confident to report*** mobile bully-victims behaviour. Similarly, most learners (63.2%)

disagreed/strongly disagreed that using M-BRS to diagnose mobile bully-victims made them *feel uneasy*. Learners' responses to open-ended question 1 reiterated this observation. Learner MM010 and MS001, who were identified as mobile bully-victim stated, *"It [M-BRS] helped me to be able to stand up for myself"*, *"I got help and support from M-BRS"*. Also, NS001 (who was identified as a victim of mobile bullying) stated, *"It [M-BRS] helped me to see that it is really important to report bullying"*.

Although learners felt timid when starting to use the M-BRS, they later realised the value of the system, as shown in responses to question 2, *"It [using M-BRS] was scary at first, but when time goes on, I found it [M-BRS] good"* (NS001), also TM002 (who was identified as a mobile bully-victim) commented, *"I was scared at first, when we had to answer questions about things we don't understand"*, and another response to open-ended question 3 reaffirmed these observations, MM003 (who was identified as a mobile bully-victim) stated *"I think what can be done is to make me feel easy"*.

Learners' responses indicated conflicting reactions regarding the easiness of the system usage. Most learners (63.1%) agreed/strongly agreed that the use of the system via mobile phones was *often difficult*. The same sentiments are shown in learners' responses to open-ended questions 2 and 3 respectively, *"Filling in the codes"* (MM010), and KM001 (who was identified as uninvolved in mobile bullying) stated, *"We can use forms instead of mobiles because some people may find it had to use phones"*. This observed difficulty may be attributed to the requirement of authentication when using the system (see section 7.4.2 – Design principle 1). On the other hand, positive perceptions were observed regarding the system's easiness. Notwithstanding the fact that the system was used after schooling hours, when learners would be heading home, all learners (100%) agreed/strongly agreed that M-BRS was *easy-to-use*. TM005 (who was identified as a victim of mobile bullying) response to question 2 supports these observations, *"I did not find any frustration from this M-BRS"*. Although the M-BRS often seemed difficult to use, as a result of the authentication requirement, the overall results indicate that M-BRS was perceived positively regarding usage easiness. Accordingly, adolescents seem very comfortable with sociodigital technologies, and easily learn novel applications (Hietajärvi *et al.*, 2020).

The acceptance of M-BRS was positive, as most learners (78.9%) agreed/strongly agreed that they would ***use personal phones*** with M-BRS. Additionally, all learners (100%) agreed/strongly agreed that the use of M-BRS should be **expanded** to other classes. This acceptance of the M-BRS is reaffirmed in learners' responses to the open-ended question 3, RS001 (who was identified as mobile bully-victim) stated, "*It [M-BRS] must be installed in every school so that bullies can be recognised themselves, so that they can get help*", also TN001 (who was identified as a victim of mobile bullying) stated, "*They must try to share this app to different schools and some small communities*", and TM002 stated, "*It [M-BRS] must be available at school or any other place, because it [M-BRS] is helpful* ". Overall, learners reported positive perceptions regarding M-BRS acceptance, usage features – easiness and psychological effects.

Table 30: Diagnosis effectiveness

	Response				Mean	Std. D
	SD	D	A	SA		
The M-BRS made me feel more confident to report mobile Bully-victims behaviour.	0	5.3	57.9	36.8	3.32	0.582
The M-BRS may increase my frequency of participation in fighting the mobile bully-victims behaviour.	10.5	21.1	36.8	31.6	2.89	0.994
Reporters' anonymity encouraged me to report mobile bully-victim behaviour.	0	15.8	52.6	31.6	3.16	0.688
The use of the M-BRS increased my understanding of mobile bully-victims behaviour.	0	10.5	42.1	47.4	3.37	0.684
The use of the M-BRS encouraged me to report bully-victim behaviour.	0	0	15.8	84.2	3.84	0.375

* Item scales codes: 1 = Strongly disagree (SD), 2 = Disagree, 3 = Agree (A), Strong agree (SA) = 4

* Standard deviation (Std. D)

Table 30 presents the analysis of *M-BRS effectiveness:* As a result of fear of punitive actions by parents or authorities, such as confiscation or losing control of mobile devices (Badenhorst 2011; Mtshazi and Kyobe 2014; Smit, 2015) children do not report cyberbullying incidents. Also, as noted by (Perren *et al.*, 2012) parents lack technological knowledge and therefore children fear that involving adults would worsen the situation (Mishna and Alaggia, 2005), or be viewed as tattletale. Similarly, victims and witnesses of cyberbullying know the steps required to report incidents, but only a few would follow through to report or seek help about cyberbullying (Paullet and Pinchot, 2019). However, it is comforting to see that most learners (94,7%) reported that using M-BRS enhanced their *confidence to report* mobile bully-victims.

Awareness initiatives about cyberbullying and its risks help to create a trusting context between victims and authorities (Perren *et al.*, 2012). Similarly, education and awareness is key to dealing with cyberbullying (Paullet and Pinchot, 2019). Hence, most learners (89.5%) agreed/strongly agreed that the use of M-BRS *increased their understanding* of mobile bully-victims behaviour. These observations are also reaffirmed in learners' responses to open-ended question 1, "*I appreciate that M-BRS helped me to be aware of bullying others, and as a thing that is not Okay or being treated badly*" (TM005), also QQ001 (who was identified as a mobile bully-victim) stated, "*They must provide the people who can help us from being bully-victims*", "*M-BRS helped me to experience the challenges of bullying others*" (TM002) and "*To help me be aware of bully-victim behaviour*" (MM003).

Anonymity is the essential enabler in reporting cyberbullying incidents, as the majority of learner "would report the incident if they could remain anonymous" (Paullet and Pinchot, 2019: 68). Most learners (84.2%) agreed/strongly agree that the *anonymity* feature enabled by M-BRS encouraged reporting mobile bully-victims. Similarly, all learners (100%) agree/strongly agreed that the use M-BRS *encouraged them to report* mobile bully-victims. In turn, more learners (68.4%) agreed/strongly agreed that using M-BRS could increase their *frequency to fight against* mobile bully-victims behaviour. Learners' responses to open-ended questions 1 corroborated these observations, NM001 (who was identified as mobile bully) specified, "*The use of the M-BRS made me feel more confident to report mobile bully-victims behaviour and also alert other people about that certain behaviour*", and "*I appreciate that it helped me to report the bully-victim*" (QQ001), and MM001 (who was identified as uninvolved in mobile bully-victim behaviour) stated, "*It [M-BRS] helps in different ways, like to report bullying and other things*".

Clearly, these observations indicate that the anonymity feature of the M-BRS helped to mitigate fear and boost confidence to report mobile bully-victims. Similarly, the M-BRS was effective in encouraging learning about and realising effects of mobile bully-victims behaviour.

Table 31: Impact

	Responses					
	SD	D	A	SA	Mean	Std. D
The use of M-BRS made me aware of mobile bully-victim behaviour.	0	0	52.6	47.4	3.47	0.513
The use of the M-BRS helped me to understand the mobile bully-victim phenomenon.	0	0	52.6	47.4	3.47	0.513
The use of the M-BRS can help me to trust the law enforcement/teachers.	0	5.3	36.8	57.9	3.53	0.612
The results of the M-BRS were accurate about my involvement in mobile bully-victims behaviour.	10.5	36.8	26.3	26.3	2.68	1.003
The use of the M-BRS helped to quickly find help against bully-victim behaviour incidents.	0	5.3	42.1	52.6	3.47	0.612
I was wrongly accused about being involved in mobile bully-victims behaviour.	15.8	26.3	26.3	31.6	2.74	1.098

* Item scales codes: 1 = Strongly disagree (SD), 2 = Disagree, 3 = Agree (A), Strong agree (SA) = 4
* Standard deviation (Std. D)

The concept of impact refers to the effect, influence, or impression made by an artefact upon participants (OED, 2016). Table 31 presents the *impact analysis of using M-BRS:* Learners may engage in cyberbullying, while attempting to have fun online, without even realising the significance of their actions on recipients (Antoniadou, Kokkinos, and Fanti, 2019). All learners (100%) agreed/strongly agreed that M-BRS ***increased their awareness*** of mobile bully-victims behaviour. Similarly, all learners (100%) agreed/strongly agreed the use of M-BRS ***helped them to understand*** the mobile bully-victim behaviour. These observations were reiterated in learners' responses to open-ended question 1, "*I appreciate that it [M-BRS] helped to know and understand more about bullying*" (TM002), "*I appreciate it because I didn't know that I was a victim of bullying. I didn't realise that I was bullying others*" (RS001), also responses to question 4, "*It was amazing experience because I got to learn about this program [M-BRS] and certain things I didn't know about*" (NM001), and MM011 (who was identified as a victim of mobile bullying) stated, "*The use of M-BRS motivated me to learn more about mobile bully-victim behaviour*".

Responses to open-ended question 2 showed that learners needed to understand the purpose of using the M-BRS. As one learner, felt the purpose of using the system was unclear, "*I didn't understand what they were going to do after they find our statuses where we are being bullies or we are the victims of bullying*" (MR001).

The lack of reported cyberbullying incidents also stem from victims' low confidence in law enforcement (Cross *et al.*, 2011). Interestingly, almost all learners (94.7%) agreed/strongly agreed the use of M-BRS could help them ***trust the law enforcement***. This observation could be attributed to the M-BRS' provision of anonymous reporting platform. Learners (52.6%) felt the ***results of M-BRS were accurate***. Most learners (94.7%) agreed/strongly agreed that using M-BRS help them to ***quickly find help*** against mobile bully-victims incidents. Response to the open-ended question 1 supported this observation, "*It [M-BRS] help people who are bullied and it gives me control in dealing with mobile bully-victims*" (MM011), "*It [M-BRS] helped me to be able to stand up for myself*" (MM010), and "*It [M-BRS] made me realise that I have been bullied all this time without even realising it*" (MM010).

More learners (57.9%) agreed/strongly agreed felt ***wrongly accused*** about being involved in mobile bully-victim behaviour. Learners' responses to open-ended 2 reiterated this observation, LM002 (who was identified as a victim of mobile bullying) stated, "*When I found out that people can accuse me of something that I didn't do*", also SM001 (who was identified as uninvolved in mobile bullying) stated, "*I found out that other people use M-BRS in a wrong way*". Since SM001 did not nominate and neither was he nominated, his comment could be as a result of other learners' sharing their results with him. However, this observation shows that retaliation could not be instigated by the use of the M-BRS and its reports, because learners' nominations were made anonymous using IDs, and learner could only see the number of nomination cast towards them.

Learners' responses to open-ended question 1 further indicated that M-BRS may help **stop mobile bully-victims behaviour**, "*Helping victims who were bullied through social media and making them be free of the mobile bullying*" (KM001), "*I appreciate that this app is very important because it will reduce bullying*" (TN001), also, in responses to question 3 MM013 (who was identified as a victim of mobile bullying) stated *"The M-BRS must go to different schools and try to reduce mobile bully-victim behaviour to other people"*, and responses to question 4 learners stated, *"M-BRS helped me and others to stop bullying each other and I thank them for that awareness that opened our eyes all"* (TM005), *"I will stop to bully other people, because the results showed me that I am a bully-victim"* (QQ001), and *"My experience with the use of M-BRS in diagnosing mobile bully-victims behaviour is that I am no longer getting bullied by other people"* (MM013).

The prevention of cyberbullying should include user empowerment through easy-to-use technology (Vandebosch, 2019). Therefore, the use of M-BRS enabled learners' reflection about mobile bully-victim behaviour. As shown in responses to additional comments request – question 4, *"I have learned that this thing is very important and it will change the life of our youth in different ways"* (LM002), *"I experienced that most of the children are being bullied by other kids"* (NS001), and *"This thing [M-BRS] is very beneficial because as a person you can realise how much do you have interest or have faith on humanity"* (TN001).

The aim of the system development was to empower learners to have control in dealing with mobile bully-victims behaviour, and seamlessly report mobile bully-victims. As suggested by Vandebosch (2019), the prevention of cyberbullying should include user empowerment through easy-to-use technology. Reporting cyberbullies or incidents should be made easy (Cox, Marczak, Teoh and Hassard, 2017). Hence the perceived usefulness, ease of use, and acceptance (willingness to continue or expand the use of artefact to other classrooms in school) of M-BRS, demonstrated the usefulness of the proposed system. Responses indicated that learners perceived the M-BRS as useful and easy to use, namely as a result of anonymity and the confidentiality. As also suggested by Paullet and Pinchot (2019), providing anonymous system for learners to report occurrences of cyberbullying is essential to addressing the behaviour. The usefulness of the systems include enabling learners to be aware and reflect on their behaviour, and empowering marginalised learners to be in control and be free to report bullies and their involvement in mobile bully-victims behaviour.

9.3. Validation

The validity and the value of a solution can be established using the demonstration or experimentation methods (Vaishnavi and Kuechler, 2015). Also, a focus group discussion was conducted in order to corroborate the results from the Evaluation 4 and validate the utility of the system to stakeholders.

9.3.1 Validation procedure

The objective of validation is to show how an artefact will be of use, without actually applying it in real-world context (Wieringa, 2014). The validation of the M-BRS was carried in a conference room at the police station. As already discussed in Section 4.6 (Sample) of Chapter 4, the participants were police officers that are responsible for social crime prevention in schools. This section presents the action research procedure and instruments in the Table 32 that were used in the validation of the artefact, as also presented in Section 8.2.1 – Evaluation procedure.

Table 32: Instruments definition

Instrument	Description
Demographic questionnaire	Questionnaire to assess the participants' knowledge and experience of the technologies and mobile bully-victim concept used in the workshop
Artefact manual	Manual to guide participants on the use of the M-BRS
Focus group discussion	Discussion to obtain participants' perceptions about the M-BRS

Step 1: Before the workshop each participant signed the consent forms and completed the demographic questionnaire, where they provided their experience regarding social crime prevention in schools, and experience about mobile bully-victims.

Step 2: The planned action research was verbally explained to participants.

Step 3: The features of the M-BRS were explained using manual, and shown by live demonstration, participants were shown how to use the M-BRS.

Step 4: Participants experimented with the M-BRS while referring to the manual or asking questions for guidance. In order enable experience of both the server and client's features of the M-BRS participants interchanged roles as police officials and school learners.

Step 5: The researcher conducted the focus group to discuss participants' perceptions about the M-BRS. Table 3 in Section 4.3.3.1 of Chapter 4 presented the route and probes for the focus group discussion.

The use of the focus group discussion was to see if the M-BRS' effects satisfied or violated requirements, and validate the proposed artefact as a solution for the stakeholders (Wieringa, 2014).

9.3.2 *Usability test*

In order reveal the utility of the M-BRS, participants were observed in the experiment using the system, in a similar way as in Evaluation 3 (see Section 7.6). The researcher observed and noted activities success rates for each *moderator* role (using the M-BRS as authority or adult not a reporter). Since *moderators* also took *subjects'* role for testing the M-BRS, *reporters'* roles could not be observed without their valid representatives. The recording of the observations was possible because the researcher did not participate either as a *moderator* or *reporter* in the usability test.

Table 33 presents success data on the use of M-BRS to diagnose mobile bully-victims in the experiment. The columns represent completed tasks for each user:

"*User column*" presents subjects for each task in the usability test.

"Create group" column presents the task to create the list of reporters to be diagnosed in the M-BRS.

"*Setup and receive connection*" columns presents the task to setup the server of the M-BRS, while client devices initiate connection request to be accepted in the server. It worth noting that connection requests are manually accepted on the server when a devise connects for the first time only, and subsequent connections are handled automatically in the server.

"*Send poll list*" column presents the task to broadcast the nomination list to all connected clients devices.

"*Check received information*" column presents the task to check if nomination and assessment were received from participants. The user must also verbally confirm with learners (in this case client device users) if they have completed the nominations and assessment.

The M-BRS report is divided into three categories, including nominations, assessments, and overall reports:

The *"Nominations report"* column consists of "Pie" and "Graph" subcategories: The *"Pie"* report column presents the task to view nomination report in a pie graph, indicating the number of identified learners according to their involvement in mobile bullying types – behaviour (bullies, bully-victims, victims, and uninvolved). The *"Graph"* report presents the task to visualise nominations report in a social network graph, according to identified learners according to their involvement in mobile bullying types.

The *"Assessments report"* column consists of "Pie" and "Details" subcategories: The "Pie" report column presents the task to view assessment report in a pie graph. The "Details" report presents the task to view individual learner report in detail, including scores for each severity assessment (impact, frequency, and content obscenity), and as well as a recommended intervention (see a sample in Figure 10).

The *"Overall report"* column presents the task to view the overall report of the diagnosis. The report includes number each learner's in- and out-degrees (nominations made and received), the identified behaviour, PageRank centrality (popularity based on in- and out-degrees), and recommended intervention which are: (1) *"Implement school bullying policy"*; (2) *"Implement school bullying policy and consider whether external support is needed"*; and (3) *"implementing school bullying policy and engaging external support"*.

Table 33: Task success rates

User	Create poll list	Setup and connect	Send poll list	Check received polls	Nominations report		Assessment report		Overview report
					Pie	Graph	Pie	Details	
HP2	S	P	S	S	S	S	S	S	S
HP6	S	S	S	P	S	S	S	S	S
HP7	S	S	S	S	S	S	S	S	S

In order to calculate the usability success rate of the experiment using the recoded codes than represent task completion status. "S" represented a complete success with a scale of 1, and "P" represented partial complete (with assistance) with a scale of 0.5, while "F" represented complete failure with a scale of 0. Then a success rate was calculated using Microsoft Excel by dividing the sum of complete and partial success by a total number of attempts.

A total of 21 attempts on the system activities were observed. Of those attempts 19 (90%) attempts were successful, while 2 (1%) were partially completed, and no total failure to complete tasks was observed. Overall, 20 (95%) out of 21 task attempts were completed successfully indicating a positive success rate of the M-BRS usability from the moderators' perspective.

9.3.3 Qualitative results (focus group)

The validation of the system also included a workshop and focus group discussion with the police, in order to assess the artefact's utility. Also, in order to gain insight regarding the utility of the Artefact in practice, a demonstration session was conducted (Ionita, Wieringa, Bullee and Vasenev, 2015). Three police officers participated in a two hours session workshop and demonstration, which aimed to stimulate feedback and discussions on the utility of the M-BRS. Table 34 presents participants profiles.

Table 34: Participants profile

ID	Gender	Age group	Rank	Experience (in years)	Knowledge of mobile bully-victim behaviour	Dealing with mobile bully-victim behaviour	Social media usage
HP2	Male	36-50	Sergeant	10	Adequate	Rarely	Never
HP6	Female	36-50	Constable	2	Minimal	Never	Frequently
HP7	Female	36-50	Sergeant	12	Adequate	Frequently	Frequently

Following the presentation about the overall function, participants were asked to use the M-BRS and later identified its usefulness. Participants provided several insights about the utility and features of the M-BRS. Table 35 presents sample responses across themes including, effectiveness, learnability, technicality, and sleekness of the M-BRS. Participants' comments showed appreciations of the M-BRS use to identify mobile bully-victim culprits, especially mitigation of learners' fear of reporting.

The analysis of comments showed participants' concerns about the memorability and technical issues about the use of the M-BRS. While participants were receptive of the M-BRS use, they indicated they would need a continuous practice with the M-BRS in order to confidently use the system in schools. HP2 (who had participated in the Evaluation 2, and indicated that he never used mobile social media) commented, *"I think I need to keep practicing with the app, so I will remember how it works, and I can easily use it in schools*", HP7 (who reported she used mobile social media frequently) also commented, *"Yes, imagine going to schools and find ourselves stuck, as if we do not know what we are doing"*.

This observation indicates that adult users may quickly forget how the system is used. This is generally the case with older users that may be resisting new technologies or need more time to learn to use new technologies (Ginsbur, *et al.*, 2017; Smith, 2013). However, participants felt the features of the M-BRS would be easy for learners if training on its use were provided. This observation is shown in the comments as HP6 (who reported she used social media frequently) stated, *"The questions are very easy and understandable"* (HP6), *and "I think the features of this app are at the level that children in school will be able to understand. If they are given explanation about how the app works, it will be much easier for them to understand and use the app"* (HP7).

Participants appreciated the ability to identify mobile bully-victim culprits using the M-BRS, which will help to provide surveillance and enables addressing the involved learners and hopefully reduce the behaviour. Participants' comments showed this observation, *"Now using the graph, I will be able to tell who is involved in this behaviour"* (HP7), and HP6 stated, *"It helps to show who is a bully at the end"* (HP6). Also, participants felt they will be able to identify patterns of learners' behaviour, and be able to intervene, as shown on the comments, *"It [M-BRS] makes it easier to find misbehaving children, and we can see who is the cause of mobile bullying or identify problematic children"* (HP7), *"This addresses an important issue so that it can be known who bully other children in classrooms"* (HP6), and *"Then we will be able to talk to that particular child"* (HP7).

Participants felt the use of the M-BRS will help learners to report incidents without fear of further victimisation, and curb the mobile bully-victim behaviour. This observation is shown in participants' comments such as, *"So, if we use the app, children will not be scared, and I think it is going to help reduce this problem of bullying"* (HP7). Another participant's comment implied that learners who know who reported on them continue victimisation outside the schools, *"Yes, sometime the bullies take the matter out of school"* (HP6). This observation showed that the use of the M-BRS would in turn mitigate fear of reporting from learners.

Table 35: Response sample across themes

Themes	Response
Effectiveness	
Culprits identification	*"Now using the graph, I will be able to tell who is involved in this behaviour" (HP7).* *"It helps to show who is a bully at the end" (HP6).* *"I feel this is helpful… " (HP7).*
Facilitates restoration	*"It [M-BRS] makes it easier to find misbehaving children, and we can see who is the cause of mobile bullying or identify problematic children" (HP7).* *"This addresses an important issue so that it can be known who bully other children in classrooms" (HP6).* *"Then we will be able to talk to that particular child" (HP7).* *"Most of the time children are being bullied, and sometimes it's just one or two of them [bullies], but other children are afraid to report them [bullies]" (HP7).*
Fear mitigation	*"Yes, sometime the bullies take the matter out of school" (HP6).* *"So, if we use the app, children will not be scared, and I think it is going to help reduce this problem of bullying" (HP7).*
Learnability	
Instruction understandability	*"The questions are very easy and understandable" (HP6).* *"I think the features of this app are at the level that children in school*
Ease of use	*will be able to understand. If they are given explanation about how the app works, it will be much easier for them to understand and use the app" (HP7).* *"I think I need to keep practicing with the app, so I will remember how it works, and I can easily use it in schools" (HP2).*
Memorability	*"I would like to keep practicing with it" (HP7).* *"Yes, imagine going to schools and find ourselves stuck, as if we do not know what we are doing" (HP7).*
Technical	
Connection	*"I don't find anything about the app frustrating (HP7).* *"Yes, as long the connection works, there is nothing to worry about" (HP6).* *"The way the app works does not waste time" (HP6).*
Design (Sleekness)	
Features	*"The results of the app were shown in a graph" (HP7).* *"I think the app is as we suggested with other colleagues in our previous meeting. The smiley faces can help to show the moods in the assessment. I think it is fine that way, and the reports are easy to find" (HP2).* *"I think the app is just fine as it is, I would not remove anything from it, because we need all these features" (HP7).* *"The smiley faces, the voting and all should remain" (HP6).* *The children will be able to nominate their bullies and then we can check who received most nominations.*
Acceptance	*"When can we have the app? We need to go to school to address cyberbullying, where they gossip about teachers or other learners" (HP7).*

Participants commented about the connection between the M-BRS server and client devices, which implied that the setting up the connections might be cumbersome. HP6 commented, *"... As long the connection works, there is nothing to worry about"*. This view was as a result of connection setup requiring when new clients use on the system for the first time. However, devices automatically connect to the same server in the subsequent uses. Another participant felt that *"the way the app works does not waste time"* (HP6). The use of the M-BRS did not waste time, as shown in this comment. Also, participants showed a determination to use the M-BRS to curb mobile bully-victims behaviour. *"When can we have the app? We need to go to school to address cyberbullying, where they gossip about teachers or other learners"* (HP7). These observations showed that participants were receptive of the M-BRS use to diagnose mobile bully-victims in schools.

The analysis of the discussion about the features of the M-BRS that participant wished to be changed, revealed that system current features were suitable and acceptable. These features included the smiley faces that to aid learners visualise answer options for the severity assessments, the polling report that showed which learners were identified as mobile bullies, bully-victims, victims and uninvolved. Participants' comments showed these observations, *"I think the app is as we suggested with other colleagues in our previous meeting. The smiley faces can help to show the moods in the assessment. I think it is fine that way, and the reports are easy to find"* (HP2). *"The smiley faces, the voting and all should remain"* (HP6). *"I think the app is just fine as it is, I would not remove anything from it, because we need all these features"* (HP7). *Particularly,* participants appreciated the report features suited their mandate to address behaviour, using the definite information about which learners were a cause of problems. HP7 stated, *"The children will be able to nominate their bullies and then we can check who received most nominations"*, as already shown in HP7 and HP6 comments about the ability of the system to identify culprits of which the results would help facilitate addressing misbehaving learners.

This validation showed that the M-BRS was efficiently effective in identifying mobile bully-victims, and guiding targeted interventions. The M-BRS also had positive usage time and easy to learn, though its memorability needed continuous practice.

9.4. Conclusion

This study followed Ashktorab's (2016; 2018) suggested framework as noted in section 5.2 for development of the M-BRS. Hence, the M-BRS was developed in keeping with the primary, secondary and tertiary prevention themes. Specifically, the design of the reporting feature kept to the primary prevention, enabling the identification of mobile bully-victim. The reporting feature of the M-BRS was also designed for secondary prevention in order to reduce identified mobile bully-victims and in turn provide control for mobile bully-victims. The *tertiary* prevention, focused on implementing intervention after harm has already occurred, by providing support to suicide inclined and depressed victims. Therefore the design of the assessment feature was in accordance with the tertiary prevention in order to aid the implementation of interventions on identified mobile bully-victims. Furthermore, the M-BRS was designed to mitigate fear and empower marginalised learners, and enable control over mobile bully-victim behaviour.

In relation to the primary prevention, the M-BRS provides anonymous reporting platform for learners, while aiding the police to identify mobile bully-victims. In turn marginalised learners are empowered to safely report mobile bully-victims, without fear of further victimisation. The anonymous reporting feature enabled learners' safety, while the police could identify and have perpetrators face consequences of their behaviour. The reporting feature of the M-BRS also enabled learners to have control over mobile bully-victim behaviour.

The assessment design enabled tertiary prevention, in order to determine the effects of mobile bully-victims and recommend a suitable intervention for addressing affected learners. The ability to assess the effects of mobile bully-victim behaviour will enable the police to further devise informed intervention to address affected learners.

The evaluation of the M-BRS employed both qualitative and quantitative data analyses methods in order to obtain richer answers to the research questions (Gilad, 2019). Qualitative data analysis helped to discover concepts and categories, while quantitative data analysis has a descriptive goal and focused on inferring characteristics between variables (Brannen, 2017). The quantitative data analysis was used to understand general patterns of mobile bully-victim behaviour, while qualitative analysis helped to make sense of results (Gilad, 2019), such that results complement each other (Tonkin-Crine *et al.*, 2015). This approach is referred to as complementarity, which in comparison to triangulation "employs different methods as a means for transcending their inherent limitations, as opposed to a concern with measurement errors" (Gilad, 2019: 23). Complementarity refers to using one set of results to enrich the other (Tonkin-Crine *et al.*, 2015). Versions of mixed methods such as complementarity transcend mere triangulation (Gilad, 2019). Hence, the combination of research methods helped to mitigate each other's flaws.

Chapter 10 – Conclusion

This chapter concludes this book by first discussing the summary of the findings obtained for the research question, and answers whether the research objectives were met. Then the contributions made in this book are presented, as well as some considerations for the development of mobile bully-victim interventions. Finally, the limitations of this study are also discussed.

10.1 Findings

The primary objective of this study was to investigate how a mobile application (app) may be developed to aid the South African Police's role to combat mobile bully-victims behaviour in high schools. Communication technologies such as social media, short messaging service, and instant messaging have increased risks of online victimisation, especially cyberbullying. Research has shown an increase of mobile phones ownership and Internet access through these devices among youths in rural areas of South Africa. As a result, high school learners are more at risk of cyberbullying. Considering the increase of cyberbullying through mobile phones, this study focused on mobile bully-victim behaviour among learners in high schools.

The literature review conducted in this study revealed that reporting of misconduct is essential, especially in South Africa where crime rate is the highest in the world (Kyobe and Lusinga, 2018). Reporting could reduce mobile bullying, however many challenges still remain thereof. Often, children choose not to report cyberbullying incidents for fear of further victimisation by perpetrators, or being grounded for wrongly using mobile phones, in turn no suitable intervention is provided. In particular, due to the anonymity affordance of technology, which enables perpetrators to conceal their identities online, the police often fail to find offenders. Similarly, if reports are brought to police, the telegraphic nature of communication on social media makes it hard to prove intentions of harm, which leaves victims at the mercy of their perpetrators. As a result learners do not see a value in reporting victimisation even if they know who their perpetrators are, because perpetrators are often not held accountable. Though compelling evidences often lack, children know their perpetrators, but need a safe platform to report their perpetrators without fear.

Therefore, as a starting point, the essential factor for the police to successfully reduce mobile bully-victims behaviour is to encourage reporting through a safe platform.

In addition, the literature review in his study examined factors that impede the police's effectiveness in the fight against mobile bully-victims behaviour in schools. The understanding about factors influencing the police's effectiveness was necessary for informing the development of a theoretical framework. Hevner, March, Park and Ram (2004) note design science research (DSR) overly emphasises technological artefacts and fail to maintain a balanced theory base, whereas technological artefacts need to be created based on applicable behavioural science theories. The theoretical framework was developed based on dominant theories, including social-ecological theory, social learning theory, social information processing theory, general strain theory, theory of planned behaviour, and role theory. These theories shed light about behavioural influences that lead children to engage in bullying. Also, the challenges to the police' involvement in curbing mobile bully-victims behaviour were examined by considering the role theory as well. The selected constructs of the theoretical framework that were deemed influential to enhance the effectiveness of law enforcement in combating mobile bully-victim behaviour include:

- Diagnosing mobile bully-victim behaviour
- Enabling safe mobile bully-victim disclosure
- Resolving mobile bully-victim behaviour incidents
- Severity assessment of mobile bully-victim behaviour
- Raising mobile bully-victim behaviour awareness instil trust on victims
- Encourage reporting mobile bully-victims behaviours

These constructs then informed the initial set of requirements for the development of a mobile app based intervention. Given that school children already use mobile phones for various purposes, and as a tool for victimisation in the hands of perpetrators, the researcher deemed suitable to develop the interventional tool on mobile platform. Hence, the researcher developed a tool called mobile bully-victim response system (M-BRS) for use by the police to provide a safe reporting platform for high school learners.

The researcher adopted the DSR methodology to guide the development of the M-BRS. In the first iteration of the design science the researcher conducted focus group discussions with the police and schoolteachers in the Eastern Free State of South Africa, in order to ascertain the suitability of the proposed conceptual framework and the resulting requirements for the M-BRS. As noted by Pittaro (2020), adults, including criminal justice professionals, hold to the adage that children will be children, and still dismiss bullying as normal childhood behaviour that disappears with age and maturity. Also, this study discovered that the police and schoolteachers do not have appropriate skills to address mobile bully-victim behaviour. Therefore, in the event that learners reported being mobile bullied the police and teachers addressed reports as a general child's feuds. Also, since the police lack adequate knowledge about mobile bullying, there have been no awareness initiatives to teach children about and encourage learners to report mobile bully-victims behaviour. In addition to the need for safe reporting platforms, these observations established the need for mobile bully-victim awareness initiative as also proposed in the conceptual framework.

The findings also showed that there are no mechanisms to detect and deter learners from mobile bully-victims behaviour in schools. In efforts to curb the mobile bully-victim behaviour, early detection is paramount (Kao *et al.*, 2019; Samara, *et al.*, 2017). However, the police and schools lack adequate mobile bully-victims identification mechanisms. As schoolteachers and the police pointed out that in an event that a learner reported mobile bullying incident, it would be difficult to establish whether the reported learner is the actual perpetrator, and bring the perpetrator to account due to insufficient evidence. This observation also indicated, as also proposed in the conceptual framework, the need for a mechanism to gather sufficient evidence through a safe reporting platform. The police (HP1 who has been involved in social crime prevention in school for 31 years) commented that if a cyberbully is found, they rely on the South African Protection from Harassment Act 17 for serious incidents, and for mild cases they use restorative justice. Although most of cyberbullying elements are criminal in nature, including violence threats, criminal intimidation, stalking, hate crimes, sexual harassments, all of which could be prosecuted if brought to court, schools should however have a greater institutional responsibility instead of focusing on criminal liability of learners (Shariff, 2008).

Additionally, both the police and the teachers agreed that there is no mechanism in place to determine the degree of harm (severity) caused by mobile bully-victims behaviour on learners. This observation necessitates the severity assessment of mobile bully-victims, as also proposed in the conceptual framework. Also, Pittaro (2020) notes the lack of knowledge in adults about bullying compels children to develop ways to defend themselves, which may include retaliation. These observations lead the researcher to conclude that the police and teachers need to be capacitated about mobile bullying especially bully-victims behaviour.

The alignment of objectives in this study with pragmatism philosophy allowed the researcher to adopt DSR approach in the development of the M-BRS artefact. The application of the DRS process model was effective in guiding the development of new and innovative artefact that underlies Information Systems. This enabled assessment and determining the fit for the app, and following the complete research cycles by considering theoretical and practical views in the development of the M-BRS.

The main findings that were discovered during the M-BRS' design and requirements evaluations include control from misuse, provision of visual cues to enable learners' understanding of assessments, and safety for learners as reporters or informant. The police suggested that the developed mobile app should not be vulnerable to misuse, particularly nominations of learners as a joke or spite. Also, the police suggested the use of smileys faces in severity assessment functions so that learners could visualise the meaning of assessment options and inform answer selection. In addition, as also proposed in the conceptual framework, the teachers and the police also felt that the app should be safe to use by protecting learners' identity in order to avoid further victimisation. Hence, the M-BRS was developed to enable anonymous reporting, such that learners would not know which of their classmates nominated them. Also, this study provided an innovative way to enable self-nominations, which helped to provide certainty of identified mobile bully-victims.

The Evaluation 4 (see Chapter 8 and 9) proved the M-BRS usable in identifying mobile bully-victims, and was well-received by learners and the police. The current study provided peer nominations validation in conjunction with self-nomination by considering in- and out-degrees to identify mobile bully-victims, bullies, and victims. Among the benefits of the artefact, learners felt empowered to come forward and report through an easy and safe platform, in turn learners felt in control against mobile bully-victims behaviour. Learners were also enabled to reflect about the effects and unacceptability of mobile bully-victims behaviour. On the other hand, the police felt that the M-BRS enabled surveillance of mobile bully-victims and cyberbullying in general. Also, the nomination and assessment results helped to implement informed interventions, and enable resolving incidents based on the evidence. The proposed artefact served as a step forward towards efforts stop mobile bully-victims behaviour and cyberbullying in general. The application of social network analysis helped not only with identifying processes underlying bullying, assisting victims or bullies behaviour, but also revealed classrooms' group structures to enable tailored interventions (Volk *et al.*, 2017). Overall, the M-BRS aided the police role to successfully identify mobile bully-victims, as well as applying well-informed interventions, while mitigating learners' fear to report and providing control over mobile bully-victims behaviour costs free.

10.2 Research contribution

This section presents discussions about research contribution of this study, starting with theoretical contribution. Then following the theoretical contribution is the methodological contribution, and concludes with the discussion of the practical contribution.

10.2.1 Theoretical contribution

The conceptual framework was developed from literature review of factors and dominant theories that influence the police's effectiveness in fighting against mobile bully-victims in high schools. This provided guidance in the development of the mobile application.

The conceptual framework developed in this study extended and tailored the "Cyberbullying Continuum of Harm" (Ashktorab, 2016), enabling inclusive and moderated diagnosis of mobile bullying categories and severity assessment. That is, not only identifying mobile bully-victims, but also bullies, victims, and uninvolved were identified. Furthermore, Gordon (2018) notes cyberbullying interventions are likely to reduce traditional bullying, since they are closely related in behaviour as well as their risk factors and dynamics. Therefore, the application of this intervention could help reduce traditional bullying. Also, moderation was necessary so that the police could oversee the identification process in order to minimise dishonest reporting. As also noted by Tłuściak-Deliowska (2018), adults' involvement is needed to complement technology mediated interventions by watching, verifying and providing support for adolescents. This framework was evaluated by developing an application that the researcher called mobile bully-victims reporting system (M-BRS).

The findings from the M-BRS evaluation showed that the developed conceptual framework provided a useful model for identification of mobile bully-victims and measurement of severity this behaviour caused on the identified learners. As shown in the comment of HP6 (who indicated that she used social media frequently) in Section 9.3.3 stated, *"This addresses an important issue so that it can be known who bully other children in classrooms"*. This evaluation proved that the framework was comprehensive not only in identifying perpetrators, but also enabled targeted intervention for the affected learners, which is helpful to reduce mobile bully-victims behaviour. Similarly, HP7 *(*who indicated that she used social media frequently*)* in Section 9.3.3 stated, *"Then we [the police] will be able to talk to that particular child"*. Also, most learners (94.7%), when responding to the survey in Section 9.2.4, indicated they would trust the police if they used the M-BRS. Furthermore, the application of conceptual framework through M-BRS fostered learners' reflection on mobile bully-victim as an unacceptable behaviour, as shown in the comment of TM002 (who was identified as a mobile bully-victim) in Section 9.2.4 stated, *"M-BRS helped me to experience the challenges of bullying others"*.

This study provided a practical way to identify and monitor mobile bully-victims behaviour in high schools, through which learners can safely report culprits. Furthermore, the severity assessment of the behaviour on the identified learners was helpful to inform a suitable intervention. This was achieved by developing a mobile application that was informed by the conceptual framework that also stemmed from literature review in this study. As already mentioned in Section 10.1, the need to develop theory-based artefacts in DSR, the researcher believes this book has paved a way in which artefacts development can be informed by theory, as a new, innovative and practical contribution to mobile bully-victim research.

10.2.2 Methodological contribution

The main methodological contribution in this study centred on the advancement of knowledge regarding the use of Design Science Research (DSR) to explore how the police role in addressing mobile bully-victims behaviour could be enhanced. This involved the development of a conceptual framework about mobile bully-victims diagnosis through literature review. The effectiveness of this framework was evaluated by developing an application that is called mobile bully-victims response system (M-BRS) in order to enable the diagnosis – identification of mobile bully-victims and severity assessment. This study affirmed the effectiveness of DSR methodology and its reliance on pragmatism as a philosophy to develop and improve technology mediated interventions for mobile bully-victims behaviour. Hence, the pragmatic nature of DSR supported the use of different methods to create a solution that is usable in real-world problems (Hevner *et al.*, 2004; Hevner, 2007; Peffers *et al.*, 2007; Peffers *et al.*, 2007).

The analysis of the quantified usability results (Chapter 8), survey, and the focus group session in Chapter 9 provided great insight into the strengths and weaknesses of the M-BRS that also informed the fit of the developed conceptual framework. Weaknesses that were discovered about M-BRS involved concerns about the connection setup task, the memorability of the functions, authentication codes. Participant felt the connection setup was cumbersome, which required selecting the server from the client device, and manually accepting connection requests on the server for devices that connected for the first time. Also, participants felt that the functions of the M-BRS could be easily forgotten if not practiced regularly. From learners' perspectives, the requirement to use authentication codes was found problematic, as learners that forgot authentication codes could not do the nominations and the severity assessment without being reminded their codes.

As shown with the Evaluation 4 (Chapter 8 and 9) of the M-BRS, this study also established the usefulness and strengths of mixed methods to enable deeper understanding of a phenomenon that was examined. For instance, the responses to quantitative items of the survey were supported with open-ended questions. Also, in order to obtain feedback about aspects of the M-BRS that were not observable, the quantified results of usability tests were supplemented with focus group discussions. Consequently, the combination of methods balanced their flaws and strengthened each other, and provided enriched accounts and insights into findings that would otherwise be fragmented.

10.2.3 Practical contribution

This study contributed practical skills to enhance the police's role in fighting mobile bully-victims behaviour by providing a safe reporting platform. That is it enabled the diagnosis of mobile bully-victims through anonymous nominations to avoid retaliation or further victimisation risks from perpetrators. Also, an approach to strengthen evidence of mobile bully-victims behaviour from different methods, including the number of nominations and PageRank centrality was revealed that might be beneficial for criminal law court cases. This was remarkable because of the difficulty to positively identify perpetrators, which often weakened evidence of reported case according to legal law requirements for prosecution (Fraser *et al.*, 2013; Volk *et al.*, 2017). Additionally, this study provided surveillance skills to monitor and control mobile bully-victims behaviour in schools, using the same reporting platform. This survellance ability also signifies the contribution of this study on technology application's ability to modify desired behaviour. As shown in following discussions, this reporting platform helped not only with identifying processes underlying mobile bully-victims behaviour, but also revealed classrooms' group structures to enable targeted and tailored interventions.

This book presented a practical way for development of policies and intervention programmes to curb mobile bully-victims behaviour. Since specific legislation that addresses bullying, including cyberbullying or mobile bullying is lacking in South Africa (CJCP, 2015; Laubscher and Vollenhoven, 2015; Reyneke and Jacobs, 2018). This study provided a way to further classify mobile bully-victims as propagators that spread the behaviour across a classroom, and retaliators that reciprocate victimisation to their perpetrators (Livingstone and Smith, 2014; Samara *et al.*, 2017). This insight is helpful in guiding policy decisions and fine-tuning interventions according to exhibited behaviour of mobile bully-victims. For instance, targeted interventions could be directed towards mobile bully-victims that exhibit propagators and retaliators behaviour. This could be helpful because the subjective norm in the theory of planned behaviour posits that individual's intention to engage in misbehaviour is influenced by other peers' behaviour (Salmivalli and Poskiparta, 2012; Smith, 2016; Tłuściak-Deliowska, 2018). This book showed a practical way to identify mobile bully-victims as propagators and retaliators, which provides guidance towards a most efficient and targeted intervention programmes. Hence, a shift was made from whole school and generalised interventions to individualised (targeted) interventions. Also, the use of relevant resources, such as using the advantage of mobile phones that learners are already familiar with, helped to limit training time for learners and the police. Since learners do not report victimisation because of fear and lack of safe reporting platforms (Kenny *et al.*, 2016; Paullet and Pinchot, 2019). This study provided skills to encourage reporting of incidents through a platform that mitigates fear by ensuring anonymity of reporters and in turn avoiding further victimisation or retaliation that is possible if perpetrators knew which of their peers reported on them. Hence, learners that were unlikely to report mobile bully-victims could find courage to do so using this platform.

This study revealed that using a suitable platform increased learners' inclination to report mobile bully-victims behaviour, which is important in identifying and preventing mobile bully-victims behaviour. Furthermore, this study provided a way to measure the severity of mobile bully-victim behaviour on learners so that suitable interventions could be devised. That was helpful since social workers are not readily available or are limited in numbers (Phillips and Cornell, 2012), as also noted in comments of LTT3 and IIT3 (section 6.3.1 – Resolving mobile bully-victim reports in Chapter 6) that soliciting help for learners in school "*takes a long time*". Hence, gauging the severity on identified individual learners was important, in order to decide whether interventions should involve professional social workers.

10.3 Future considerations

The recommendations in this book commend the South African Police Service (SAPS) together with the Department of Basic Education (DBE) to put in place interventions to address mobile bully-victims behaviour in schools. The high rate of crime and violence in South African schools requires effective strategies to encourage reporting as the primary avenue to reducing violence, and capacitating the SAPS and DBE personnel with skills to deal with cyberbullying, especially mobile bully-victims, as a factor that fans school violence (You and Lim, 2016). Furthermore, teachers and the police need to be provided with tools to examine the potential liability of online posting, as well as lawful rights and accountabilities of all involved parties (Shariff and Eltis, 2017). Also, research appraisal is needed for the law enforcement officials so that they can gain understanding about the changes of communication norms among digital natives and the complex characterisation of cyberbullying (Shariff and Eltis, 2017). In turn, the police could cascade knowledge to learners about cyberbullying and its consequences. As also noted by Gordon (2018), cyberbullying interventions focus on raising awareness, cautioning learners about legal consequences of inappropriate online conduct and it's negative effects. The finding showed that due to lack of knowledge about cyberbullying, schoolteachers and the police attended to incidents based on their seriousness, or when perpetrators can be positively identified. Additionally, the researcher encourages the development of new technological interventions that are suitable for the diverse cultural context of South Africa.

It is noteworthy that, due to the number of people that have access to Internet and could fall victims of abuse, legal courts in America were not ready to deal with large influx of cyberbullying cases, which led to out of court settlements (Shariff, 2008). Also, the American courts have been pressured to prosecute cases, but they have considered the maturity level of teenagers and dismissed charges of non-consensual distribution of pictures online (Shariff, 2015). Similarly, there is a lack of cyberbullying legislation in South Africa (Laubscher and Vollenhoven, 2015; Reyneke and Jacobs, 2018). However, the impact of peer-to-peer cyberbullying such as defamation of character could be far-reaching even negatively influencing potential employment of the victims in the future (Shariff, 2008). For example, being labelled as a paedophile on social media by peers at school, and later when the victim applies for work, employers could find out about this on social media and treat the application with contempt. This implies that as an alternative the DBE and the SAPS need to provide policies that adequately enable addressing and reducing cyberbullying incidents in schools. This observation also calls for attention to the need to capacitate teachers and the police about cyberbullying and in turn cascade information to learners.

Future studies should pay attention on enhancing the memorability of the interventional tools such as the mobile bully-victim application that was developed in this study. Studies should also focus on design for varied mobile phone, in order to avoid interchanging client devices between participants, and in turn avoid the use of authentication codes as a way to track participants' information.

10.4 Limitations

The findings in this study were based on the newly developed theoretical framework and the mobile application resulting from that framework. Since mobile bully-victim involves sensitive topics, as also noted by Hoover and Morrow (2015) that recollection of unpleasant experience also affects participant interest in the research, while other participants may feel empowered to share their experience and help to address their challenges. In addition, as a result of convenient sampling that relied on voluntary participation and limited availability of participants, the numbers of participants that took part in this were limited. This study collected data from both black and white ethnicity groups of the police, but all schoolteachers and learners were of black ethnicity. Therefore, future large-scale studies should aim for adequate ethnicity groups' representation and schools from across various safety zones to test the theoretical framework, in so doing more insight regarding cultural differences on learners reporting behaviour can be discovered. This will also provide confirmation and establishment of the proposed framework's contribution.

Also, the time allocated for school learners to participate in the use of the mobile application was limited in order to avoid disturbance of learning, and to enable learners to get home on time and safely. Since the use of the developed mobile bully-victims response system (M-BRS) required moderation by an official and used only four client devices, survey features to examine the acceptance and usability of the M-BRS were not embedded on the system in order to save time. Therefore, the researcher relied on a manual survey to examine the usability of the mobile application. However, the diagnosis's reports that were created through the mobile application helped to infer the M-BRS' utility.

Despite the limited sample sizes, the empirical results of the M-BRS, including a survey, focus group, and social network analysis established the artefact's utility. This study was the first of its kind to evaluate a mobile bully-victims mitigation tool through a direct and moderated reporting platform to identify mobile bully-victims, bullies, victims, and uninvolved, as well as assessing the severity of the mobile bully-victim behaviour for provision of informed intervention. Overall the findings of this study are limited to making projections and predictions to assist future researches.

References

Aggarwal, A., Sharma, C., Jain, M., & Jain, A. (2018). Semi Supervised Graph Based Keyword Extraction Using Lexical Chains and Centrality Measures. *Computation Systems, 22*(4), 1307-1315.

Ahmed, Z., Ganti, S. K., & Kyhlbäck, H. (2010). Design artefacts, design principles, problems, goals and importance. *In Fourth International Conference of Statistical Sciences,*Pakistan.2008;15:57-68 *arXiv preprint arXiv:1008.1322.*

Antoniadou, N., Kokkinos, C. M., & Fanti, K. A. (2019). Traditional and cyber bullying/victimization among adolescents: examining their psychosocial profile through latent profile analysis. *International Journal of Bullying Prevention*, 1(2), 85-98.

Antoun, C. (2015), "Who are the Internet users, mobile Internet users, and mobile mostly Internet users? Demographic differences across Internet- use subgroups in the U.S," in *Mobile Research Methods: Opportunities and Challenges of Mobile Research Methodologies*, D. Toninelli, D., Pinter, R. and de Pedraza, P. (Eds). London, U.K.: Ubiquity Press, pp. 99-117.

Ashktorab, Z. (2018). "The Continuum of Harm" Taxonomy of Cyberbullying Mitigation and Prevention. In J. Gobeck (Ed). *Online Harrasment, Human–Computer Interaction Series* (pp. 211-227). Switzerland: Springer.

Ashktorab, Z., & Vitak, J. (2016). Designing cyberbullying mitigation and prevention solutions through participatory design with teenagers. In *Proceedings of the 2016 CHI Conference on Human Factors in Computing Systems*, May 2016. (pp. 3895-3905).

Auemaneekul, N., Powwattana, A., Kiatsiri, E., & Thananowan, N. (2019). Investigating the mechanisms of theory of planned behavior on Cyberbullying among Thai adolescents. *Journal of Health Research, 34*(1), 42-55.

Auerbach, C. F., & Silverstein, L. B. (2003). *An introduction to coding and analysis: Qualitative data.* New York, NY: New York University.

Bækgaard, L. (2015). Conceptual model of artefacts for design science research. *Proceedings of the 21st Americas Conference on Information Systems, Fajardo, Puerto Rico.* Americas Conference on Information Systems, 2015.

Baskerville, R., & Pries-Heje, J. (2010). Explanatory design theory. *Business & Information Systems Engineering, 2*(5), 271-282.

Bastien, J. C. (2010). Usability testing: some current practices and research questions. *International journal of medical informatics*, 4(3), 547-551.

Bazeley, P. (2013). Qualitative data analysis: Practical strategies. Los Angeles, Sage.

Benbasat, I., & Zmud, R. W. (2003). The identity crisis within the IS discipline: Defining and communicating the discipline's core properties. *MIS quarterly*, 27(2), 183-194.

Beskow, L. M., Fullerton, S. M., Namey, E. E., Nelson, D. K., Davis, A. M., & Wilfond, B. S. (2012). Recommendations for ethical approaches to genotype-driven research recruitment. *Human genetics*, *131*(9), 1423-1431.

Bhattacherjee, A. (2012). Social science research: Principles, methods, and practices. (http://scholarcommons.usf.edu/oa_textbooks/3/). Retrieved on 12 October 2017.

Bishop, F. L. (2015). Using Mixed Methods Research Designs In Health Psychology: An Illustrated Discussion From A Pragmatist Perspective. *British Journal Of Health Psychology, 20(1)*, 5-20.

Blakey, J. M., Glaude, M., & Jennings, S. W. (2019). School and program related factors influencing disclosure among children participating in a school-based childhood physical and sexual abuse prevention program. *Child abuse & neglect, 96(2019)*, 104092.

Bonett, D. G., & Wright, T. A. (2015). Cronbach's alpha reliability: Interval estimation, hypothesis testing, and sample size planning. *Journal of Organizational Behaviour*, *36*(1), 3-15.

Boone, H.N. & Boone, D.A. (2012). Analysing Likert data. *Journal of Extension,* 50(2), 1-5.

Bower, P., Brueton, V., Gamble, C., Treweek, S., Smith, C. T., Young, B., & Williamson, P. (2014). Interventions to improve recruitment and retention in clinical trials: a survey and workshop to assess current practice and future priorities. *Trials*, *15*(1), 1-9.

Brandtner, P., Helfert, M., Auinger, A., & Gaubinger, K. (2015). Conducting focus group research in a design science project: Application in developing a process model for the front end of innovation. *Systems, Signs & Actions*, *9*(1), 26-55.

Brannen, J. (Ed.). (2017). *Mixing methods: Qualitative and quantitative research.* New York, Routledge.

Braun V & Clarke V. (2006). Using thematic analysis in psychology. *Qualitative research in psychology, 3*(2), 77-101.

Braun, R., Benedict, M., Wendler, H., & Esswein, W. (2015). Proposal for requirements driven design science research. In *International Conference on Design Science Research in Information Systems* (pp. 135-151). Springer, Cham.

Brewer, G., & Kerslake, J. (2015). Cyberbullying, self-esteem, empathy and loneliness. *Computers in human behaviour*, 48 (2015), 255-260.

Brier, S. (2015). Cybersemiotics and the reasoning powers of the universe: philosophy of information in a semiotic-systemic transdisciplinary approach. *Green Letters, 19*(3), 280-292.

Brin, S. & Page, L. (1998). The anatomy of a large-scale hypertextual Web search engine. *Computer Networks and ISDN Systems*, 30(7), 107-117.

Brink, R. (2018). A multiple case design for the investigation of information management processes for work-integrated learning. *International Journal of Work-Integrated Learning, 19*(3), 223-235.

Broll, R., & Huey, L. (2015). "Just being mean to somebody isn't a police matter": Police perspectives on policing cyberbullying. *Journal of school violence, 14*(2), 155-176.

Bryant, A. (2017). Grounded theory and grounded theorizing: Pragmatism in research practice. New York: Oxford University Press.

Bujang, M. A., Omar, E. D., & Baharum, N. A. (2018). A review on sample size determination for Cronbach's alpha test: a simple guide for researchers. *The Malaysian journal of medical sciences: MJMS, 25*(6), 85-99.

Bukowski, W. M., & Sippola, L.K. (2001). Groups, individuals, and victimization: A view of the peer system. In J. Juvonen & S. Graham (Eds.), *Peer harassment in school: The plight of the vulnerable and victimized* (pp.355-377). New York: Guilford.

Burton, P. (2016). Bullying and cyberbullying in Southern Africa. In United Nations (Ed). *Ending the torment: Tackling bullying from the schoolyard to cyberspace.* New York, NY: United Nations. (https://violenceagainstchildren.un.org/sites/violenceagainstchildren.un.org/files/documents/publications/tackling_bullying_from_schoolyard_to_cyberspace_low_res_fa.pdf). Retrieved on 12 October 2017.

Campean, I. F., & Yildirim, U. (2017). Enhanced sequence diagram for function modelling of complex systems. *Procedia* CIRP, *60*, 273-278. (https://www.sciencedirect.com/science/article/pii/S2212827117300549) Retrieved on 12 September 2019

Carter, N., Bryant-Lukosius, D., DiCenso, A., Blythe, J., & Neville, A. J. (2014). The use of triangulation in qualitative research. *Oncology Nursing Forum*, 41(5), 545-457.

Centre For Justice And Crime Prevention (CJCP). (2015). Online Child Safety: South African Law. (http://www.cyberbullying.org.za/south-african-law.html) Retrieved 03 April 2017.

Chandra L, Seidel, S. & Gregor, S. (2015) Prescriptive knowledge in IS research: conceptualizing design principles in terms of materiality, action, and boundary conditions. In: 48th Hawaii International Conference on System Sciences, Kauai. IEEE, pp 4039-4048

Charmaz, K. (2014). Constructing grounded theory. 2nd Ed. London: Sage.

Chen, P., Xie, H., Maslov, S., & Redner, S. (2007). Finding scientific gems with Google's PageRank algorithm. *Journal of Informetrics, 1*(1), 8-15.

Cheng, L. C. (2016). The mobile app usability inspection (maui) framework as a guide for minimal viable product (mvp) testing in lean development cycle. In *Proceedings of the 2nd International Conference in HCI and UX Indonesia* April 13 - 15, 2016. (pp. 1-11).

Chetty, K., Qigui, L., Gcora, N., Josie, J., Wenwei, L., & Fang, C. (2017). Bridging the digital divide: measuring digital literacy. Economics Discussion Papers, No 2017-69. Kiel Institute for the World Economy. *(http://www.economicsejournal.org/economics/discussionpapers/2017-69)* Retrived 17 March 2018.

Chia, C., Choo, K. K., & Fehrenbacher, D. (2017). How cyber-savvy are older mobile device users? In Au M.H., Choo K.-K. R. (Eds.), Mobile security and privacy; Chapter 4. Waltham, MA: Syngress/Elsevier, pp. 67-83

Chorbev, I., Trajkovik, V., Goleva, R. I., & Garcia, N. M. (2017). Cloud based smart living system prototype. In Dobre, C., Mavromoustakis, C., Garcia, N., Goleva, R. & Mastorakis, G (Eds), *Ambient assisted living and enhanced living environments* (pp. 147-170) New York: Elsevier, Butterworth-Heinemann.

Cillessen, A. H. & Marks, P. E. L. (2017). Methodological choices in peer nomination research. In P. E. L. Marks & A. H. N. Cillessen (Eds.), *New directions in peer nomination methodology. New directions for child and adolescent development 157*, 21-44.

Cillessen, A. H. (2011). Toward a theory of popularity. In A. H. N. Cillessen, D. Schwartz & L. Mayeux (Eds.), *Popularity in the peer system* (pp. 273-299). New York, NY: Guilford Press.

Clifton, A., & Webster, G. D. (2017). An introduction to social network analysis for personality and social psychologists. *Social Psychological and Personality Science, 8*(4), 442-453.

Coie, J. D., Dodge, K. A., & Coppotelli, H. (1982). Dimensions and types of social status: A cross-age perspective. *Developmental psychology, 18*(4), 557-570.

Cole, F.L. 1988. Content Analysis: Process And Application. *Clinical Nurse Specialist 2*(1),53-57.

Conboy, K., Gleasure, R., & Cullina, E. (2015). Agile design science research. In *International Conference on Design Science Research in Information Systems* (pp. 168-180). Springer, Cham.

Contandriopoulos, D., Larouche, C., Breton, M., & Brousselle, A. (2018). A sociogram is worth a thousand words: proposing a method for the visual analysis of narrative data. *Qualitative Research, 18*(1), 70-87

Conti, M., Delmastro, F., Minutiello, G., & Paris, R. (2013). Experimenting opportunistic networks with WiFi Direct. In *2013 IFIP Wireless Days (WD)* (pp. 1-6). IEEE.

Cook, C. R., Williams, K. R., Guerra, N. G., Kim, T. E., & Sadek, S. (2010). Predictors of bullying and victimization in childhood and adolescence: A meta-analytic investigation. *School Psychology Quarterly, 25*(2), 65-83.

Coon, J. K., & Travis III, L. F. (2012). The role of police in public schools: A comparison of principal and police reports of activities in schools. *Police Practice and Research, 13*(1), 15-30.

Cox, T., Marczak, M., Teoh, K., & Hassard, J. (2017). New directions in intervention: cyber-bullying, schools and teachers. In McIntyre T., McIntyre S., Francis D. (Eds), *Educator Stress* (pp. 411-435). Cham: Springer.

Creswell, J. (2009). Research Design: Qualitative, Quantitative, And Mixed Methods Approaches. 3rd Ed. London: Sage.

Cronbach, L. (1951). Coefficient alpha and the internal structure of
tests. *Psychomerika, 16*(3), 297-334.

Cunliffe, A. L., & Alcadipani, R. (2016). The politics of access in fieldwork:
Immersion, backstage dramas, and deception. *Organizational Research
Methods, 19*(4), 535-561.

Cysneiros, L. M., do Prado Leite, J. C. S., & Neto, J. D. M. S. (2001). A framework
for integrating non-functional requirements into conceptual
models. *Requirements Engineering, 6*(2), 97-115.

Dasgupta, K. (2019). Youth response to state cyberbullying laws. *New Zealand
Economic Papers, 53*(2), 184-202.

De Nooy, W., Mrvar, A., & Batagelj, V. (2018). Exploratory social network analysis
with Pajek: Revised and expanded edition for updated software. New York:,
Cambridge University Press.

De Vasconcelos, J. B., Gouveia, F. R., & Kimble, C. (2016). An organisational
memory information system using ontologies. In Atas da Conferência da
Associação Portuguesa de Sistemas de Informação, *3*(3).
(http://revista.apsi.pt/index.php/capsi/article/download/378/354)
Retrieved on 7 May 2018.

Deleuze, G., & Guattari, F. (1994). *What is philosophy?* London: Verso.

DeSmet, A., Aelterman, N., Bastiaensens, S., Van Cleemput, K., Poels, K.,
Vandebosch, H., ... & De Bourdeaudhuij, I. (2015). Secondary school educators'
perceptions and practices in handling cyberbullying among adolescents: A
cluster analysis. *Computers & Education, 88*, 192-201.
(http://www.sciencedirect.com/science/article/pii/S0360131515001268)
Retrieved on 18 May 2018.

Divisi, D., Di Leonardo, G., Zaccagna, G., & Crisci, R. (2017). Basic statistics with
Microsoft Excel: a review. *Journal of Thoracic Disease, 9*(6), 1734.

Dobre, C., Mavromoustakis, C.X., Garcia, N.M., Mastorakis, G., & Goleva, R.I.
(2017). Introduction to the AAL and ELE Systems. In Ambient Assisted Living
and Enhanced Living Environments, Principles, Technologies and Control (pp. 1-
16). New York: Elsevier.

Dutot, A, Guinand, F., Olivier, D., & Pigné, Y. (2007). *GraphStream: A tool for
bridging the gap between complex systems and dynamic.* Proceedings of Emergent

Properties in Natural and Artificial Complex Systems (EPNACS) (pp. 63-72). Dresden, Germany: Springer.

Ellis, T. J., & Levy, Y. (2010). A guide for novice researchers: Design and development research methods. In *Proceedings of Informing Science & IT Education Conference (InSITE)* (Vol. 10, pp. 107-118), Cassino, Italy.

Fan, M., Yu, L., & Bowler, L. (2016). Feelbook: A social media app for teens designed to foster positive online behavior and prevent cyberbullying. In *Proceedings of the 2016 CHI Conference Extended Abstracts on Human Factors in Computing Systems* (pp. 1187-1192). New York, NY, USA.

Farib, A., Asadullah, S. & Mior Nasir, M-N. (2017). Artefact evaluation in information system design science research: social constructivism environment. *Science International. (Lahore), 29*(5),1059-1064.

Farmer, T. W., Petrin, R. A., Robertson, D. L., Fraser, M. W., Hall, C. M., Day, S. H., & Dadisman, K. (2010). Peer relations of bullies, bully-victims, and victims: The two social worlds of bullying in second-grade classrooms. *The Elementary School Journal, 110*(3), 364-392.

Flora, H. K., & Chande, S. V. (2013). A review and analysis on mobile application development processes using agile methodologies. *International Journal of Research in Computer Science, 3*(4), 9.

Freeman, L. (1979). Centrality in social networks: Conceptual clarification. *Social Networks, 1*(3),215-239.

Fruchterman, T. M. J., & Reingold, E. M. (1991). Graph drawing by force-directed placement. Software: *Practice and Experience, 21*(11), 1129-1164. https://doi.org/10.1002/spe.4380211102

Gacenga, F., Cater-Steel, A., Toleman, M., & Tan, W. G. (2012). A proposal and evaluation of a design method in design science research. *Electronic Journal of Business Research Methods, 10*(2), 89-100.

Gass, O. & Maedche, A. (2011). Enabling end-user- driven data interoperability - a design science research project. In *Proceedings of the 17th Americas Conference on Information Systems (AMCIS 2011), Detroit, USA.*

Gibson, M., & Arnott, D. (2007). The use of focus groups in Design Science Research. *ACIS 2007 Proceedings.* 14. (https://aisel.aisnet.org/acis2007/14). Retrieved 7 June 2018.

Gigliotti, L. M., & Fopma, S. J. (2019). Low survey response! Can I still use the data?. *Human Dimensions of Wildlife*, *24*(1), 71-79.

Gilad, S. (2019). Mixing qualitative and quantitative methods in pursuit of richer answers to real-world questions. *Public Performance & Management Review*, 1-25. (https://doi.org/10.1080%2F15309576.2019.1694546) Retrieved 17 February 2020.

Ginsburg, H. J., Cameron, R., Mendez, R. V., & Westhoff, M. (2017). Helping others use social media: age stereotypes when estimating learners' success. *Psychology, Society, & Education*, *8*(1), 1-12.

Goldkuhl, G. (2012). Pragmatism vs. interpretivism in qualitative information systems research. *European journal of information systems, 21*(2), 135-146.

Goodhue, D. L., Klein, B. D., & March, S. T. (2000). User evaluations of IS as surrogates for objective performance. *Information & Management, 38*(2), 87-101.

Goodno NH 2011. How public schools can constitutionally halt cyberbullying: A model cyberbullying policy that considers first amendment, due process, and fourth amendment challenges. The Wake Forest Law Review, 46:641-700. (http://wakeforestlawreview.com/wpcontent/uploads/2014/10/Goodno_LawRev iew_1.11.Pdf) Retrieved on 17 March 2015.

Gordon, J, U., ed. (2018). *Bullying Prevention and Intervention a School: Integrating Theory and Research into Best Practices*. Cham, Switzerland: Springer Publishers.

GraphStream Team. (2010). GraphStream. (http://graphstream-project.org/) Retrieved 12 February 2018.

Gregor, S., & Hevner, A. R. (2013). Positioning And Presenting Design Science Research For Maximum Impact. *MIS Quarterly*, *37*(2), 337-355.

Grunspan, D. Z., Wiggins, B. L., & Goodreau, S. M. (2014). Understanding classrooms through social network analysis: A primer for social network analysis in education research. *Cell Biology Education, 13*(2), 167-178.

Gupta, S., Bostrom, R. P., & Huber, M. (2010). End-user training methods: what we know, need to know. *ACM SIGMIS Database: The DATABASE for Advances in Information Systems, 41*(4), 9-39.

Gutiérrez, J. H., Astudillo, C. A., Ballesteros-Pérez, P., Mora-Melià, D., & Candia-Véjar, A. (2016). The multiple team formation problem using

sociometry. *Computers & Operations Research, 75*, 150-162.
(http://www.sciencedirect.com/science/article/pii/S0305054816301198
) Retrieved on 07 March 2019.

Hair, J.F., Black, W.C., Babin, B.J., & Anderson, R.E. (2014). Multivariate Data
Analysis. 7th Ed. Edinburgh Gate, Harlow: Pearson Education Limited.

Hall, R.H., Collier, H.L., Thomas, M.L. & Hilgers, M. G. (2005). A Student
Response System for Increasing Engagement, Motivation, and Learning in
High Enrolment Lectures. In *Americas Conference on Information Systems* (p.
255).
(http://lite.mst.edu/media/research/ctel/documents/hall_et_al_srs_amcis_procee
dings.pdf) Retrieved on 07 March 2019.

Hawley, P. H., & Williford, A. (2015). Articulating the theory of bullying
intervention programs: Views from social psychology, social work, and
organizational science. *Journal of Applied Developmental Psychology*, 37, 3-
15. (https://doi.org/10.1016%2Fj.appdev.2014.11.006) Retrieved on 07
March 2019.

Hawley, P. H., Stump, K. N., & Ratliff, J. (2011). Sidestepping The Jingle Fallacy:
Bullying, Aggression, And The Importance Of Knowing The Difference. In D.
L. Espelage & S. Swearer (Eds.), *Bullying in North American schools* (2nd ed.,
pp. 101-115). New York, NY: Routledge.

Heeringa, S. G., West, B. T., & Berglund, P. A. (2010). *Applied survey data analysis.*
2nd Ed. Florida: Taylor and Francis Group.

Hevner, A. R. (2007). A three-cycle view of design science research, *Scandinavian
Journal of Information Systems 19* (2), 87-92.

Hevner, A. R., March, S. T., Park, J. & Ram, S. (2004). Design Science In
Information Systems Research. *MIS Quarterly, 28*(1), 75-105.

Hevner, A., & Chatterjee, S. (2010). *Design research in information systems: theory
and practice. Integrated Series in Information Systems.* Heidelberg London:
Springer.

Hevner, A., March, S. T., Park, J., & Ram, S. (2004). Design Science Research in
information systems. *MIS Quarterly, 28*(1), 75-105.

Hietajärvi, L., Lonka, K., Hakkarainen, K., Alho, K., & Salmela-Aro, K. (2020). Are
schools alienating digitally engaged students?: Longitudinal relations between

digital engagement and school engagement. *Frontline Learning Research, 8*(1), 33-55.

Hoover, S. M., & Morrow, S. L. (2015). Qualitative Researcher reflexivity: A follow-up study with female sexual assault survivors. *Qualitative Report, 20*(9), 1476-1489.

Howe, K. R. (1988). Against The quantitative-qualitative incompatibility book: or dogmas die hard. *Educational Researcher, 17*(8), 10-16.

Howison, J., Wiggins, A., & Crowston, K. (2011). Validity issues in the use of social network analysis with digital trace data. *Journal of the Association for Information Systems, 12*(12), 767-797.

Huitsing, G., & Veenstra, R. (2012). Bullying in classrooms: Participant roles from a social network perspective. *Aggressive behaviour, 38*(6), 494-509.

Iivari, J. (2015). Distinguishing and contrasting two strategies for design science research. *European Journal of Information Systems, 24*(1), 107-115

Iivari, J.: (2007). A paradigmatic analysis of Information Systems as a Design Science. *Scandinavian Journal of Information Systems, 19*(2), 39-63.

Ioannou, A., Blackburn, J., Stringhini, G., De Cristofaro, E., Kourtellis, N., & Sirivianos, M. (2018). From risk factors to detection and intervention: a practical proposal for future work on cyberbullying. *Behaviour & Information Technology, 37*(3), 258-266.

Ionita, D., Wieringa, R., Bullee, J. W., & Vasenev, A. (2015). Tangible modelling to elicit domain knowledge: an experiment and focus group. In *International Conference on Conceptual Modeling* (pp. 558-565). Springer, Cham.

Jafarkarimi, H., Saadatdoost, R., Tze Hiang Sim, A. L. E. X., & Mei, J. H. (2017). Determinant factors of cyberbullying: An application of theory of planned behavior. *Journal of Theoretical & Applied Information Technology, 95*(23), 6472-6482.

Johnson, J., & Henderson, A.. (2002). Conceptual models: begin by designing what to design. *Interactions, 9*(1). 25-32.

Johnson, R. B., & Onwuegbuzie, A. J. (2004). Mixed Methods Research: A research paradigm whose time has come. *Educational Researcher, 33*(7), 14-26.

Johnson, T., & Owens, L. (2003). Survey response rate reporting in the professional literature. In 58th Annual Meeting of the American Association for Public Opinion Research, (pp. 127-133), Nashville.

Jolliffe, D., & Farrington, D. P. (2011). Is low empathy related to bullying after controlling for individual and social background variables?. *Journal of adolescence, 34*(1), 59-71.

Juan, A., Zuze, L., Hannan, S., Govender, A., & Reddy, V. (2018). Bullies, victims and bully-victims in South African schools: Examining the risk factors. South African Journal of Education, *38*(1), S1-S10

Jungherr, A., Schoen, H., Posegga, O., & Jürgens, P. (2017). Digital trace data in the study of public opinion: An indicator of attention toward politics rather than political support. *Social Science Computer Review, 35*(3), 336-356.

Juvonen, J., & Graham, S. (2014). Bullying in schools: The power of bullies and the plight of victims. *Annual review of psychology, 65*(1), 159-185.

Kandola, B. (2012). Focus Groups. In G. Symon, G., Ca ssell, C. (Eds.), *Quantitative Organizational Research* (pp. 259-274), London: Sage,

Kangas, E., & Kinnunen, T. (2005). Applying user-centered design to mobile application development. *Communications of the ACM, 48*(7), 55-59.

Kao, H. T., Yan, S., Huang, D., Bartley, N., Hosseinmardi, H., & Ferrara, E. (2019). Understanding Cyberbullying on Instagram and Ask. fm via Social Role Detection. In *Companion Proceedings of The 2019 World Wide Web Conference* (pp. 183-188).

Kaplan-Mor, N., Glezer, C., & Zviran, M. (2011). A comparative analysis of end-user training methods. *Journal of Systems and Information Technology 13*(1), 25-42.

Karokola, G., Kowalski, S., & Yngström, L. (2012). Secure e-Government Services: Protection Profile for Electronic Voting–A Case of Tanzania. In *Proceedings of the IST-Africa 2012 Conference* (pp. 1-13).

Kaufman, L., & Rousseeuw, P. J. (2009). *Finding groups in data: An introduction to cluster analysis*. New Jersey:John Wiley & Sons.

Kenny, R., Dooley, B., & Fitzgerald, A. (2016). Developing mental health mobile apps: exploring adolescents' perspectives. *Health informatics journal, 22*(2), 265-275.

Kight, R., & Gram-Hansen, S. B. (2019, April). Do Ethics Matter in Persuasive Technology?. In *International Conference on Persuasive Technology* (pp. 143-155). Springer, Cham.

Kirmani, M. (2017). Agile methods for mobile application development: A comparative analysis. *International Journal of Advanced Research in Computer Science, 8*(5), 1200-1205.

Knight J. (2019). The need for improved ethics guidelines in a changing research landscape. *South African Journal of Science, 115*(11-12), 1-3.

Koelsch, L. E. (2013). Reconceptualizing the member check interview. *International Journal of Qualitative Methods, 12*(1), 168-179.

Koppenhagen, N., Gaß, O., & Müller, B. (2012). Design Science Research in Action-Anatomy of Success Critical Activities for Rigor and Relevance. In Proceedings of European Conference on Information Systems (ECIS) (pp. 1-12).

Koppenhagen, N., Katz, N., Maedche, A., & Müller, B. (2011). How do procurement networks become social? Design principles evaluation in a heterogeneous environment of structured and unstructured interactions. Proceedings of Thirty Second International Conference on Information Systems proceedingd, Shanghai.

Kornbluh, M. (2015). Combatting challenges to establishing trustworthiness in qualitative research. *Qualitative Research in Psychology, 12*(4), 397-414.

Kowalski, R. M., Giumetti, G. W., Schroeder, A. N., & Lattanner, M. R. (2014). Bullying In The Digital Age: A Critical Review And Meta-Analysis Of Cyberbullying Research Among Youth. *Psychological Bulletin, 140*(4), 1073–1137.

Kowatsch, T., Volland, D., Shih, I., Rüegger, D., Künzler, F., Barata, F., ... & Gindrat, P. (2017). Design and evaluation of a mobile chat app for the open source behavioural health intervention platform MobileCoach. In *International Conference on Design Science Research in Information System and Technology* (pp. 485-489). Springer, Cham.

Krueger, R. A. & Casey M. A. (2015*). Focus groups: A practical guide for applied research*. Califonia, Sage.

Kyobe, M., & Lusinga, S. (2018). Factors in reporting mobile victimization in South African schools. In *Bullying Prevention and Intervention at School* (pp. 119-137). Cham: Springer.

Kyobe, M., Mimbi, L., Nembandona, P., & Mtshazi, S. (2018). Mobile bullying among rural South African students: Examining the applicability of existing theories. *The African Journal of Information Systems, 10*(2), 85-104.

Lameck, W. U. (2013). Sampling design, validity and reliability in general social survey. *International Journal of Academic Research in Business and Social Sciences, 3*(7), 212-218.

Laubscher, M., & Van Vollenhoven, W. (2015). Cyberbullying: Should schools choose between safety and privacy? *Potchefstroom Electronic Law Journal 18*(6), 2219.

Lee, K. (2007). User-participatory idea generation for usability Testing of Information Appliances. *Korea Advanced Institute of Science and Technology.* pp.297-304.

Lereya, S. T., Copeland, W. E., Zammit, S., & Wolke, D. (2015). Bully/victims: a longitudinal, population-based cohort study of their mental health. *European child & adolescent psychiatry, 24*(12), 1461-1471.

Lessig, L. (2000). Code and other laws of cyberspace. Basic Books, New York.

Leung, B. P., & Silberling, J. (2006). Using sociograms to identify social status in the classroom. *The California School Psychologist, 11*(1), 57-61.

Lewis, J. R. (1991c). *User satisfaction questionnaires for usability studies: 1991 manual of directions for the ASQ and PSSUQ* (Tech. Report 54.609). Boca Raton, Florida, International Business Machines Corporation.

Lewis, J. R. (1992). Psychometric evaluation of the post-study system usability questionnaire: The PSSUQ. In *Proceedings of the Human Factors and Ergonomics Society Annual Meeting* (Vol. 36, No. 16, pp. 1259-1260). Sage CA: Los Angeles, CA: SAGE Publications.

Lewis, J. R. (1995). IBM computer usability satisfaction questionnaires: psychometric evaluation and instructions for use. *International Journal of Human-Computer Interaction, 7*(1), 57-78.

Lewis, R. E., & Winkelman, P. (2017). *Lifescaping practices in school communities: Implementing action research and appreciative inquiry.* New York, NY, Routledge.

Li, Z., Xu, W., Zhang, L., & Lau, R. Y. (2014). An Ontology-Based Web Mining Method For Unemployment Rate Prediction. Decision Support Systems, 66(2014), 114-122.

Lightenberg, W., Pei, Y., Fletcher, G., & Pechenizkiy, M. (2018, April). Tink: A temporal graph analytics library for apache flink. In *Companion Proceedings of the The Web Conference 2018*(pp. 71-72).

Livingstone, S., & Smith, P. K. (2014). Annual research review: Harms experienced by child users of online and mobile technologies: The nature, prevalence and management of sexual and aggressive risks in the digital age. *Journal of Child Psychology and Psychiatry, 55*(6), 635-654.

Long, T. & Johnson, M. 2000. Rigour, reliability and validity research. *Clinical Effectiveness in Nursing, 4*(1):30-37.

Lowdermilk, T. (2013). *User-centered design: a developer's guide to building user-friendly applications*. Califonia: O'Reilly Media, Inc.

Ludema, J. D., Cooperrider, D. L., & Barrett, F. J. (2006). Appreciative inquiry: The power of the unconditional positive question. In Reason, P. & Bradbury, H. (Eds.), *Handbook of Action Research* (pp. 189-199). Thousand Oaks, CA: Sage.

Lukka, K. (2003). The constructive research approach. In Ojala, L. Hilmola, O. P. (Eds). *Case study research in logistics. Publications of the Turku School of Economics and Business Administration*, Series B, 1 (pp. 83-101).

Ma, X., Yan, B., Chen, G., Zhang, C., Huang, K., Drury, J., & Wang, L. (2013). Design and implementation of a toolkit for usability testing of mobile apps. *Mobile Networks and Applications, 18*(1), 81-97.

Malhotra, R., & Bahl, L. (2017). A defect tracking tool for open source software. In *2017 2nd International Conference for Convergence in Technology (I2CT)* (pp. 901-905). IEEE.

Malterud, K., Siersma, V. D., & Guassora, A. D. (2016). Sample size in qualitative interview studies: guided by information power. *Qualitative health research, 26*(13), 1753-1760.

March, S.T., Smith, G.F. (1995). Design and natural science research on information technology. *Decision support systems, 15*(4), 251-266.

Masitsa, M. G. (2011). Exploring safety in township secondary schools in the Free State province. *South African Journal of Education, 31*(2), 163-174.

Mazzone, E., Read, J., & Beale, R. (2008). Understanding children's contributions during informant design. *In proceedings of the 22nd British HCI Group Annual Conference on People and Computers: Culture, Creativity, Interaction, 2* (pp. 61-64).

Mazzone, E., Xu, D., & Read, J. C. (2007). Design in evaluation: reflections on designing for children's technology. *In proceedings of the 21st British HCI Group Annual Conference on People and Computers: Culture, Creativity, Interaction, 2* (pp. 153-156). BCS Learning & Development Ltd.

McCarthy, M. (2014). Cyberbullying laws and First Amendment rulings: Can they be reconciled. *Mississippi Law Journal, 83(1)*, 805-.834.

Meritam, P., Ryvlin, P., & Beniczky, S. (2018). User-based evaluation of applicability and usability of a wearable accelerometer device for detecting bilateral tonic–clonic seizures: A field study. *Epilepsia, 59*(S1), 48-52.

Mertens, D. (2010). *Research and Evaluation in Education and Psychology.* Thousand Oaks: Sage.

Mfutso-Bengo, J., Ndebele, P., & Masiye, F. (2008). Disseminating research results to research participants and their communities. *Malawi Medical Journal, 20*(2), 64-66.

Miles, M. B., & Huberman, A. M. (1994). *Qualitative data analysis: an expanded sourcebook.* Thousand Oaks, CA, Sage.

Miles, M. B., Huberman, A. M., & Saldaña, J. (2014). *Qualitative data analysis: A methods sourcebook.* 3rd Ed. Thousand Oaks, CA: Sage.

Mishna, F., & Alaggia, R. (2005). Weighing the risks: A child's decision to disclose peer victimization. *Children and Schools, 27*(4), 217-226.

Mishra, P., Pandey, C. M., Singh, U., Gupta, A., Sahu, C., & Keshri, A. (2019). Descriptive statistics and normality tests for statistical data. *Annals of cardiac anaesthesia, 22*(1), 67-72.

Morales, A. (2020). Public's perception of law enforcement in schools. (https://scholarworks.merrimack.edu/cgi/viewcontent.cgi?article=1015&context=crm_studentpub) Retrieved on 12 March 2020.

Morgan, D. L. (2007). Paradigms lost and pragmatism regained: Methodological implications of combining qualitative and quantitative methods. *Journal Of Mixed Methods Research, 1*(1), 48-76.

Mtsweni, J., Biermann, E., & Pretorius, L. (2014). iSemServ: A model-driven approach to developing semantic web services. *South African Computer Journal, 52*(1), 55-70.

Mugagga, P. K. B., & Winberg, S. (2015). Sound source localisation on Android smartphones: A first step to using smartphones as auditory sensors for training AI systems with Big Data. In *AFRICON 2015* (pp. 1-5), IEEE.

Mullis, I. V. S., Martin, M. O., Foy, P., & Hooper, M. (2016b). *TIMSS advanced 2015 international results in advanced mathematics and physics*. Boston, Boston College, TIMSS and PIRLS International Study Center.

Mutti, S., Bacis, E., & Paraboschi, S. (2015). Sesqlite: Security enhanced sqlite: Mandatory access control for android databases. In *Proceedings of the 31st Annual Computer Security Applications Conference* (pp. 411-420).

MyBroadband. (2013). South Africa's Internet Access Stats Revealed. (https://mybroadband.co.za/news/internet/85165-south-africas-internet-access-statsrevealed.html) Retrieved on 17 May 2017.

Myers, C. A., & Cowie, H. (2019). Cyberbullying across the lifespan of education: Issues and interventions from school to university. *International Journal of Environmental Research and Public Health, 16*(7), 1217-1231.

Ndyave, Z. C., & Kyobe, M. (2019). Mobile bully-victim behaviour on Facebook: The case of South African students. In *2019 IEEE 10th Annual Information Technology, Electronics and Mobile Communication Conference (IEMCON)*(pp. 0743-0749). IEEE.

Neilsen, J. (2001). Success rate: The simplest usability metric. (https://www.nngroup.com/articles/success-rate-the-simplest-usability-metric/) Retrieved on 30 March 2020.

Niehaves, B., Ortbach, K., & Tavakoli, A. (2012). On the relationship between the IT Artefact and Design Theory: The case of Virtual Social Facilitation.In Peffers, K., Rothenberger, M., & Kuechler, b. (Eds). *Design Science in Information Systems: Advances in Theory and Practice. 7th International Conference*, DESRIST (2012), Las Vegas, NV,USA, May 2012.

Nielsen, J. (1997). The use and misuse of focus groups. *Software, Institute of Electrical and Electronics Engineers (IEEE) Software, 14*(1), 94-95.

Nocentini, A., Zambuto, V., & Menesini, E. (2015). Anti-bullying programs and Information and Communication Technologies (ICTs): A systematic review. *Aggression and Violent Behaviour, 23(2015)*, 52-60.

O'Raghallaigh, P., Sammon, D., & Murphy, C. (2012). Using Focus Groups to Evaluate Artefacts in Design Research. In *Proceedings of the 6th European*

Conference on Information Management and Evaluation, edited by T. Nagle, University of Cork, Ireland (pp. 251-257).

Odora, R. J., & Matoti, S. N. (2015). The nature and prevalence of cyber bullying behaviors among South African high school learners. *International Journal of Educational Sciences, 10*(3), 399-409.

Oldenburg, B., Van Duijn, M., & Veenstra, R. (2018). Defending one's friends, not one's enemies: A social network analysis of children's defending friendship, and dislike relationships using XPNet. *PloS one, 13*(5).

Oscar, R., Ola, L., Robert, K., & Markus, H. (2018). Negotiations and research bargains: bending professional norms in the effort to gain field access. *International Journal of Qualitative Methods, 17*(1). (https://journals.sagepub.com/doi/pdf/10.1177/1609406918770033) Retrieved on 03 May 2019.

Östberg, V., Modin, B., & Låftman, S. B. (2018). Exposure to school bullying and psychological health in young adulthood: A prospective 10-year follow-up study. *Journal of school violence, 17*(2), 194-209.

Ouellet-Morin, I., & Robitaille, M.-P. (2018). Stronger than Bullying, a mobile application for victims of bullying: Development and initial steps toward validation. *Reducing Cyberbullying in Schools*, 159-174. (https://dx.doi.org/10.1016/b978-0-12-811423-0.00012-2) Retrived on 11 June 2019.

Pabian, S., & Vandebosch, H. (2014). Using the theory of planned behaviour to understand cyberbullying: The importance of beliefs for developing interventions. *European Journal of Developmental Psychology, 11*(4), 463-477.

Pampaka, M., Hutcheson, G., & Williams, J. (2016). Handling missing data: analysis of a challenging data set using multiple imputation. *International Journal of Research & Method in Education, 39*(1), 19-37.

Parker, A., & Tritter, J. (2006). Focus group method and methodology: current practice and recent debate. *International Journal of Research & Method in Education, 29*(1), 23-37.

Parra, O., España, S., & Panach, J. I. (2017). Extending and validating gesture user interface (gestUI) using technical action research. In *2017 11th International Conference on Research Challenges in Information Science (RCIS)* (pp. 341-352). IEEE.

Partington, D (Ed). (2002). Essential Skills for Management Research. Thousand Oaks: SAGE.

Patas, J., Milicevic, D., & Goeken, M. (2011). Enhancing design science through empirical knowledge: Framework and application. In *International Conference on Design Science Research in Information Systems* (pp. 32-46). Springer, Berlin, Heidelberg.

Patil, S., & Palshikar, G. K. (2013). Surveycoder: A system for classification of survey responses. In *International Conference on Application of Natural Language to Information Systems* (pp. 417-420). Springer, Berlin, Heidelberg.

Paullet, K., & Pinchot, J. (2019). Behind the screen where today's bully plays: Perceptions of college students on cyberbullying. *Journal of information systems education, 25*(1), 63-69.

Peffers, K, Tuunanen, T, Rothenberger, M.A. & Chatterjee, S. (2007). A Design Science Research Methodology for Information Systems Research. *Journal of Management Information Systems, 24*(3), 45-77.

Peffers, K., Rothenberger, M., Tuunanen, T., & Vaezi, R. (2012). Design science research evaluation. In International Conference on Design Science Research in Information Systems (pp. 398-410). Springer, Berlin, Heidelberg.

Peffers, K., Tuunanen, T., & Niehaves, B. (2018). Design science research genres: introduction to the special issue on exemplars and criteria for applicable design science research. *European Journal of Information Systems, 27*(2), 129-139.

Peffers, K., Tuunanen, T., Rothenberger, M. A., & Chatterjee, S. (2007). A Design Science Research methodology for Information Systems research. *Journal Of Management Information Systems, 24*(3), 45-77.

Pellegrini, A. D., Long, J. D., Solberg, D., Roseth, C., DuPuis, D., Bohn, C., & Hickey, M. (2010). Bullying and social status during school transitions. In S. R. Jimerson, S. M. Swearer, & D. L. Espelage (Eds.), *Handbook of bullying in schools: An international perspective* (pp. 199–210). New York, NY: Routledge.

Peña-Ayala, A. (2014). Educational data mining: A survey and a data mining-based analysis of recent works. *Expert Systems with Applications, 41*(4), 1432-1462.

Phillips, A. W., Friedman, B. T., & Durning, S. J. (2017). How to calculate a survey response rate: Best practices. *Academic Medicine, 92*(2), 269.

Phillips, B., Steward, C., Hardy, B., & Marsicano, C. (2015). Android programming: The big nerd ranch guide. 2nd Ed. Indianapolis, Pearson Technology Group.

Pittaro, M. (2020). Cyberbullying in adolescence: Victimization and adolescence. In *Developing Safer Online Environments for Children: Tools and Policies for Combatting Cyber Aggression* (pp. 131-154). IGI Global

Polit, D.F., & Hungler, B.P. (1999). Nursing research. principles and methods. 6th Ed. Philadelphia, New York, Baltimore: J.B. Lippincott.

Ponelis, S., Renaud, K., Venter, I., & de la Harpe, R. (2015). Deploying Design Science Research in graduate computing studies in South Africa. *In AIS Electronic Library (AISeL). Twenty First Americas Conference on Information Systems, Puerto Rico* (pp. 1-11).

Porter, G., Hampshire, K., Milner, J., Munthali, A., Robson, E., De Lannoy, A., ... & Abane, A. (2016). Mobile phones and education in Sub-Saharan Africa: From youth practice to public policy. *Journal of International Development, 28*(1), 22-39.

Prat, N., Comyn-Wattiau, I., & Akoka, J. (2014). Artifact evaluation in Information Systems Design-Science Research: A holistic view. *Proceedings of the 18th Pacific Asia Conference on Information Systems* (p. 23).

Prinsloo, I. J. (2005). How safe are South African schools? *South African Journal Of Education,* 25(1), 5-10.

Public Safety Canada. (2018). Overview of approaches to address bullying and cyberbullying. (https://www.publicsafety.gc.ca/cnt/rsrcs/pblctns/2018-ddrss-bllyng-cybrbllyng/2018-ddrss-bllyng-cybrbllyng-en.pdf) Retrieved 16 March 2019.

Rajathi, A., & Chandran, P. (2015). *SPSS for You*. Chennai: MJP Publishers.

Ramaprasad, A., Syn, T., & Thirumalai, M. (2014). An ontological map for meaningful use of healthcare information systems (Muhis). In *HEALTHINF 2014: Proceedings of the International Conference on Health Informatics,* M. Bienkiewicz, C, Verdier, G. Plantier, T. Schultz, A. Fred and H/ Gamboa, Eds: Scitepress.

Reichertz, J. (2007). Abduction: e logic of discovery in grounded theory. In A. Bryant &. K. Charmaz (Eds.), e Sage Handbook of Grounded Theory (pp. 214-228). London: Sage.

Reyneke, M. J., & Jacobs, L. (2018). Can legal remedy be used to address bullying and cyberbullying in South African schools? *Polish Journal of Educational Studies,* 71(1), 66-80.

Robinson, E. (2013). Parental involvement in preventing and responding to cyberbullying. *Family Matters, 2013*(92), 68-76. (https://search.informit.com.au/documentSummary;dn=442274761799511;res=IELFSC) Retrieved 3 March 2018.

Rodkin, P. C., Espelage, D. L., & Hanish, L. D. (2015). A relational framework for understanding bullying: developmental antecedents and outcomes. *American Psychologist, 70*(4), 311-321.

Rodríguez, P., Partanen, J., Kuvaja, P., & Oivo, M. (2014). Combining lean thinking and agile methods for software development: A case study of a finnish provider of wireless embedded systems detailed. In *2014 47th Hawaii International Conference on System Sciences* (pp. 4770-4779). IEEE.

Ryan, J. B., Katsiyannis, A., Counts, J. M., & Shelnut, J. C. (2018). The growing concerns regarding school resource officers. *Intervention in School and Clinic, 53*(3), 188-192.

Rytioja, M., Lappalainen, K., & Savolainen, H. (2019). Behavioural and emotional strengths of sociometrically popular, rejected, controversial, neglected, and average children. *European Journal of Special Needs Education, 34*(5), 557-571.

Salah, D., Paige, R. F., & Cairns, P. (2014). A systematic literature review for agile development processes and user centred design integration. In *Proceedings of the 18th International Conference on Evaluation and Assessment in Software Engineering* (pp. 1-10).

Saldaña, J. (2013). *The coding manual for qualitative researchers.* 2nd ed. Thaousant Oaks, CA: Sage.

Salmivalli, C., & Peets, K. (2011). Bullies, Victims, And Bully-Victim Relationships In Middle Childhood And Early Adolescence. In K. H. Rubin, W. M. Bukowski, & B. Laursen (Eds.), *Handbook Of Peer Interactions, Relationships, And Groups* (pp. 322–340). New York, NY: Guilford.

Salmivalli, C., & Poskiparta, E. (2012). KiVa antibullying program: Overview of evaluation studies based on a randomized controlled trial and national rollout in Finland. *International Journal of Conflict and Violence, 6*(2), 294-302.

Samara, M., Burbidge, V., El Asam, A., Foody, M., Smith, P. K., & Morsi, H. (2017). Bullying and cyberbullying: their legal status and use in psychological assessment. *International Journal of Environmental Research and Public Health, 14*(12), 1449.

Santos, J. R. A. (1999). Cronbach's alpha: A tool for assessing the reliability of scales. *Journal of Extension, 37*(2), 1-5.

Saqr, M., Fors, U., & Nouri, J. (2018). Using social network analysis to understand online Problem-Based Learning and predict performance. *PloS one, 13*(9), e0203590.

Sargeant, J. (2012). Qualitative Research Part II: Participants, analysis, and quality assurance. *Journal of Graduate Medical Education, 4*(1), 1-3.

Saunders, M.N.K. (2012). Choosing research participants. In Symon, G., & Cassell, C. (Eds.). *Qualitative Organizational Research: Core Methods and Current Challenges, pp. 35–52.*

Sauro, J. (2019). 10 things to know about the post study system usability questionnaire (https://measuringu.com/pssuq/) Retrieved on 03 February 2020.

Schnall, R., Rojas, M., Travers, J., Brown III, W., & Bakken, S. (2014). Use of design science for informing the development of a mobile app for persons living with HIV. In *AMIA Annual Symposium Proceedings* (Vol. 2014, p. 1037). American Medical Informatics Association

Schulze, K., & Krömker, H. (2010). A framework to measure user experience of interactive online products. In *Proceedings of the 7th International Conference on Methods and Techniques in Behavioral Research* (pp. 1-5).

Schwartz, D. (2000). Subtypes Of Victims And Aggressors In Children's Peer Groups. Journal of Abnormal Child Psychology, 28, 181–192.

Schwartz, D., Proctor, L. J. and Chien, D. H. (2001). The Aggressive Victim of Bullying: Emotional and Behavioral Dysregulation as a Pathway to Victimization by Peers. In Juvonen, J., & Graham, S. (Eds.), *Peer harassment in school: The plight of the vulnerable and victimized.* Guilford Press.

Sentse, M., Kretschmer, T., & Salmivalli, C. (2015). The longitudinal interplay between bullying, victimization, and social status: Age-related and gender differences. *Social Development, 24*(3), 659-677.

Shariff, S. (2008). *Cyber-bullying: Issues and solutions for the school, the classroom and the home.* New York, NY: Routledge.

Shariff, S. (2015). *Sexting and cyberbullying: Defining the line for digitally empowered kids.* New York, NY: Cambridge University Press.

Shariff, S., & Chan, K. (2013). Canada needs a sweeping strategy to fight cyberbullying. (https://www.theglobeandmail.com/opinion/canada-needs-a-sweeping-strategy-to-fight-cyberbullying/article15505007/). Retrieved on 22 August 2019

Shariff, S., & Eltis, K. (2017). Addressing online sexual violence: An opportunity for partnerships between law and education. *Education & Law Journal, 27*(1), 99-112.

Shieh, B. S. (2016). *Cyberpal: A mobile resource for cyberbullying* (Doctoral book, Pepperdine University).

Shinde, S. S., Shukla, S., & Chitre, D. K. (2013). Secure e-voting using homomorphic technology. *International Journal of Emerging Technology and Advanced Engineering, 3*(8), 203-206.

Simon, J. (2015). *Distributed Epistemic Responsibility In A Hyperconnected Era.* In *The Onlife Manifesto* (pp. 145-159). Cham: Springer .

Singh, A. M. (2017). Bridging the digital divide: the role of universities in getting South Africa closer to the global information society. *South African Journal of Information Management. 6(2)*. a303.

Smit, D. M. (2015). Cyberbullying in South African and American schools: A legal comparative study. *South African Journal of Education, 35*(2), 1-11.

Smith, M. L. (2006). Overcoming theory-practice inconsistencies: Critical realism and Information Systems Research. *Information And Organization, 16*(3), 191-211.

Smith, P. K. (2016). School-based interventions to address bullying. *Eesti Haridusteaduste Ajakiri. Estonian Journal of Education, 4*(2), 142-164.

Smith, P. K. (2019). Research on cyberbullying: strengths and limitations. In H. Vandebosch & L. Green (Eds), *Narratives in Research and Interventions on Cyberbullying among Young People* (pp. 9-27). Springer, Cham.

Smith, P. K., Bauman, S., & Wong, D. (2019). Challenges and opportunities of anti-bullying intervention programs. *International Journal if Environmental Resources Public Health, 16*(10), 1810.

Smith, P. K., Cowie, H., Olafsson, R. F., & Liefooghe, A. P. (2002). Definitions of bullying: A comparison of terms used, and age and gender differences, in a Fourteen–Country international comparison. *Child development, 73*(4), 1119-1133.

Smith, P. K., Mahdavi, J., Carvalho, M., Fisher, S., Russell, S., & Tippett, N. (2008). Cyberbullying: Its nature and impact in secondary school pupils. *Journal of child psychology and psychiatry, 49(4), 376-385.*

Sonnenberg, C., & vom Brocke, J. (2012). Evaluations in the science of the artificial – reconsidering the build-evaluate pattern in Design Science Research. *In: International Conference on Design Science Research in Information Systems and Technology* (pp. 238–297). Berlin, Heidelberg: Springer.

Souma, W., & Jibu, M. (2018). Progress of studies of citations and PageRank. *Scientometrics* (pp. 213-231). (https://www.intechopen.com/books/scientometrics/progress-of-studies-of-citations-and-pagerank) Retrieved on 20 April 2019.

South African Government Gazette (2013). Protection of Personal Information Act. (https://www.justice.gov.za/inforeg/docs/InfoRegSA-POPIA-act2013-004.pdf) Retrieved on 13 March 2019.

Spizzirri, L. (2011). Justification and application of eigenvector centrality. *Algebra in Geography: Eigenvectors of Network.* (http://geza.kzoo.edu/~erdi/patent/b-leo.pdf) Retrieved on 17 May 2019.

Statistics South Africa's General Household Survey. (2017). General Household Survey. (http://www.statssa.gov.za/publications/P0318/P03182016.pdf) Retrieved on 12 July 2019.

Stratton-Berkessel, R. (2010). *Appreciative inquiry for collaborative solutions: 21 strength-based workshops.* New York:John Wiley & Sons.

Sturm, B., & Sunyaev, A. (2019). Design principles for systematic search systems: a holistic synthesis of a rigorous multi-cycle design science research journey. *Business & Information Systems Engineering, 61*(1), 91-111.

Sturm, B., Schneider, S., & Sunyaev, A. (2015). Leave no stone unturned: introducing a revolutionary meta-search tool for rigorous and efficient systematic literature searches. Association for Information Systems, Research-in-Progress Papers. Paper 34.

Symon, G. & Cassell, C (2012). *Qualitative Organizational Research: Core Methods and Current Challenges.* London, SAGE Publications Ltd.

Tan, X. (2017). A new extrapolation method for PageRank computations. *Journal of Computational and Applied Mathematics, 313,* 383-392.

(http://www.sciencedirect.com/science/article/pii/S0377042716304034)
Retrieved on 22 May 2018.

Tan, Z., Jamdagni, A., He, X., Nanda, P., & Liu, R. P. (2013). A system for denial-of-service attack detection based on multivariate correlation analysis. *IEEE transactions on parallel and distributed systems, 25*(2), 447-456.

Tavakol, M., & Dennick, R. (2011). Making sense of Cronbach's alpha. *International journal of medical education*, 2: 53-55. (https://www.ncbi.nlm.nih.gov/pmc/articles/PMC4205511/) Retrieved 6 February 2020.Taylor-Powell, E. (2003). *Analysing quantitative data.* (http://www.uaex.edu/support-units/program-staff-development/docs/Analyzing%20Quantitative%20Data.pdf) Retrieved on 27 June 2014.

Tezci, E., & İçen, M. (2017). High School students' social media usage habits. *Online Submission, 8*(27), 99-108.

Theocharis, D., & Bekiari, A. (2017). Applying social network indicators in the analysis of verbal aggressiveness at the school. *Journal of Computer and Communications, 5*(07), 169–181.

Thompson, E. M. (2019). Understanding bullying and the necessity for prevention and intervention in schools. *Honors Program Liberty University, Unpublished book.*

Tłuściak-Deliowska, A. (2018). Using technology to prevent peer (cyber)bullying and antisocial behavior. *International Journal of Pedagogy, Innovation and New Technologies, 5*(1), 32-43.

Toepoel, V., & Funke, F. (2018). Sliders, visual analogue scales, or buttons: Influence of formats and scales in mobile and desktop surveys. *Mathematical Population Studies, 25*(2), 112-122.

Tonkin-Crine, S., Anthierens, S., Hood, K., Yardley, L., Cals, J. W., Francis, N. A., ... & Butler, C. C. (2015). Discrepancies between qualitative and quantitative evaluation of randomised controlled trial results: achieving clarity through mixed methods triangulation. *Implementation Science, 11*(1), 1-8.

Toribio-Guzmán, J. M., García-Holgado, A., Pérez, F. S., García-Peñalvo, F. J., & Martín, M. F. (2017). Usability evaluation of a private social network on mental health for relatives. *Journal of Medical Systems, 41*(9), 137.

Tremblay, M. C., Hevner, A. R., & Berndt, D. J. (2010). Focus groups for artifact refinement and evaluation in design research. *Communications of the Association for Information Systems, 26*(27), 599-618.

Ttofi, M. M., & Farrington, D. P. (2011). Effectiveness of school-based programs to reduce bullying: A systematic and meta-analytic review. *Journal of Experimental Criminology, 7*(1), 27-56.

Tullis, T. S., & Stetson, J. N. (2004). A comparison of questionnaires for assessing website usability. In *Usability professional association conference* (pp. 1-12). Minneapolis, Minnesota.

Turber, S., & Smiela, C. (2014). A business model type for the Internet of things. *In* M. Avital, J. M. Leimeister and U. Schultze (Eds.), *Proceedings of the 22nd European Conference on Information Systems (ECIS 2014)*, , Tel Aviv, Israel.

Turner, C. W., Lewis, J. R., & Nielsen, J. (2006). Determining usability test sample size. *International Encyclopedia of Ergonomics and Human Factors, 3*(2), 3084-3088.

Ursachi, G., Horodnic, I. A., & Zait, A. (2015). How reliable are measurement scales? External factors with indirect influence on reliability estimators. *In 7th International Conference on Globalization and Higher Education in Economics and Business Administration* (pp. 679-686).

Vacek, J., Vonkova, H., & Gabrhelík, R. (2017). A successful strategy for linking anonymous data from students' and parents' questionnaires using self-generated identification codes. *Prevention Science, 18*(4), 450-458.

Vaishnavi, V. K., & Kuechler, W. (2015). *Design science research methods and patterns: innovating information and communication technology. 2ⁿᵈ Ed*. Boca Raton, London: Crc Press.

van der Zwaan, J. M., Dignum, V., Jonker, C. M., & van der Hof, S. (2014). On technology against cyberbullying. In *Responsible Innovation 1* (pp. 369-392). Springer, Dordrecht.

van Dijk, A., Poorthuis, A. M., & Malti, T. (2017). Psychological processes in young bullies versus bully-victims. *Aggressive Behavior, 43*(5), 430-439.

Van Griethuijsen, R. A. L. F., van Eijck, M. W., Haste, H., den Brok, P. J., Skinner, N. C., Mansour, N., … BouJaoude, S. (2014). Global patterns in students' views of science and interest in science. *Research in Science Education, 45*(4), 581-603.

Vandebosch, H. (2019). Cyberbullying prevention, detection and intervention. In *Narratives in Research and Interventions on Cyberbullying among Young People* (pp. 29-44). Cham: Springer.

Varshney, U. (2012). An approach for smart artefacts for mobile advertising. In *International Conference on Design Science Research in Information Systems* (pp. 147-151). Berlin, Heidelberg: Springer.

Venable, J., & Baskerville, R. (2012). Eating our own cooking: Toward a more rigorous design science of research methods. *Electronic Journal of Business Research Methods, 10*(2), 141-153.

Venable, J., Pries-Heje, J. & Baskerville, R. (2012) A Comprehensive Framework for Evaluation in Design Science Research. In K. Peffers, M. Rothenberger & B. Kuechler (Eds.), *Design Science Research in Information Systems. Advances in Theory and Practice*, 7286(2012),423-438. Berlin / Heidelberg, Springer.

Venable, J., Pries-Heje, J., & Baskerville, R. (2016). FEDS: A framework for evaluation in Design Science Research. *European Journal of Information Systems, 25*(1), 77-89.

Volk, A. A., Dane, A. V., & Marini, Z. A. (2014). What is bullying? A theoretical redefinition. *Developmental Review, 34*(4), 327-343.

Volk, A. A., Veenstra, R., & Espelage, D. L. (2017). So you want to study bullying? Recommendations to enhance the validity, transparency, and compatibility of bullying research. *Aggression and violent behavior, 36*, 34-43. (http://www.sciencedirect.com/science/article/pii/S1359178917302112) Retrieved on 15 April 2020.

Vom Brocke, J., & Buddendick, C. (2006). Reusable conceptual models–requirements based on the design science research paradigm. In *Proceedings of the First International Conference on Design Science Research in Information Systems and Technology (DESRIST)* (pp. 576-604). Claremont, CA, United States of America.

Wahyuni, D. (2012). The research design maze: Understanding paradigms, cases, methods and methodologies, *Journal of Applied Management Accounting Research, 10*(1), 69-80.

Walliman, N. (2001). *Your research project: a step-by-step guide for the first-time researcher*. 2nd Ed. London: Sage.

Walls, J. G., Widmeyer, G. R., & El Sawy, O. A. (1992). Building an information system design theory for vigilant EIS. *Information Systems Research, 3*(1), 36-59.

Wang, R., Perez-Riverol, Y., Hermjakob, H., & Vizcaíno, J. A. (2015). Open source libraries and frameworks for biological data visualisation: A guide for developers. *Proteomics, 15*(8), 1356-1374.

Warburton, N. (2013). *Philosophy: The basics.* London: Routledge.

Wasserman, S., & Faust, K. (1994). *Social network analysis: Methods and applications.* Cambridge, England: Cambridge University Press.

Wegge, D., Vandebosch, H., Eggermont, S., & Pabian, S. (2016). Popularity through online harm: The longitudinal associations between cyberbullying and sociometric status in early adolescence. *The Journal of Early Adolescence, 36*(1), 86-107.

Wieringa, R. J. (2014). *Design science methodology for information systems and software engineering.* London: Springer.

Wieringa, R., & Moralı, A. (2012). Technical action research as a validation method in Information Systems Design Science. In *International Conference on Design Science Research in Information Systems* (pp. 220-238). Berlin, Heidelberg: Springer.

Wijayanto, A. W., & Murata, T. (2017). Flow-aware vertex protection strategy on large social networks. In *Proceedings of the 2017 IEEE/ACM International Conference on Advances in Social Networks Analysis and Mining 2017* (pp. 58-63).

Williams, A. (2003). How to… Write and analyse a questionnaire. *Journal of Orthodontics, 30*(3), 245-252.

Wisniewski, P., Ghosh, A. K., Xu, H., Rosson, M. B., & Carroll, J. M. (2017). Parental control vs. teen self-regulation: Is there a middle ground for mobile online safety? In *Proceedings of the 2017 ACM Conference on Computer Supported Cooperative Work and Social Computing* (pp. 51-69).

Wohlin, C., Runeson, P., Höst, M., Ohlsson, M. C., Regnell, B., & Wesslén, A. (2012). *Experimentation in software engineering.* Berlin Heidelberg: Springer.

Wolfe, D. A & Jaffe, P. G. 1999. Emerging strategies in the prevention of domestic violence. *The future of children,* 9(3), 133-144.

Xiao, Y., Liu, H., & Li, H. (2017). Integration of the forced-choice questionnaire and the Likert scale: a simulation study. *Frontiers in Psychology, 8,* 806. (https://doi.org/10.3389%2Ffpsyg.2017.00806) Retrieved 28 March 2018.

Xie, X., Zhao, F., Xie, J., & Lei, L. (2016). Symbolization of mobile phone and life satisfaction among adolescents in rural areas of China: Mediating of school-related relationships. *Computers in Human Behavior*, *64*, 694-702. (http://www.sciencedirect.com/science/article/pii/S074756321630543X) Retrieved on 2 November 2018.

Yaghmale, F. 2009. Content validity and its estimation. *Journal of Medical Education* 3(1): 25-27.

Yakubu, M., Ngene, C.U. & Gambo, Y. (2017). Modified Math Client-Server Application for E-Learning. *International Journal of Computer Applications*, *170(4)*, 0975-8887.

You, S., & Lim, S. A. (2016). Longitudinal Predictors Of Cyberbullying Perpetration: Evidence From Korean Middle School Students. *Personality and Individual Differences*, 89, 172-176. (https://doi.org/10.1016%2Fj.paid.2015.10.019) Retrieved on 6 February 2018.

Zhang, F., You, Z., Fan, C., Gao, C., Cohen, R., Hsueh, Y., & Zhou, Z. (2014). Friendship quality, social preference, proximity prestige, and self-perceived social competence: Interactive influences on children's loneliness. *Journal of School Psychology*, *52*(5), 511-526.

Zorrilla, M., & de Lima Silva, M. (2019). Sociograms: An effective tool for decision making in social learning. *Technology, Knowledge and Learning*, *24*(4), 659-681.

Appendices

Appendix 1: Focus group route and probes

Exploratory focus group A route and probes

Route	Probe
Opening	1. Tell us your name, which area (sector) you work in, and what you enjoy most about crime prevention in schools.
Introduction	2. How did you learn about the mobile bully-victim behaviour?
Transition	3. Think back when you first learned about the mobile bully-victim behaviour. What were your first impressions?
Key	4. In your opinion, what causes lack of reported cases of mobile bully-victim behaviour to police?
	5. What do you think can be done to encourage learners to come forward and report mobile bully-victim behaviour?
	6. How can learners who are affected by mobile bullying behaviour helped?
Ending	7. Suppose you were attending a complaint about mobile bully-victim in school. What would you do?
	8. Suppose the complainant's evidence is inconclusive. What would you do?
	9. Using names and pupil's recollections of bullying experiences are possible risks of participating in this study. Can you identify any other risks?

Exploratory focus group B route and probes

Route	Probe
Opening	1. Tell us your name, which area (sector) you work in, and what you enjoy most about crime prevention in schools.
Introduction	2. How did you learn about the mobile bully-victim behaviour?
Transition	3. Think back when you first learned about the mobile bully-victim behaviour. What were your first impressions?
Key	4. What information would you need to positively identify mobile bully-victims among pupils in class?
	5. How can poll results be presented?
	6. What features of an app can be used to obtain confirmation of mobile bully-victims nomination?
Ending	7. How should poll results be presented on the app? Details of identified mobile bully-victims can include
	8. We want you to help us further develop and evaluate the app. We want to know how to improve the functions of the app. Is there anything we should have talked about but didn't?

Confirmatory focus group A route and probes used in the evaluation of the M-BRS

Route	Probe
Opening	Tell us your name, which area (sector) you work in, and what you enjoy most about crime prevention in schools.
Introduction	What was the first thing that came to mind when you used the app?
Transition	Think back when you first used the mobile app as a bully-victims diagnosis tool. What were your first impressions?
Key	What was using the app features (definition and instructions, or questions) like for you?
	What was particularly frustrating about the app?
	What was particularly helpful about the app?
Ending	If you could rearrange the app's diagnosis process. What would you do?
	If you could pick one feature between the **nomination**, and **confirmation** and **assessment** to fight mobile bully-victim behaviour. Which one would you pick?

Appendix 2: Evaluation questionnaire

University of Cape Town
Department of Information Systems

Questionnaire:	Towards a mobile application to aid law enforcement in diagnosing and preventing mobile bully-victim behaviour in Eastern Free State High schools of South Africa

Dear participant

Thank you for taking time to complete this questionnaire. Your feedback will provide understanding about your experiences with the Mobile Bully-victim Response System (M-BRS) that you used in the schools. This questionnaire should take about 10 minutes to complete.

Any information that is obtained in connection with this questionnaire and that can be identified with you will be treated completely anonymous. Your completion of this questionnaire will be regarded as consent to use your feedback for the purposes of the research.

Participation is voluntary. Your decision whether or not to complete this questionnaire will have no bearing on you.

Instructions: Please circle your selected answers.

<table>
<tr><td colspan="4" align="center">Section 1 – Demographic information</td></tr>
</table>

Tell us more about yourself:

1. **Gender:**   Male   Female   prefer not to answer
2. **Age:**   12-14   15-17   18+
3. **Do you own a smart phone?**   Yes   No
4. **How often do you use social media such as Facebook, Whatsapp, Google talk and Twitter on your phone?**   never   rarely   frequently

<table>
<tr><td colspan="5" align="center">Section 2 – Using the M-BRS</td></tr>
</table>

On a scale of 1 - 4, please select the number that best represents your belief about each statement:

	Strongly disagree	Disagree	Agree	Strongly agree
1. The use of the M-BRS made me feel more confident to report mobile Bully-victims behaviour.	1	2	3	4
2. I often had difficulty in using M-BRS via mobile phone.	1	2	3	4
3. The use of the M-BRS in diagnosing mobile bully-victims behaviour made me feel uneasy.	1	2	3	4
4. If possible I would also use my personal mobile phone with M-BRS.	1	2	3	4

University of Cape Town
Department of Information Systéms

5.	The M-BRS was easy to use.	1	2	3	4
6.	The use of the M-BRS should be expanded to other classes and schools.	1	2	3	4

Section 3 – Diagnosis of bully-victims through M-BRS use

On a scale of 1 - 4, please select the number that best represents your belief about each statement:

		Strongly disagree	Disagree	Agree	Strongly agree
1.	The M-BRS helped me increased my involvement in fighting mobile bully-victim behaviour.	1	2	3	4
2.	The M-BRS increased my frequency of participation in fighting the mobile bully-victims behaviour.	1	2	3	4
3.	Reporters' anonymity encouraged me to report mobile bully-victim behaviour.	1	2	3	4
4.	The use of the M-BRS increased my understanding of mobile bully-victims behaviour.	1	2	3	4
5.	The use of the M-BRS encouraged me to report bully-victim behaviour incidents.	1	2	3	4

Section 4 – Impact of M-BRS use

On a scale of 1 - 4, please select the number that best represents your belief about each statement:

		Strongly disagree	Disagree	Agree	Strongly agree
1.	The use of M-BRS made me aware of mobile bully-victim behaviour.	1	2	3	4
2.	The use of the M-BRS helped me to understand the mobile bully-victim phenomenon.	1	2	3	4
3.	If the police used the M-BRS, I would trust them to help me against mobile bully-victims behaviour.	1	2	3	4
4.	The results of the M-BRS were accurate about my involvement in mobile bully-victims behaviour.	1	2	3	4

If you have questions about this study please do not hesitate to call or email:
Researcher: Fani Radebe (RDBFAN002)   Supervisor: Professor Michael Kyobe
Phone: 076 296 3289   Phone: 021 650 2597
Email: RDBFAN002@myuct.ac.za   Email at michael.kyobe@uct.ac.za

This study has been reviewed and approved by ethical review committee of the University of Cape Town. Feel free to contact Salah Kabanda, email: salah.kabanda@uct.ac.za, Tel: 0 21 650 4253 should you have any queries or complaints.

2

University of Cape Town
Department of Information Systems

5.	The use of the M-BRS helped to quickly find help against bully-victim incidents.	1	2	3	4
6.	The use of the M-BRS reinforced mobile bully-victim behaviour awareness.	1	2	3	4
7.	I was wrongly accused about being involved in mobile bully-victims behaviour.	1	2	3	4

Section 5 – Personal experiences with M-BRS

1. What did you appreciate about the use of the M-BRS?

____
____
____

2. What did you find frustrating about the use of the M-BRS?

____
____
____

3. What do you think can be done to improve the way in which the M-BRS was used to diagnose mobile bully-victim behaviour?

____
____
____

4. Please provide any additional comment(s) about your experience with the use of M-BRS in diagnosing mobile bully-victims behaviour?

____
____
____

Thank you for taking the time to complete this questionnaire!

If you have questions about this study please do not hesitate to call or email:

Researcher: Fani Radebe (RDBFAN002) Supervisor: Professor Michael Kyobe
Phone: 076 296 3289 Phone: 021 650 2597
Email: RDBFAN002@myuct.ac.za Email at michael.kyobe@uct.ac.za

This study has been reviewed and approved by ethical review committee of the University of Cape Town. Feel free to contact Salah Kabanda, email: salah.kabanda@uct.ac.za, Tel: 0 21 650 4253 should you have any queries or complaints.

3

Appendix 4: M-BRS server user guide

M-BRS Server App

User Guide

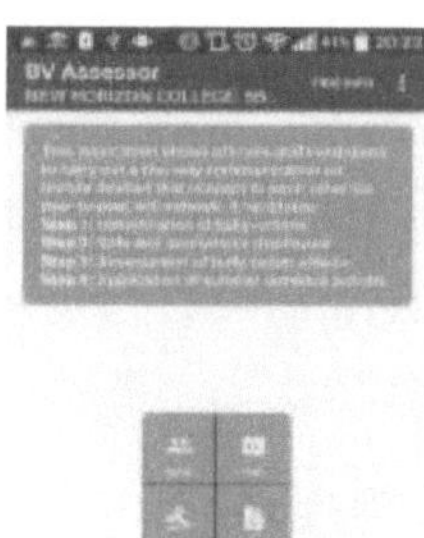

Getting To Know Sever Functions
Menu Bar:
1. HIDE INFO / SHOW INFO menu option, to *display* or *hide* the description view.
2. Filter in the overflow menu, to select school and class grade, press the.

Server Functions:
1. App description (*Top field*), to view the purpose of the app.
2. Admin button (*Top-left button*), to *register*, *update* details, or *delete* candidates, *press* the.
3. Poll button (*Top-right*), to *start* nomination session, press the. (Requires the WIFI Direct Connection).
4. Assessment matrix button (*Bottom-left*), to *start* confirmation of nomination, and assessment matrix of, *press* the. (Requires the WIFI Direct Connection).
5. Report button (*Bottom-right*), to *view* assessment results.

Step 1: Setting Filter
At this step, you can *enter* the institution name and grade level. This step launches automatical when using the app for the first time.

1. To set / select school, type school name in the INSTITUTION field.
2. To set / select class, type grade level and extension (5B, for an example) in the GRADE field.

Step 2: Candidate Administration
At this step, you can *add*, *update* or *delete* candidates using Menu Bar options, and view candidates list.

To *view* the description of the admin function
1. *Press* the SHOW INFO from the overflow menu option.

To *hide* the description of the admin function
1. *Press* the HIDE INFO from the overflow menu option.

To *view* added candidates
1. *See* list the in the main screen.

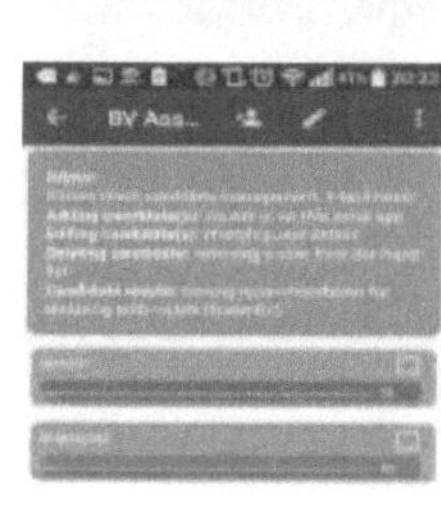

To *register* candidates
1. *Press* the Plus icon on the menu options, and then do one of the following. (See the Step 3: Registering Candidate(s) Step to complete registerring candidates).

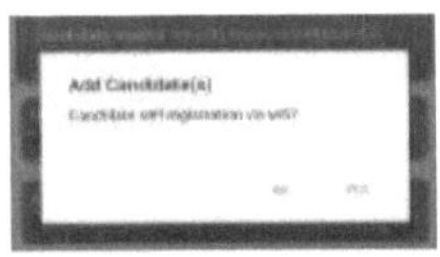

Step 3: Registering Candidate(s)

At this step, you can select the registration mode (WIFI or Embeded Function).

To register candidate via WIFI
1. *Select* YES on the *Add Candidate(s) dialog.*

OR

To register new candidates through the embeded function
1. *Select* NO on the *Add Candidate(s)* dialog.

   (*See the* Capture Details *section to complete the registration process*)

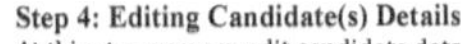

Step 4: Editing Candidate(s) Details

At this step, you can edit candidate details.

To *edit* existing candidates details
1. *Select* the cadidate on the list
2. *Press* the Pen icon on the menu options.

   (*See the* Capture Details *section to complete the editing process*)

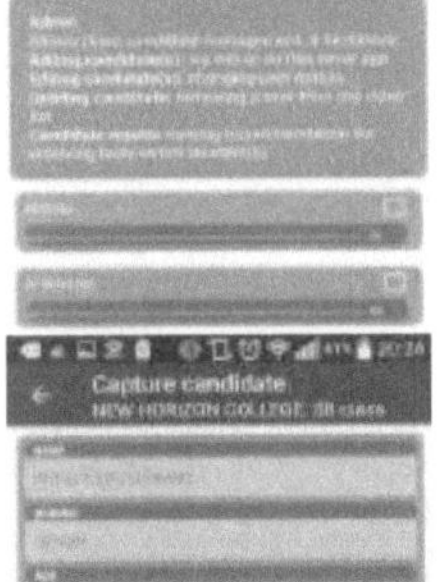

Step 5: Capture Detail

At this step, you can enter or edit candidate name, gender and age.

To *capture* candidate's or *edit* candidate's details:
1. *Enter* initials and Surname in the NAME field,
2. *Enter* Gender in the GENDER field,
3. *Enter* Age in the AGE field,
4. Then, *press* the ADD button to save the information.

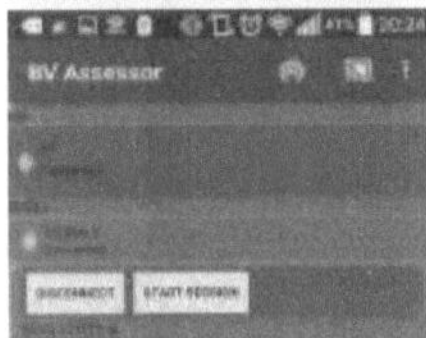

Step 6: Connecting / Disconnecting WIFI Direct

At this step, you can allow clients to connect to the server, and then start poll or assessment matrix session, once all available clients have connected to this server.

Allowing clients to connect
1. *Ensure* that the device's WIFI is enabled.
   Ensure that all candidates know the device name on which the BV-Assessor Server in running.

Starting the pooling or assessment matrix session
1. *Verify* that all client devices (candidate devices) on the list are connected.
2. *Press* the START SESSION button

Disconnecting clients from poll or assessment matrix session
1. *Press* the DISCONNECT button, to release clients devices from a session.

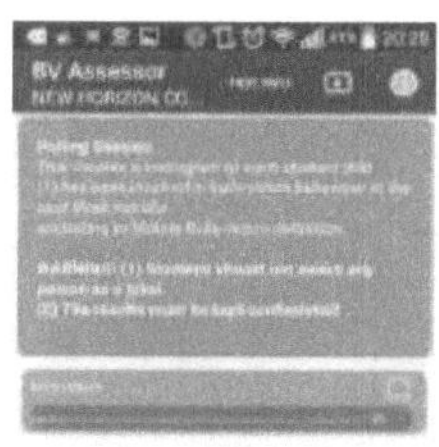

Step 7: Polling Session

At this step, (1) you can send the list of candidates to connected clients, to facilitate polling, (2) allow candidate to send back nominees from the list (nomination), (3) and save polls results.

To send class list to client devices,

1. *Press* the SEND icon on the menu option. (All connected client devices should have the list).

Nominations
2. Each candidate progress bar on the list is automatically updated for each nomination.

To saving polls (once all candidates finish nominations)

1. *Press* the SAVE icon on the menu option.

Step 8: Assessment Matrix Session

At this step, (1) you can send the list of candidates to connected clients, to facilitate assessment matrix, (2) allow candidate to send feedback.
Note:
- Only candidates who have not yet completed the assessment for the current session are listed.
- If the list is emty, not candidates need assessment.
- Candidates whose assessment is received are check, using the checkbox on the right.

To send class list (All connected client devices should have the list)

1. *Press* the SEND icon on the menu option.

Saving assessment matrix
1. The Assessment Matrix information is *saved automatically.*

Step 9: Viewing / Sending Report

At this step, (1) you can view reports for each selected session, (2) feedback details for candidates, and (3) send report.

Selecting session number and viewing the assessment matrix chart.
To view a session results chart,
1. *Press* the SESSION NUMBER on the menu option.
2. *Select* the SESSION NUMBER on the drop-down list.

Viewing Assessment Matrix results *for the selected session.*
To view candidate assessment matrix results

1. *Press* the GAVEL icon on the menu option.
   (See the Step 10: Viewing Assessment Matrix Results Step section for viewing results).

Sending the report *of the selected session*
To send report

1. *Press* the SEND icon on the menu option.
2. *Select* the available e-mail app from the dialog.

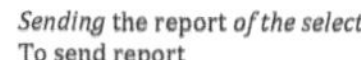

(*See* Selecting E-Mail App *for selecting e-mail app*).

3. *Select* the SEND icon on the menu option of the e-mail app. (*See* Step11: Selecting E-Mail App Step and Sending Report *Step* to complete the sending report task).

Step 10: Viewing Assessment Matrix Results
At this step, you can view the results of the assessment metrix to provide guidance on assisting candidates in dealing with the bully-victim effects and incidents.

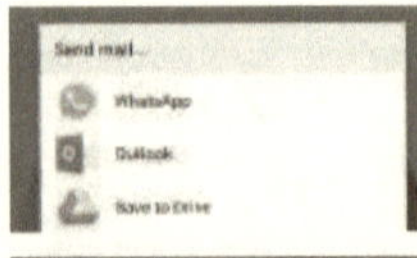

To proceed to next item
1. *Swipe-left* to proceed to the next item.

To return to previous item
2. *Swipe-right* to proceed to the next item.

Step 11: Selecting E-Mail App
At this step, you can select an e-mail app for sending the report.

To *select* the available e-mail app from the dialog.
1. *Press* the e-mail app from the dialog.
   (Outlook, Gmail, E-mail, etc.)

Step 12: Sending Report
At this step, you can view the report file on attachment of the composed e-mail and send the e-mail. (Requires Internet access).

To view the report file
1. *View* the attached report file

To send report
2. *Press* the SEND icon on the menu option.

The address is automatically set.

Appendix 5: M-BRS client user guide

M-BRS Client App

User Guide

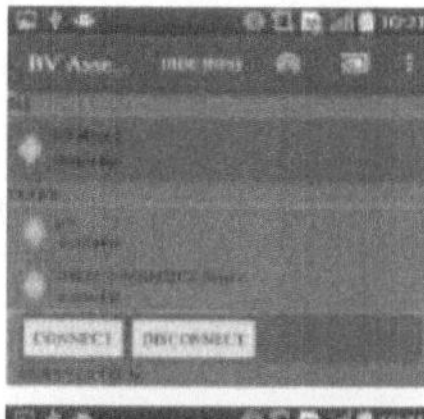

Getting To Know BV-Assessor Client Menu Bar

At the Menu Bar you can hide or display the definition of mobile bully-victim, connecting to the server, and the instructions for the polling session.

To hide of display information

1. Press HIDE INFO / SHOW INFO menu option, to *display* or *hide* the description view.

To refresh connection
1. *Press* the CONNECT button.

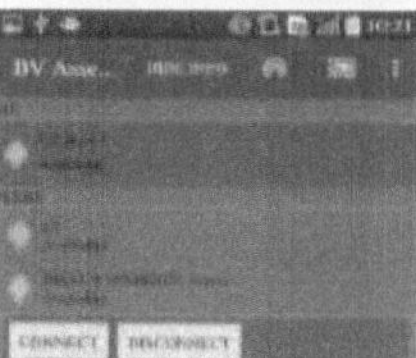

Step 1: WIFI Connection

At this step, (1) you can discover avalable peers on WIFI, (2) find the device name of the BV-assessr server, (3) and select the device by name to connect with. If the connection fails, you can refresh it.

To discover to server
2. *Press* the CONNECT icon on the menu option. 

Identifying the BV-Assessor sever device name.
2. Ask the instructor for the name of the server.

Do Step 2 and 3 to select and connect to server, only if your device is connecting for the first time.
To select the server
3. *Press* the name of the server on the list, (the CONNECT and DISCONNECT buttons will appear).

To connect to server
4. *Press* the CONNECT button.

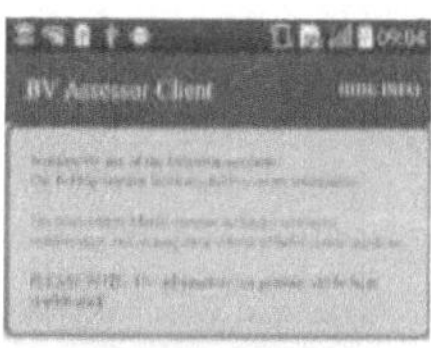

Step 2: Waiting for Session Information

Once the connection has been established, the *Waiting for session* screen will appear, showing details of poll and assessment matrix sessions.

At this step you can wait for a session to be started by server.

Step 3: Authentication

At this step, you can authenticate into the polling session.

To authenticate

1. *Insert* you ID code in the ID field (replace asterisks), and your name will be automatically shown in the Name field.

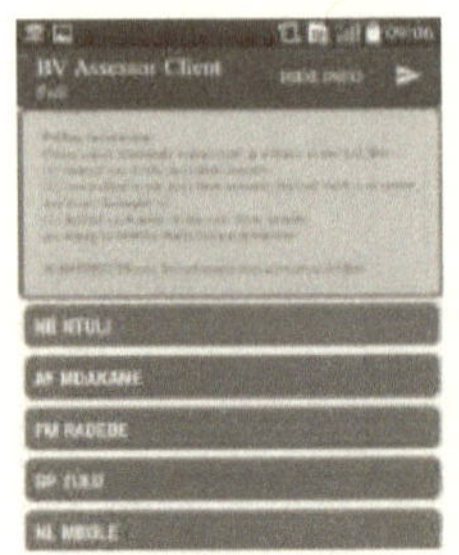

Step 4: Polling Session

At this step, you can select names of your classmate that you perceive as bully-victim and send it to the server.

To nominate classmates
2. *Select* the classmate's *name* from the class list.

To send the name
3. *Press* SEND icon on menu options. 

    A "*Sent*" confirmation will be displayed.

Repeat Step 1 and 2, if there are other names that you want to select. Otherwise, if you are done with clear the list.

To clear the list
4. *Press* the BACK button on the device.

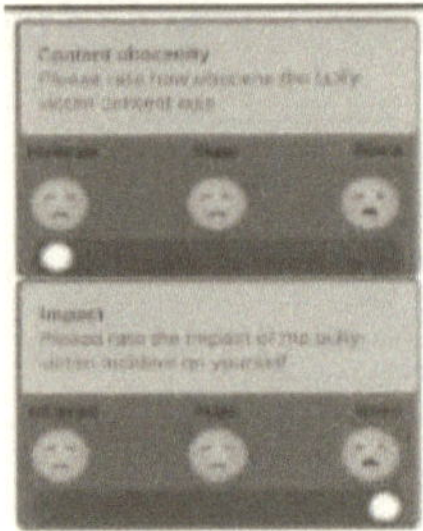

Step 5: Selecting Confirmation Response

At this step, you can confirm, deny your nominations, and procees to next items.

To deny your nomination
1. *Check* the Unlikely smiley face, if you disagree.

If you are undecide
2. *Check* the Unsure smiley face, if you are not sure.

To confirm your nomination as true
3. *Check* the Likely smiley face, if you agree.

To proceed to next item
1. *Swipe-up* to proceed to the next item. 

Step 6: Completing Severity Assessment

At this step, you can rate and provide the severity of mobile bully-victim effects that you have experienced.

To rate the Severity effects
1. *Tap* the Moderate smiley face, if you feel the incident had moderate effects.
2. *Tap* the Major smiley face, if you feel the incident had major effects.
3. *Tap* the Severe smiley face, if you feel the incident had severe effects.

To proceed to next item
1. *Swipe-up* to proceed to the next item. 

To return to previous item
2. *Swipe-down* to proceed to the next item. 

Step 9: Assessment Items Description

At this step, you can view the description of assessment items.

To view descriptions
1. *Tap* the DESCRIPTION item on menu options.

To close descriptions
2. *Tap* the BACK button of the device.

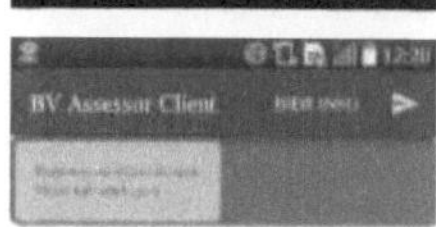

Step 10: Resending Assessment Matrix Feedback

At this step, you can resent feedback, if a confirmation was not received. If the feedback could not be sent, an error message will be display, requiring a resend action.

To resend feedback
3. *Press* SEND icon on menu options.

A *"Sent"* confirmation will be displayed.

Appendix 6: Consent letter to South African Police Service

University of Cape Town
Department of Information Systems

25 March 2019

South African Police Department

Dear Sir/Madam

RE: Towards a mobile application to aid law enforcement in diagnosing and preventing mobile bully-victim behaviour in Eastern Free State High schools of South Africa

My name is Fani Radebe and I am conducting a study towards doctoral degree with the University of Cape Town (UCT). This study is based on the role of law enforcement, particularly South African Police who are responsible for crime prevention in schools, in curbing mobile bully-victim behaviour across Eastern Free State. The main aim of this study is to develop a mobile application (app) that can assist the police to diagnose mobile bully-victim behaviour in schools. The study is led by Professor Michael Kyobe at UCT in the Department of Information Systems and is funded by the National Research Foundation. The information that will be gathered through this study will help to shed light on the mobile bully-victim phenomenon.

Mobile bully-victim behaviour is one form of electronic bullying that is relatively new. It involves the use of technology applications such as email, chat rooms, instant messaging and small text messages. This form of bullying often goes unnoticed, however bully-victims face higher risks of poor conduct, academic, and peer relationship problems, as well as substance abuse. Victims, institutions and parents are unaware of how to deal with it and there is limited knowledge of its legal and social implications.

I request your permission to conduct this study in your organization with personnel who are responsible for social crime prevention in schools. This study is solely used to evaluate utility and efficacy of the app, which consists of two stages:
(1) Participants will be provided with training on the use of the app. The police will be asked to diagnose pupils' involvement in mobile bully-victim behaviour using the app. The first step of this process includes anonymous peer-nomination or self-report by pupils who are involved in the mobile bully-victim behaviour. While the nominations of mobile bully-victims are completely anonymous, that is pupils will not know who nominated (accused) them. It is possible that pupils may wrongfully nominate (accuse) others, perhaps as a joke. However the second step of the process, which validates the nominations, affords each nominee an opportunity to deny or assent to nominations without any compulsion or penalty. In the validation process pupils will be requested to recall and share their bully-victim experiences, which may cause emotional disturbance. Hence counselling for pupils will be provided through the Social Development Department to handle emotional distress risks that may arise because of false accusations and bully-victim incidents recollection. In the final step pupils may be invited for remedial help based on the app's report. Additionally consent from parents, school principals and police personnel will be requested in writing before the study commences.

(2) The personnel will also be requested to share their experience regarding the use of the app to diagnose mobile bully-victims. The testing procedure, and questionnaire and focus group guide for data collection are attached. Please be assured that no other information whether personal or that can bring the department into disrepute will be collected or disseminated.

If you have questions about this study please do not hesitate to call or email:

Researcher: Fani Radebe (RDBFAN002)	Supervisor: Professor Michael Kyobe
Tel: 076 296 3289	Tel: 021 650 2597
Email: RDBFAN002@myuct.ac.za	Email at michael.kyobe@uct.ac.za

This study has been reviewed and approved by ethical review committee of the University of Cape Town. Feel free to contact Salah Kabanda, email: salah.kabanda@uct.ac.za, Tel: 0 21 650 4253 should you have any queries or complaints.

University of Cape Town
Department of Information Systems

The benefits of taking part in this study include raising awareness about mobile bully-victim behaviour, and encouraging pupils to report incidents. Additionally the study will help to provide the app to equip law enforcement in fighting the mobile bully-victim behaviour.

I hope that my request will find favour with you. For further information please do not hesitate to contact Mr Fani Radebe or Professor Michael Kyobe.

Fani Radebe

Signature Removed

Appendix 7: Consent letter to Department of Basic Education

University of Cape Town
Department of Information Systems

09 July 2018

Department of Education

Dear Sir/Madam

Re: Towards a mobile application to aid law enforcement in diagnosing and preventing mobile bully-victim behaviour in Eastern Free State High schools of South Africa

My name is Fani Radebe and I am conducting a study towards doctoral degree with the University of Cape Town (UCT). This study is based on the role of law enforcement, particularly South African Police who are responsible for crime prevention in schools, in curbing mobile bully-victim behaviour across Eastern Free State. The main aim of this study is to develop a mobile application (app) that can assist the police to diagnose mobile bully-victim behaviour in schools. The study is led by Professor Michael Kyobe at UCT in the Department of Information Systems and is funded by the National Research Foundation. The information that will be gathered through this study will help to shed light on the mobile bully-victim phenomenon.

Mobile bully-victim behaviour is one form of electronic bullying that is relatively new. It involves the use of technology applications such as email, chat rooms, instant messaging and small text messages. This form of bullying often goes unnoticed, however bully-victims face higher risks of poor conduct, academic, and peer relationship problems, as well as substance abuse. Victims, institutions and parents are unaware of how to deal with it and there is limited knowledge of its legal and social implications.

I request your permission to conduct this study in schools. This study is solely used to evaluate utility and efficacy of the app, which consists of two stages:
(1) Participants will be provided with training. Then police will be asked to diagnose pupils' involvement in mobile bully-victim behaviour using the app. The first step of this process includes anonymous peer-nomination or self-report by pupils who are involved in the mobile bully-victim behaviour. While the nominations of mobile bully-victims are completely anonymous, that is pupils will not know who nominated (accused) them. It is possible that pupils may wrongfully nominate (accuse) others, perhaps as a joke. However the second step of the process, which validates the nominations, affords each nominee an opportunity to deny or assent to nominations without any compulsion or penalty. Also pupils will be requested to recall and share their bully-victim experiences, which may cause emotional disturbance. Therefore counselling for pupils will be provided through the Social Development Department to handle emotional distress risks that may arise because of false accusations and bully-victim incidents recollection. In the final step pupils may be invited for remedial help based on the app's report. Additionally consent from parents, school principals and police personnel will be requested in writing before the study commences.

(2) Participants will also be requested to share their experience regarding the use of the app to diagnose mobile bully-victims. The questionnaire for the data that will be collected is attached. Please be assured that no other information whether personal or that can bring the department into disrepute will be collected or disseminated.

If you have questions about this study please do not hesitate to call or email:
Researcher: Fani Radebe (RDBFAN002)   Supervisor: Professor Michael Kyobe
Tel: 076 296 3289   Tel: 021 650 2597
Email: RDBFAN002@myuct.ac.za   Email at michael.kyobe@uct.ac.za

This study has been reviewed and approved by ethical review committee of the University of Cape Town. Feel free to contact Salah Kabanda, email: salah.kabanda@uct.ac.za, Tel: 0 21 650 4253 should you have any queries or complaints.

1

University of Cape Town
Department of Information Systems

I hope that my request will find favour with you. For further information please do not hesitate to contact Mr Fani Radebe or Professor Michael Kyobe.

Fani Radebe

Signature Removed

Appendix 8: Consent letter to School principals

University of Cape Town
Department of Information Systems

30 July 2018

Dear Principal

RE: Towards a mobile application to aid law enforcement in diagnosing and preventing mobile bully-victim behaviour in Eastern Free State High schools of South Africa

My name is Fani Radebe and I am conducting a study towards doctoral degree with the University of Cape Town (UCT). This study is based on the role of law enforcement, particularly South African Police who are responsible for crime prevention in schools, in curbing mobile bully-victim behaviour across Eastern Free State. The main aim of this study is to develop a mobile application (app) that can assist the police to diagnose mobile bully-victim behaviour in schools. The study is led by Professor Michael Kyobe at UCT in the Department of Information Systems and is funded by the National Research Foundation. The information that will be gathered through this study will help to shed light on the mobile bully-victim phenomenon.

Mobile bully-victim behaviour is one form of electronic bullying that is relatively new. It involves the use of technology applications such as email, chat rooms, instant messaging and small text messages. Using these technologies victims are harmed psychologically and emotionally by spreading lies, sending insults, and exclusion from social groups. This form of bullying often goes unnoticed, however bully-victims face higher risks of poor conduct, academic, and peer relationship problems, as well as substance abuse. Victims, institutions and parents are unaware of how to deal with it and there is limited knowledge of its legal and social implications.

I request your permission to conduct this study in your school. This study is solely used to evaluate utility and efficacy of the app, which consists of two stages:
(1) Participants will be provided with training on the use of the app. Then police will be asked to diagnose pupils' involvement in mobile bully-victim behaviour using the app. The first step of this process includes confidential peer-nomination and self-report by pupils who are involved in the mobile bully-victim behaviour. While the nominations of mobile bully-victims are confidential, that is pupils will not know who nominated (accused) them. It is possible that pupils may wrongfully nominate (accuse) others, perhaps as a joke. However the second step of the process, which validates the nominations, affords each nominee an opportunity to deny or assent to nominations without any compulsion or penalty. Also pupils will be requested to recall and share their bully-victim experiences, which may cause emotionally disturbance. Therefore counseling for pupils will be provided through the Social Development Department to handle emotional distress risks that may arise because of false accusations and bully-victim incidents recollection. In the final step pupils may be invited for remedial help based on the app's report. Additionally consent from your child (please see the attached form for your perusal), the school principal and police personnel will be requested in writing before the study commences.

(2) Pupils will also be requested to share their experiences regarding the use of the app to diagnose mobile bully-victims. Please be assured that no other information whether personal or that can lead to victimisation of pupils or bring disrepute to school will be collected or publicly divulged.

If you have questions about this study please do not hesitate to call or email:
Researcher: Fani Radebe (RDBFAN002)   Supervisor: Professor Michael Kyobe
Tel: 076 296 3289   Tel: 021 650 2597
Email: RDBFAN002@myuct.ac.za   Email at michael.kyobe@uct.ac.za

This study has been reviewed and approved by ethical review committee of the University of Cape Town. Feel free to contact Salah Kabanda, email: salah.kabanda@uct.ac.za, Tel: 0 21 650 4253 should you have any queries or complaints.

1

University of Cape Town
Department of Information Systems

The benefits of taking part in this study include raising awareness about mobile bully-victim behaviour, and encouraging pupils to report incidents. Additionally the availability of the app will help to equip the law enforcement in fighting bully-victim behaviour.

I hope that my request will find favour with you. For further information please do not hesitate to contact Mr Fani Radebe or Professor Michael Kyobe.

Fani Radebe

Signature Removed

If you have questions about this study please do not hesitate to call or email:

Researcher: Fani Radebe (RDBFAN002)   Supervisor: Professor Michael Kyobe
Tel: 076 296 3289   Tel: 021 650 2597
Email: RDBFAN002@myuct.ac.za   Email at michael.kyobe@uct.ac.za

This study has been reviewed and approved by ethical review committee of the University of Cape Town. Feel free to contact Salah Kabanda, email: salah.kabanda@uct.ac.za, Tel: 0 21 650 4253 should you have any queries or complaints.

2

University of Cape Town
Department of Information Systems

Study details

Please read the details of the study and, if you agree to the details, sign on the provided space.

Please note the following information about the study:

- Permission to conduct this study in schools has been granted by the South African Police department and the department of education.
- Parents' consent to involve their children in this study will be requested.
- Participation is completely voluntary, and participants may withdraw from the study at any time, if they wish so.
- The time to answer questionnaires will not exceed 10 minutes and the interviews will not exceed 45 minutes. Please be assured that utmost care will be taken not to divulge any personal information and identity of participants. Participants also have the right to skip any particular question or questions if they do not wish to answer them.
- Participants will be provided training on the use of the app in phase II and III.
- During the diagnosis process, pupils will use the app to nominate other pupils who are involved in mobile bully-victim behaviour. It is possible that pupils will wrongfully accuse each other, perhaps as a joke. However each child can deny or assent to accusations without any compulsion or penalty. Also pupils will be requested to recall and share their bully-victim experiences, which may cause emotional disturbance. Therefore counselling for pupils will be provided through the Social Development Department to handle emotional distress risks that may arise because of false accusations and bully-victim incidents recollection. The app's report will also be used to invite the affected pupils for remedial help.
- The diagnosis process will last for 25 minutes, and you are requested to keep nominated pupils' names and reports of the app confidential.
- The diagnosis will have no bearing whatsoever on pupils' schooling.
- While the collected information will be released in research reports or publications. Any information that is obtained in connection with this study that can be identified with the participant will be treated completely anonymous.

University of Cape Town
Department of Information Systems

Study: Towards a mobile application to aid law enforcement in diagnosing and preventing mobile bully-victim behaviour in Eastern Free State High schools of South Africa

School Principal Consent Form

I have read the information explaining the purpose of the research project and understand that:

- Permission to conduct this study in schools has been granted by the South African Police department and the department of education.
- Parents' consent to involve their children in this study will be requested.
- Participation is completely voluntary, and participants may withdraw from the study at any time, if they wish so.
- The time to answer questionnaires will not exceed 10 minutes and the interviews will not exceed 45 minutes. Please be assured that utmost care will be taken not to divulge any personal information and identity of participants. Participants also have the right to skip any particular question or questions if they do not wish to answer them.
- Participants will be provided training on the use of the app in phase II and III.
- During the diagnosis process, pupils will use the app to nominate other pupils who are involved in mobile bully-victim behaviour. It is possible that pupils will wrongfully accuse each other, perhaps as a joke. However each child can deny or assent to accusations without any compulsion or penalty. Also pupils will be requested to recall and share their bully-victim experiences, which may cause emotional disturbance. Therefore counselling for pupils will be provided through the Social Development Department to handle emotional distress risks that may arise because of false accusations and bully-victim incidents recollection. The app's report will also be used to invite the affected pupils for remedial help.
- The diagnosis process will last for 35 minutes, and you are requested to keep nominated pupils' names and reports of the app confidential.
- The diagnosis will have no bearing whatsoever on pupils' schooling.
- While the collected information will be released in research reports or publications. Any information that is obtained in connection with this study that can be identified with the participant will be treated completely anonymous.

Your signature on this form will be regarded as assent to approach teachers and pupils to participate in this study, and to use their feedback for the purposes of the research.
Please sign in the provided spaces and return the signed page.

Initials and Surname (Principal)   Signature   Date

If you have questions about this study please do not hesitate to call or email: 4
Researcher: Fani Radebe (RDBFAN002)   Supervisor: Professor Michael Kyobe
Tel: 076 296 3289   Tel: 021 650 2597
Email: RDBFAN002@myuct.ac.za   Email at michael.kyobe@uct.ac.za

This study has been reviewed and approved by ethical review committee of the University of Cape Town. Feel free to contact Salah Kabanda, email: salah.kabanda@uct.ac.za, Tel: 0 21 650 4253 should you have any queries or complaints.

Appendix 9: Consent letter to learners' parents and/or guardians

University of Cape Town
Department of Information Systems

30 July 2018

Dear Parent/Guardian

Re: Towards a mobile application to aid law enforcement in diagnosing and preventing mobile bully-victim behaviour in Eastern Free State High schools of South Africa

My name is Fani Radebe and I am conducting a study towards doctoral degree with the University of Cape Town (UCT). This study is based on the role of law enforcement, particularly South African Police who are responsible for crime prevention in schools, in curbing mobile bully-victim behaviour across Eastern Free State. The main aim of this study is to develop a mobile application (app) that can assist the police to diagnose mobile bully-victim behaviour in schools. The study is led by Professor Michael Kyobe at UCT in the Department of Information Systems and is funded by the National Research Foundation. The information that will be gathered through this study will help to shed light on the mobile bully-victim phenomenon.

Mobile bully-victim behaviour is one form of electronic bullying that is relatively new. It involves the use of technology applications such as email, chat rooms, instant messaging and small text messages. Using these technologies victims are harmed psychologically and emotionally by spreading lies, sending insults, and exclusion from social groups. This form of bullying often goes unnoticed, however bully-victims face higher risks of poor conduct, academic, and peer relationship problems, as well as substance abuse. Victims, institutions and parents are unaware of how to deal with it and there is limited knowledge of its legal and social implications.

I request your permission to involve your child in this study at school. This study is solely used to evaluate utility and efficacy of the app, which consists of two stages:

(1) Your child will be provided with training on the use of the app. Then police will be asked to diagnose pupils' involvement in mobile bully-victim behaviour using the app. The first step of this process includes confidential peer-nomination or self-report by pupils who are involved in the mobile bully-victim behaviour. While the nomination of mobile bully-victims is confidential, that is pupils will not know who nominated (accused) them. It is possible that pupils may wrongfully nominate (accuse) others, perhaps as a joke. However the second step of the process, which validates nominations, affords each nominee an opportunity to deny or assent to nominations without any compulsion or penalty. Also pupils will be requested to recall and share their bully-victim experiences, which may cause emotionally disturbance. Therefore counselling for pupils will be provided through the Social Development Department to handle emotional distress risks that may arise because of false accusations and bully-victim incidents recollection. In the final step pupils may be invited for remedial help based on the app's report. Additionally consent from your child (please see the attached form for your perusal), the school principal and police personnel will be requested in writing before the study commences.

(2) Your child will also be requested to share his/her experience regarding the use of the app to diagnose mobile bully-victims. Please be assured that no other information whether personal or that can lead to victimisation of your child will be collected or publicly divulged.

<table>
<tr><td>

If you have questions about this study please do not hesitate to call or email:

Researcher: Fani Radebe (RDBFAN002)
Tel: 076 296 3289
Email: RDBFAN002@myuct.ac.za

</td><td>

Supervisor: Professor Michael Kyobe
Tel: 021 650 2597
Email at michael.kyobe@uct.ac.za

</td><td>1</td></tr>
<tr><td colspan="3">

This study has been reviewed and approved by ethical review committee of the University of Cape Town. Feel free to contact Salah Kabanda, email: salah.kabanda@uct.ac.za, Tel: 0 21 650 4253 should you have any queries or complaints.

</td></tr>
</table>

The benefits of taking part in this study include raising awareness about mobile bully-victim behaviour, and encouraging pupils to report incidents. Additionally the availability of the app will help to equip the law enforcement in fighting bully-victim behaviour.

I hope that my request will find favour with you. For further information please do not hesitate to contact Mr Fani Radebe or Professor Michael Kyobe.

Fani Radebe

Signature Removed

If you have questions about this study please do not hesitate to call or email:
Researcher: Fani Radebe (RDBFAN002)   Supervisor: Professor Michael Kyobe
Tel: 076 296 3289   Tel: 021 650 2597
Email: RDBFAN002@myuct.ac.za   Email at michael.kyobe@uct.ac.za

This study has been reviewed and approved by ethical review committee of the University of Cape Town. Feel free to contact Salah Kabanda, email: salah.kabanda@uct.ac.za, Tel: 0 21 650 4253 should you have any queries or complaints.

2

University of Cape Town
Department of Information Systems

Study details

Please read the details of the study, if you agree to the details, sign on the provided space.

Please note the following information about the study:
- Permission to conduct this study in schools has been granted by the department of education.
- Pupils' consent to participate in this study will be requested.
- Participation is completely voluntary, and participants may withdraw from the study at any time, if they wish so.
- The time to answer questionnaires will not exceed 10 minutes. Please be assured that utmost care will be taken not to divulge any personal information and identity of participants. Participants also have the right to skip any particular question or questions if they do not wish to answer them.
- Participants will be provided training on the use of the app.
- During the diagnosis process, pupils will use the app to nominate other pupils who are involved in mobile bully-victim behaviour. It is possible that pupils will wrongfully accuse each other, perhaps as a joke. However each child can deny or assent to accusations without any compulsion or penalty. Also pupils will be requested to recall and share their bully-victim experiences, which may cause emotional disturbance. Therefore counselling for pupils will be provided through the Social Development Department to handle emotional distress risks that may arise because of false accusations and bully-victim incidents recollection. The app's report will also be used to invite the affected pupils for remedial help.
- The diagnosis process will last for 25 minutes, and participants are requested to keep nominated pupils' names and reports of the app confidential.
- The diagnosis will have no bearing whatsoever on pupils' schooling.
- While the collected information will be released in research reports or publications. Any information that is obtained in connection with this study that can be identified with the participant will be treated completely anonymous.

If you have questions about this study please do not hesitate to call or email:
Researcher: Fani Radebe (RDBFAN002)   Supervisor: Professor Michael Kyobe
Tel: 076 296 3289   Tel: 021 650 2597
Email: RDBFAN002@myuct.ac.za   Email at michael.kyobe@uct.ac.za

This study has been reviewed and approved by ethical review committee of the University of Cape Town. Feel free to contact Salah Kabanda, email: salah.kabanda@uct.ac.za, Tel: 0 21 650 4253 should you have any queries or complaints.

3

University of Cape Town
Department of Information Systems

Study: Towards a mobile application to aid law enforcement in diagnosing and preventing mobile bully-victim behaviour in Eastern Free State High schools of South Africa

Parent/Guardian Consent Form

I have read the project information explaining the purpose of the research project and participation, and understand that:

- Permission to conduct this study in schools has been granted by the department of education.
- Pupils' consent to participate in this study will be requested.
- Participation is completely voluntary, and participants may withdraw from the study at any time, if they wish so.
- The time to answer questionnaires will not exceed 10 minutes. Please be assured that utmost care will be taken not to divulge any personal information and identity of participants. Participants also have the right to skip any particular question or questions if they do not wish to answer them.
- Participants will be provided training on the use of the app.
- During the diagnosis process, pupils will use the app to nominate other pupils who are involved in mobile bully-victim behaviour. It is possible that pupils will wrongfully accuse each other, perhaps as a joke. However each child can deny or assent to accusations without any compulsion or penalty. Also pupils will be requested to recall and share their bully-victim experiences, which may cause emotional disturbance. Therefore counselling for pupils will be provided through the Social Development Department to handle emotional distress risks that may arise because of false accusations and bully-victim incidents recollection. The app's report will also be used to invite the affected pupils for remedial help.
- The diagnosis process will last for 25 minutes, and participants are requested to keep nominated pupils' names and reports of the app confidential.
- The diagnosis will have no bearing whatsoever on pupils' schooling.
- While the collected information will be released in research reports or publications. Any information that is obtained in connection with this study that can be identified with the participant will be treated completely anonymous.

> If you understand the provided information and wish for your child to participate in this study, please provide your name, your child's name and surname, and sign in the provided spaces. Also remember that your child's participation is voluntary and may be discontinued at any time, if you wish so. **Please return the signed form.**

I (Parent/Guardian's initials and surname) ____ have read and understand the information given in this document and I consent that my child

(Child's name and surname) ____ may participate in this study.

____
Signature (Parent / Guardian)

____
Date

If you have questions about this study please do not hesitate to call or email:

Researcher: Fani Radebe (RDBFAN002)
Tel: 076 296 3289
Email: RDBFAN002@myuct.ac.za

Supervisor: Professor Michael Kyobe
Tel: 021 650 2597
Email at michael.kyobe@uct.ac.za

This study has been reviewed and approved by ethical review committee of the University of Cape Town. Feel free to contact Salah Kabanda, email: salah.kabanda@uct.ac.za, Tel: 0 21 650 4253 should you have any queries or complaints.

4

Project title:

Towards a mobile application to aid law enforcement in diagnosing and preventing mobile bully-victim behaviour in Eastern Free State High schools of South Africa

06/11/2018

id. 10537323

by **Fani Radebe** in **Commerce Faculty Ethics Application 2018**

rdbfan002@myuct.ac.za

Original submission

06/11/2018

UCT Student / Staff Number	**RDBFAN002**
Degree Being Studied (For Students Only)	**PhD**
Cellphone Number / UCT Extention	**0762973289**
UCT Email Address	**rdbfan002@myuct.ac.za**
Alternative Email Address	**fmradebe@hotmail.com**
1. PROJECT DETAILS	
Principal Researcher/s:	**rdbfan002@myuct.ac.za**
Status of Applicant	**PhD Student**
Please specify "Other"	
Supervisor Name (For Students Only) :	**Professor Michael Kyobe**
Supervisor email address	**michael.kyobe@uct.ac.za**
Department:	**Department of Information Systems**

Co-researcher(s)
Names:

Co-researcher(s)
Email Addresses:

Review Track   **Expedited**

Motivation for an Expedited Review

I am requesting expedited review because I am resubmitting the application, addressing previously raised concerns. My application in the Department of Education to conduct the study and collect data in schools requires ethical clearance from the university first. I also hope to roll out the study in schools mid August.

Brief description of the research project

The aim of this study is to develop a mobile application that can assist law enforcement agents to diagnose mobile bully-victim behaviour in schools. Mobile bully-victim behaviour is one form of electronic bullying that is relatively new. It involves the use of mobile technology applications such as email, chat rooms, instant messaging and small text messages. Victims, institutions and parents are unaware of how to deal with it and there is limited knowledge of its legal and social implications.

The diagnosis process includes peer nominations and self-report of pupils who are involved in the mobile bully-victim behaviour. A validation process, so pupils can deny or assent to accusations, and measuring the degree of bully-victim effects on pupils. Confirmed bully-victims will be warned about the effects of bullying and be encouraged to abandon the behaviour.

Study Procedure
This study consists of three phases including an inference on teachers and police's nuances in resolving pupils misconduct especially mobile bully-victim behaviour in order to inform study design. As well as role-playing by teachers for assessing the apps utility and efficacy, and live roll out of the app with police. Permission from South African Police Department and Free State Education Department has been requested. Also participation consent in phase 1-3 for SAPS, teachers, and pupils are tiered in one form, while parents and school principals' forms are separate.

Phase 1
Focus groups with teachers and police, who are responsible for social crime prevention, will be conducted to inform study design. Information will be elicited regarding the involvement of teachers, police and parents, and approaches used to handle pupils misconduct in schools (the Focus_Group_Guide A document provides questions). At least six participants will be solicited using purposeful sampling. The police that will be involved are those that are designated for social crime prevention in schools, as well as intermediate and high school teachers.

Phase 2

The application test, the Mobile Bully-victim Diagnosis Process document (attached) provides details and step-by-step procedure. In order to alleviate the risk of involving police in the live testing of the application, teachers will be requested to take part in the study as role players, and to enable the app's utility and efficacy testing. The teachers that have been identified in phase 1 will be requested to participate in this phase, as well as pupils who own mobile phones.

Data collection will involve questionnaire and focus group with teachers only (please see the attached Questionnaire_Teachers_and_Police, and Focus_Group_Guide B document).

Phase 3
Live roll out of the app with police over 6 months and follow-ups to solicit perceptions on the use of the app. The questionnaire that was used with teachers will be reused with police, and focus group (please see the attached Focus_Group_Guide B) will be included. This will phase also concludes the study. The police that have been identified in phase 1 will be requested to participate in this phase, as well as pupils who own mobile phones.

Data collection: (please select)	**Interviews** **Questionnaire** **Other***
*Other - please specify below	**Developed application reports including statistical data about number of pupils who participated in each diagnosis session. The number nominated pupils, as well as the number and names of positively identified bully-victims.**

File Upload

Education_Department_Permission_Request.pdf

Parent_Guardian_Consent_Form.pdf

SAP_Teacher_Pupil_Consent.pdf

SAPS_Department_Permission_Request.pdf

School_Principal_Permission_Request.pdf

Social_Development_Department_Permission_Request.pdf

Focus_Group_Guide_A.pdf

Focus_Group_Guide_B.pdf

Mobile_Bully-victim_Diagnosis_Process.pdf

Questionnaire_Pupils.pdf

Questionnaire_Teachers_and_Police.pdf

Research_Proposal_EiRC.pdf

Have you attached a **Yes**
research proposal
with research
methodology?

2. PARTICIPANTS

2.1 Please indicate **Education sector / Academic sector**
below the affiliations **Other***
of participants from
the list below :

* Other - Please **South African Police Service (SAPS)**
specify below

2.2 Please describe **Consent form will provide participants full knowledge of the risks and**
how you plan to **benefits of participation so they can freely choose to participants.**
protect the **Permission from parents/guardians for vulnerable participants will be**
participants **requested in writing, describing risks of participation. Since this**
study uses pupils names and nominations, confidentiality of
participants' information will always be kept, and in reports of
findings as well. After data analysis the information about the study
will be provided back to the participants to verify if it resembles their
experience. Also, codes will be used in places of real identities when
participants' opinion is represented in reports.

Should pupils experience harm as a result of this study, counselling
will be provided through the Social Development Department. Also
teachers participation in the study is included to reduces the risk of
using students' names with police.

2.3 Does the **No**
research
discriminate against
participation by
individuals, or
differentiate between
participants, on the
grounds of gender,
race or ethnic group,
age range, religion,
income, handicap,
illness or any similar
classification?

2.4 Does the research require the participation of socially or physically vulnerable people (children, aged, disabled, etc.) or legally restricted groups?	**Yes**
2.5 Will you be able to secure the informed consent of all participants in the research? (In the case of children, will you be able to obtain the consent of their guardians or parents?)	**Yes**
2.6 Will any confidential data be collected or will identifiable records of individuals be kept?	**Yes**
2.7 In reporting on this research is there any possibility that you will not be able to keep the identities of the individuals involved anonymous?	**No**
2.8 Are there any foreseeable risks of physical, psychological or social harm to participants that might occur in the course of the research?	**Yes**
2.9 Does the research include making payments or giving gifts to any participants?	**No**

2.10 Race / Ethnicity - Are you asking a question about race/ethnicity in your questionnaire?	No
Which race categories have been used?	
2.13 Gender - Are you asking a question about gender in your questionnaire?	Yes
2.14 If you answered Yes to 2.13 - Have you included the option: "Prefer not to answer" as part of your gender question?	Yes
* If you have selected "No" in 2.14, please explain why	
3. PROVISION OF SERVICES	
3.1 Does your research involve the provision of services to communities?	No
* If your answer is YES, please provide a brief description below:	
3.2 Is the community expected to make decisions for, during or based on the research?	No
*If your answer is YES, please provide a brief description below:	

3.3 At the end of the research will any economic or social process be terminated or left unsupported, or equipment or facilities used in the research be recovered from the participants or community?

Yes*

*If your answer is YES, please provide a brief description below

The application used to diagnose mobile bully-victims will be removed from participants' mobile phones.

3.4 Will any service be provided at a level below the generally accepted standards?

No

*If your answer is YES, please provide a brief description

4. ORGANISATIONAL PERMISSION

4.1 If your research is being conducted within a specific organisation, please state how organisational permission has been/will be obtained:

Permission is being requested from Police Department and Department of Education.

4.2 Have you attached the letter from the organisation granting permission? (please select)

No but it will be obtained before commencing the research

4.2.1 If you have selected "Yes" in the question above please upload a the letter granting permission.

SAPS_CONSENT_FORM_.pdf

4.3 Are you making use of UCT students as respondents for your research?	**No**
4.4 Have you already contacted the Department of Student Affairs for permission?	**No**
Please upload DSA approval form here	
4.5 Are you making use of UCT staff as respondents for your research?	**No**
4.6 If yes, have you contacted Executive Director: Human Resources for permission ?	**No**
4.7 Was approval granted?	**No**
Contact Details	**Executive Director: Human Resources - Miriam.Hoosain@uct.ac.za** **Executive Director: Student Affairs - Moonira.Khan@uct.ac.za**

5. INFORMED CONSENT

| 5.1 What type of consent will be obtained from study participants? | **Written Consent**
Anonymous survey questionnaire (covering letter required and no consent form needed)) |
| 5.2 How and where will consent/permission be recorded? | **The participants' signature will be collected through consent forms that provide details about the study.** |

6. CONFLICT OF INTEREST

6.1 Is there any existing or potential conflict of interest between a research sponsor, academic supervisor, other researchers or participants?	**No**

6.2 Will information that reveals the identity of participants be supplied to a research sponsor, other than with the permission of the individuals?	**No**

6.3 Does the proposed research potentially conflict with the research of any other individual or group within the University?	**No**

6.4 Are you aware of any other conflict of interest that you would like to declare ?	**No**

If you have answered YES to any of these questions, please describe how you plan to address these issues (Questions 6.1 - 6.4)

7. RISK TO PARTICIPANTS

7.1 Does the
proposed research
pose any physical,
psychological, social,
legal, economic, or
other risks to study
participants you can
foresee, both
immediate and long
range? (please
select)

Yes*

* If YES, please
answer the following
questions:

7.2 Describe in detail
the nature and extent
of the risk and
provide the rationale
for the necessity of
such risks

Pupils names will be used for the mobile bully-victim diagnosis process, to nominate other pupils who are perceived as mobile bully-victims. It is possible that pupils might be falsely accused. Also pupils will be requested to recollect their bullying experiences that may lead to emotional distress.
1) The diagnosis process allows nominated pupils to deny or assent to accusations.
2) Counselling will be provided through the Social Development Department.

The rationale for this process is to provide a platform for pupils to report mobile bully-victim behaviour, install trust on pupils that the law enforcement can address bullying incidents. Since the reporting is done confidentially, pupils may feel safe to disclose mobile bullying behaviour. The study will also inform suitable surveillance mechanism against mobile bully-victim behaviour for police.

7.3 Outline any
alternative
approaches that
were or will be
considered and why
alternatives may not
be feasible in the
study

Teachers participation in the study is included to reduce the risk of using students' names with police. Alternatively, a self-report by pupils would be considered. While the possibility of false accusations is eliminated, the biasness and subjectivity of self-report may lead to incongruent findings in the diagnosis of mobile bully-victim behaviour.

| 7.4. Outline whether and why you feel that the value of information to be gained outweighs the risks | **Bully-victims face higher risks of poor conduct, academic, and peer relationship problems, as well as substance abuse. There is a great need for understanding police's involvement in curbing mobile bully-victim behaviour that are targeted along general intervention such as school polices. Also evidence-based studies about cyberbullying are need in order to discover the children lived experiences in schools. This study will pave a way to practically infer police involvement, role and challenges in curbing mobile bully-victim behaviour. Pupils will be empowered to disclose mobile bullying and find help, while they gain knowledge about unacceptable behaviour when using mobile technologies.** |

I certify that I have read the the Commerce Faculty Ethics in Research policy (http://www.commerce.uct.ac.za/Pages/ComFac-Downloads)

true

I hereby undertake to carry out my research in such a way that

*** there is no apparent legal objection to the nature or the method of research; and
* the research will not compromise staff or students or the other responsibilities of the University;
* the stated objective will be achieved, and the findings will have a high degree of validity;
* limitations and alternative interpretations will be considered;
* the findings could be subject to peer review and publicly available; and
* I will comply with the conventions of copyright and avoid any practice that would constitute plagiarism.**

Sign off

Supervisor has seen the application

Supervisor has seen the application

true

Signature

COM_Ethics_Signatories_2018_-_RDBFAN002-2.pdf

8. CHECKLIST - Please complete the section below.

A full copy of a research proposal or a literature review with methodology is attached

true

Interview schedules / cover letters / questionnaires / forms and other materials used	**true**
Organisational consent letter / UCT student or staff approval letter	**false**
On your cover letter to your questionnaire have you included the following?	
1. The circular UCT Logo - Please see http://www.uct.ac.za/images/uct.ac.za/about/intro/logo/logocircless.gif	**true**
2. A sentence explaining the aim of the research	**true**
3. Sentences of a similar nature to below must be included in the cover letter or consent form:	**true**
List of sentences	*** This research has been approved by the Commerce Faculty Ethics in Research Committee.** *** Your participation in this research is voluntary. You can choose to withdraw from the research at any time.** *** The questionnaire will take approximately X minutes to complete** *** You will not be requested to supply any identifiable information, ensuring anonymity of your responses.** **OR** *** Due to the nature of the study you will need to provide the researchers with some form of identifiable information however, all responses will be confidential and used for the purposes of this research only.** *** Should you have any questions regarding the research please feel free to contact the researcher (insert contact details).**
4. Have you scanned in your signature for the last section of the form?	**true**